Packing Death in Australian Literature

Packing Death in Australian Literature: Ecocides and Eco-Sides addresses Australian Literature from ecocritical, animal studies, plant studies, indigenous studies, and posthumanist critical perspectives. The book's main purpose is twofold: to bring more sustained attention to environmental, vegetal, and animal rights issues, past and present, and to do that from within the discipline of literary studies. Literary studies in Australia continue to reflect disinterest or not enough interest in critical engagements with the subjects of Australia's oldest extant environments and other beings beside humans. *Packing Death in Australian Literature: Ecocides and Eco-Sides* foregrounds the vegetal and nonhuman animal populations and contours of Australian Literature. Critical studies relied on in *Packing Death in Australian Literature: Ecocides and Eco-Sides* include books by CA. Cranston and Robert Zeller, Simon C. Estok, Bill Gammage, Timothy Morton, Bruce Pascoe, Val Plumwood, Kate Rigby, John Ryan, Wendy Wheeler, and Cary Wolfe. The selected literary texts include work by Merlinda Bobis, Eric Yoshiaki Dando, Nugi Garimara, Francesca Rendle-Short, Patrick White, and Evie Wyld.

Iris Ralph holds a B.Sc. (Pharmacology), Monash University; B.A. (English), San Francisco State University; M.A. (English) and Ph.D. (English), the University of Texas at Austin; and Graduate Diploma in TESOL & Literacy, Victoria University. Dr. Ralph currently teaches in the English Department of Tamkang University. She joined the faculty in 2009 as an Assistant Professor and was promoted to Associate Professor in 2016. Dr. Ralph has published many journal articles and book chapters that focus on ecocritical and environmental concerns.

Routledge Studies in World Literatures and the Environment

Climate and Crises
Magical Realism as Environmental Discourse
Ben Holgate

Ecocriticism and the Semiosis of Poetry
Holding on to Proteus
Aaron Moe

Christina Rossetti's Environmental Consciousness
Todd O. Williams

Ecoprecarity
Vulnerable Lives in Literature and Culture
Pramod K. Nayar

The Environment on Stage
Scenery or Shapeshifter?
Julie Hudson

Ecofictions, Ecorealities and Slow Violence in Latin America and the Latinx World
Ilka Kressner, Ana María Mutis and Elizabeth M. Pettinaroli

Modernism in the Green
Public Greens in Modern Literature and Culture
Edited by Julia E. Daniel and Margaret Konkol

Packing Death in Australian Literature
Ecocides and Eco-Sides
Iris Ralph

For more information about this series, please visit: https://www.routledge.com

Packing Death in Australian Literature

Ecocides and Eco-Sides

Iris Ralph

NEW YORK AND LONDON

First published 2021
by Routledge
605 Third Avenue, New York, NY 10017

and by Routledge
2 Park Square, Milton Park, Abingdon, Oxon, OX14 4RN

First issued in paperback 2022

Routledge is an imprint of the Taylor & Francis Group, an informa business

Publisher's Note
The publisher has gone to great lengths to ensure the quality of this reprint but points out that some imperfections in the original copies may be apparent.

Library of Congress Cataloging-in-Publication Data
A catalog record for this title has been requested

ISBN 13: 978-0-367-56568-8 (pbk)
ISBN 13: 978-0-367-56567-1 (hbk)
ISBN 13: 978-1-003-09839-3 (ebk)

DOI: 10.4324/9781003098393

Typeset in Sabon
by codeMantra

To my mother, Elvera Pascoe Ralph, my sister, Anthula Maria Ralph, my brother, Eric Kodjo Ralph, my brother, Daniel Ralph, and my husband, Peter I-min Huang

Contents

Acknowledgments

The beginnings of this book trace to 2005, to the inaugural conference of the Association for the Study of Literature and Environment-Australia and New Zealand (ASLE-ANZ), now called the Association for the Study of Literature, Environment and Culture-Australia and New Zealand (ASLEC-ANZ). My thanks go to the conference organizers, especially to Kate Rigby, the president of ASLE-ANZ in 2005. My equal thanks go to CA. Cranston, a future president of ASLEC-ANZ. Kate and CA greatly encouraged and supported me in my hopes to find a teaching and research position when I was a fledgling scholar and my future was uncertain. I also thank many other ASLEC-ANZ current and former members. They include Vanessa Bible, Tom Bristow, Charles Dawson, Anne Elvey, Luke Fischer, Cathy Fitzgerald, David Fonteyn, Jennifer Hamilton, Lesley Instone, Deborah Jordan, Eileen Joy, Grace Moore, Alanna Myers, Siobhan O'Sullivan, Perdita Phillips, Elspeth Probyn, Susan Pyke, Libby Robin, Deborah Bird Rose, Ariel Salleh, Lorraine Shannon, Victoria Team, Mark Tredinnick, Evelyn Tsitas, and Jessica White. In addition, I thank the following people who are current or former ASLEC-ANZ members: Susan Hawthorne, Barbara Holloway, Miriel Lenore, and John Ryan. I learned more about the publishing company Spinifex Press, founded by Susan Hawthorne and Renate Klein, when Susan invited me in 2014 to the book launch of Diane Bell's *Ngarrindjeri Wurruwarrin: A World That Is, Was, and Will Be*. The memorable event led me to other Spinifex publications and to writing about several of them in this book. I met Barbara Holloway in 2014 at the 5th ASLEC-ANZ biennial conference held at Australia National University (ANU) and am grateful to her for generously sharing her work with me. I am also grateful to Miriel, whom I met in 2012 at the 4th ASLEC-ANZ biennial conference held at RMIT University and Monash University. Miriel's poetry collection, *in the garden*, set me on the path to embark on research in the area of critical plant studies and so to meet and learn about the work of John Ryan and other critical plant studies scholars. I met John at the 5th ASLEC-ANZ biennial conference and thank him equally for his conversations and sharing his work with me.

I thank many current and former members of the Association for the Study of Literature and Environment in the United States (ASLE). Foremost among these individuals are Simon C. Estok and Scott Slovic. I am extraordinarily grateful to them for their constant encouragement and support of me over the years. I thank Amy McIntyre for her help on many occasions. I thank Joni Adamson, Greta Gaard, Ursula K. Heise, Serenella Iovino, Xinmin Liu, Patrick Murphy, Serpil Oppermann, Catriona Sandilands, Doug Vakoch, Priscilla Wald, and Ann Fisher-Wirth.

I thank many current and former members of ASLE-UKI (ASLE-United Kingdom and Ireland) for my meetings and conversations with them. Some of these meetings and conversations also were brief, squeezed in mostly at tea breaks at conferences, but they helped me greatly in my own thinking. Foremost among the many people to whom I owe thanks for their support, which led to, in addition to this book, publication outcomes in the form of book chapters and journal articles, are Terry Gifford, Axel Goodbody, Richard Kerridge, John C. Parham, Adeline Johns-Putra, and Wendy Wheeler.

In addition to thanking current and former members of ASLEC-ANZ, ASLE, and ASLE-UKI, I thank current and former members of ASLE-Taiwan, ASLE-India, ASLE-Japan, and ASLE-Korea. Many people whom I met at one or more of the conferences of these associations encouraged and supported me in my research for this book. I thank most of all I-ping Liang (梁一萍), the current president of ASLE-Taiwan. I-ping has steadfastly encouraged and supported me over the years, between now and 2009, when I moved to Taiwan and took up a teaching position at Tamkang University. I give thanks also to Bruce Allen, Hannes Bergthaller, Chia-ju Chang (張嘉如), Yalan Chang (張雅蘭), Hong Chen (陳紅), Xiangzhan Cheng (程相占), Shiuhhuah Serena Chou (周序樺), Kiu-Wai Chu (朱翹瑋), Kim-won Chung, Catherine Diamond, Don Gilleland, Patricia Haseltine, Hsinya Huang (黃心雅), Rose Hsiu-li Juan (阮秀莉), Shuyuan Lu (魯樞元), Emerald Kuo (古綺玲), Young-Hyun Lee, Bei Liu (劉蓓), Ken Noda, Swarnalatha Rangarajan, Lili Song (宋麗麗), Nuo Wang (王諾), Xiaohua Wang (王曉華), Qi-qi Wei (韋清琦), Winnie Yee, and Masami Yuki.

I thank Paul Cappucci, Christopher MacGowan, and Daniel Morris for their support of me in my research on William Carlos Williams. That research included ecocritical studies of Williams and helped me in my subsequent research for this book about Australian literature.

I thank my former teachers at the University of Texas at Austin (UT-Austin) for supporting and encouraging me many years ago, when I was pursuing a doctoral degree in the English Department and researching and writing about American Literature. My especial thanks go to my dissertation advisor, Brian A. Bremen, and my four dissertation committee members, Phillip Barrish, the late Anthony Hilfer and Wayne Lesser, and Ann Reynolds. I thank Jane Hilfer in memory of

Tony Hilfer, who was my M.A. thesis adviser as well as one of my dissertation committee members. Tony first introduced me to and encouraged me to pursue work in the area of ecocriticism. I thank the English Department of UT-Austin in memory of Wayne Lesser, who magnanimously championed many students and whose seminars on literary theory and criticism aided me immensely in my research. I also thank the English Department in memory of the late Don Graham. I enrolled in Professor Graham's Australian Literature class in 2005, the last year of my graduate studies at UT-Austin. I kept my notes for that class and added to them over the years. In addition to the ASLE-ANZ inaugural conference that I attended in 2005, Don's class was one of the first seeds of this book.

I thank Lucia Chen (陳小雀) and Mei-hua Sung (宋美瑾), former deans of the College of Foreign Languages and Literatures of Tamkang University, and Wan Bao Wu (吳萬寶), the current dean. I am grateful to Professors Sung, Chen, and Wu for guiding me through and helping me to fulfill the various administrative requirements related to my research projects, the main outcome to date of which is this book. I also thank Yu-fen Tai (戴毓芬), Associate Professor, Spanish Department, Tamkang University, for her friendship and support. I thank many of my colleagues in the English Department, College of Foreign Languages, Tamkang University. I owe thanks above all to Yi-Ti Lin (林怡弟), the current Chair of the English Department. I am deeply grateful to Yi-Ti for her support, friendship, advice, guidance, and encouragement. I also thank Iain Brown, Carrie Chang (張雅慧), Pei-yun (Jill) Chen (陳佩筠), Chin-jau Chien (錢欽昭), Yi-Tso (Amanda) Chien (簡伊佐), Yung-yu (Ernest) Huang (黃永裕), Chia-chen Kuo (郭家珍), Shizen Ozawa, Yu-ching Tseng (曾郁景), Ai-lin Wang (王藹玲), and Ya-chu (Karen) Yang (楊雅筑) for their support and friendship.

I am grateful to the Ministry of Science and Technology (MOST) in Taiwan for a generous research grant awarded to me in 2016, when I first proposed this book project. I am grateful to the individuals at MOST who read my project proposal and gave the thumbs up to it.

I thank Victor Sherwood in memory of my friend and University Melbourne alumnus Andrea Sherwood. We picked fruit in the summers in the late 1970s and early 1980s at the Knolls' farm in Hoddles Creek, Victoria, Australia and talked about books through the staves, stalks, thorns, and leaves. I thank Martin Ramsay, a fellow fruit-picker and literature scholar. I thank, in memory of Willard Goodwin, his dear cousins Katy and Greg Belt. I thank Stephen Farrell, Amanda Wauchope, Robert Menzies, and Helen Vassallo for their great friendship as well. I thank my mother, Elvera Pascoe Ralph, my older brother Eric Kodjo Ralph, my sister Anthula Maria Ralph, and my younger brother Danny Ralph for, for as long as I can remember, their great and steadfast love and support. I thank with equally great measure and feeling my husband,

Peter I-min Huang. I will cherish always his love for and support of me, and his inestimable contribution to establishing and supporting ecocriticism in China and Taiwan.

I thank the environments that supported me and that I let down growing up in the United States and Australia: the creeks and orchards in Billerica, Massachusetts; the birch trees and black eyed susans in East Lempster, New Hampshire; the pine trees, unwilling roped-in colonizers and leftovers from a pine plantation, at the back of 6 Anglo Court in Mooroolbark, Victoria, Australia; the paddocks over the back fences of another street there, 3 Erskine Ridge; the lone gum trees.

Permissions

The author thanks Ateneo de Manila University for permission to print a revised version of "Packing Death in Australian Literature." This article appears in the journal *Kritika Kultura* (vols. 33/34, 2019/2020, pp. 618–640). Ateneo de Manila University gives permission only for the first printing, and permission must be obtained for each subsequent reprint. The application for and approval of this permission contain all the terms relating to the said permission to reprint.

The author thanks the publishers and editors of the journals (listed here) for permission to print revised material from the following publications: "Australian Tongue and Ag-gag Law," *AJE: Australasian Journal of Ecocriticism and Cultural Ecology*, vol. 6, Summer 2016/2017, pp. 50–61, published in the former outlet journal of the Association for the Study of Literature, Environment, and Culture-Australia and New Zealand (ASLEC-ANZ); "The Systemic Approach, Biosemiotic Theory, and Ecocide in Australia," *CLCWeb: Comparative Literature and Culture*, vol. 16, no. 4, Dec. 2014, published by Perdue University Press; "Patrick White's *Riders in the Chariot*: a green flaw in the crystal glass," *Colloquy/Text Theory Critique*, No. 12, Nov. 2006, pp. 28–42, published by the Literary and Cultural Studies Graduate Research Program of Monash University; "Ecophobia and the Porcelain Porcine Species," *ISLE: Interdisciplinary Studies in Literature and Environment*, vol. 26, no. 2, Spring 2019, pp. 401–412, published by Oxford University Press.

The author thanks Spinifex Press for permission to cite words and lines from the poetry collection *Cow* by Susan Hawthorne; and Wakefield Press for granting permission to cite in their entirety two poems ("the oak" and "the living fossil") from the poetry collection *in the garden* by Miriel Lenore.

1 Introduction

Australian Ecocriticism and Animal Studies

This book addresses plants and animals in Australia and its literature. The floral subjects of the book mostly refer to pre-1788 species; the fauna refers to pre- and post-1788 animals inclusive of the animals conceived and slaughtered in industrial farming facilities and hunted and killed in rural areas and remote bush. I write about these subjects from the critical perspectives of animal studies, ecocriticism, ecofeminism, environmental history, plant studies, and posthumanism. My purpose in doing so is to add to other studies of Australian literature that sustain the cynosure of beings that as a society we more often than not neglect, dismiss, exclude, and exterminate under lightweight and threadbare, speciesist, moral, and ethical frameworks. The words "packing death" in the title of this study refer to those frameworks, or to the all but thoughtless commercial packing, and packaging, of ecocide (killing of the environment) in Australia. In Australian English slang ("Strine"), "packing death" is a common expression for fear or anxiety. The words mean that here, too, and they mean states of trepidation in both nonhuman beings and human beings. The words "packing death" in this study also refer to the literary record of ecocide and so to the eco-sides of that record, for along with death this record reflects the many efforts, often accompanied by mammoth losses and against great odds, to slow and even halt many ecocidal policies and practices.

CA. Cranston and Robert Zeller's edited *The Littoral Zone: Australian Contexts and Their Writers* is one of the most important studies for scholars interested in bringing attention to and supporting work in defense of Australia's beings beside humans. Contributors to the anthology examine such iconic authors as Jack Davis, Randolph Stow, Dorothy Hewett, Tim Winton, Ray Lawler, Robert Gray, Miles Franklin, Oodgeroo Noonucaal, and Judith Wright in the context of the writers' portraits of and relationships with such environments as the wheat belt in Western Australia, the limestone plains of New South Wales, the McPherson Range that straddles Queensland and New South Wales, the tropics of North Queensland, and the island of and seas around

Tasmania. The last four environments mentioned might also be called natural or ecogenic (nonhuman-made) environments in order to distinguish them from human-made or anthropogenic environments, which include the wheat belt in Western Australia. Natural environments have not been intensely cultivated or otherwise significantly transformed by humans to the extent that they have become more anthropogenic. The word "environment" in this study usually refers to such environments, and the words "nature" and "natural" in this study thus refer to things and beings that are relatively more ecogenic than anthropogenic. However, the given distinction, and many others like it that divide ecogenic and anthropogenic matter, caves in with the slightest of poking and prodding. The distinction assumes in effect that humans and their anthropogenic extensions are not part of the environment, or are not environmental. Colonial powers nefariously relied on this assumption and claim to rationalize the seizure of the Australian environment in 1788. It was not until 1992, the year Australia's High Court recognized Aboriginal rights to land after Eddie Koiki Mabo successfully claimed "uninterrupted ownership of his people's traditional land at Mer Island," that the Australian government admitted, if only on an anthropocentrically logical grounds of admission, "the falsehood of the claim" that Australia was *terra nullius* (Heiss and Minter 6). Since then, the government has only marginally entertained the idea that the environment itself has rights and is not merely a tabula rasa waiting to be written into existence by the human.

Australia's oldest people understood that the natural world was full of creatures, individuals, groups, existences, histories, creativities, choices, wills, joys, and sorrows; they chose, therefore, to cooperate with rather than beat that world into submission. Such cooperation allowed their own species, the human species, to thrive alongside other species. The oldest Australians did not irresponsibly control or interfere in the ecogenic agencies of those species to the extent that later generations of Australian people desired and sought to oversee the environment. A minority of Australians today are paying heed to and promoting pre-1788 human–environment relationships. Cranston and Zeller's ecocritical study *The Littoral Zone* exemplifies such relationships in Australian literary studies contexts.

Environmental historian Bill Gammage's *The Biggest Estate on Earth: How Aborigines Made Australia*, indigenous studies scholar Bruce Pascoe's *Dark Emu. Black Seeds: Agriculture or Accident?*, ecocritic Kate Rigby's *Dancing with Disaster: Environmental Histories, Narratives, and Ethics for Perilous Times*, and regenerative agriculturalist Charles Massey's *Call of the Reed Warbler* also make up the small, but significant, body of criticism that recognizes how and why Australia's oldest people gave country a fair go. These authors lay out and point to evidence for the careful management of the island-continent of Australia and its smaller islands and marine environments by humans, "the people of 1788," Gammage's descriptive for the oldest Australian people, before the arrival of "newcomers," Gammage's term for Australia's colonial-settler people, in 1788. After that fateful year, large areas of the Australian continent and its isles were mismanaged out of a mixture of antipathy, greed, and sheer ignorance.

Mark Tredinnick's edited *A Place on Earth: An Anthology of Nature Writing from Australia and North America*, Tom Bristow's *The Anthropocene Lyric: An Affective Geography of Poetry, Person, Place*, and Graham Huggan and Helen Tiffin's *Postcolonial Ecocriticism: Literature, Animals, Environment* are additional important key texts for scholars interested in the subject of fairer relations between humans and the environment in the context of Australian literary studies. Tredinnick writes about the influence of place on the poetry of Tim Winton, Charmian Clift, Barbara Blackman, and Patrice Newell. Bristow focuses on "place perception," "more-than-human worlds," and "Anthropocene emotion" in his discussion of a selection of British and Australian poets, the latter group of which include John Kinsella. Huggan and Tiffin, analyzing the ideological links between genocide and ecocide and racism and speciesism, and arguing that genocide and ethnocentrism are inseparable from ecocide and speciesism, discuss the work of Judith Wright, Oodgeroo Noonuccal, J. M. Coetzee, and Peter Goldsworthy (the last author of whom is represented in the penultimate chapter of the present study).[1]

Green Sense: The Aesthetics of Plants, Place and Language and *Posthuman Plants: Rethinking the Vegetal World through Culture, Art, and Poetry* are two studies of the plants of southwestern Australia by critical plant studies scholar John Ryan. They are important texts for scholars of Australian literature who are interested in human–environment relationships in Australian literary studies contexts. Working through principles of "cultural botany" and "cultural ecology," Ryan discusses such plant texts as William Hart-Smith's (1911–1990) poem about the "iconic red and green flower," the kangaroo paw (Mangles paw, *Anigozanthos manglesii*), a plant that has been the floral emblem of Western Australia since 1960 and once grew "thick on the sides of the road" (*Posthuman Plants* 113); poems by Judith Wright (1915–2000) about the many orchid species that thrived before the advent of Anglo-Europeans (115); Andrew Lansdown's (1954–) "A Few Weeks Later I Returned to Find," a poem about the grasstree or balga (*Xanthorrhea preissii*), "a primordial and profoundly slow-growing" tree species that has a lifespan of 500 years and was decimated when pastoralists from England and other countries in Europe arrived in Australia and embarked on the agricultural transformation of the southwest region of Australia (xi, 120); Charles Harpur's (1813–1868) poetic tributes to the casuarina (or she oak or swamp oak) (117); and a poem by John Kinsella (1963–)

about a pincushion lily plant (belonging to the *Borya* species) that is commonly called a "resurrection plant" because of its ability to survive long periods of drought (121). In commenting on these and other plants in his work, Ryan makes an argument that parallels the claims of Gammage, Pascoe, and Rigby: newcomers by and large misunderstood, took for granted, dismissed, or too lightly recognized both the astonishing pre-1788 vegetal power of Australia and the work of the people of 1788 who respected and cultivated that power.

In *The Green Thread: Dialogues with the Vegetal World*, an anthology coedited by Patrícia Vieira, Monica Gagliano, and John Ryan, the editors and other contributors explore the ways in which histories of ecophobia and ecocide intersect with those of racism, xenophobia, and sexism. Guinevere Narraway and Hannah Stark make that argument (in the chapter entitled "Vital Plants and Despicable Weeds in Ray Lawrence's *Lantana*") in the specific context of director Ray Lawrence's film *Lantana* (adapted from the play *Speaking in Tongues* by Andrew Bovell), the main trope of which refers to a plant that has been "largely condemned" for being one of Australia's 20 "most invasive imported plants" and now is classified as a "Weed of National Significance" (183). The authors critique the "usual discursive encoding [of lantana] as unproductive weed" (183) toward understanding how and why plants are enlisted in the articulation of "political attitudes toward foreignness" and "difference" (Vieira, Gagliano, and Ryan xvii).

For environmental humanities scholars who are interested in animal studies publications that address the question of human animal–nonhuman animal relationships in Australian cultural, if not manifestly Australian literary, contexts, Adrian Franklin's *Animal Nation* is a noteworthy study.[2] Franklin is critical of what he calls "eco-nationalism," or the "mutually reinforcing symmetry between nationalism and ecology" (4). He rejects the claim that "any lasting notion of Australian nationhood must arise from an intimate understanding of Australian ecosystems" (Flannery qtd. in Franklin 4).[3] His argument is "Australian nationhood" must be understood essentially in symbolic and social terms (25).

The arguments that I make in the present study go against the grain of Franklin's contention; they also owe to it in the sense that Franklin usefully alerts one to the concern of superficial green initiatives and rhetoric that pit affluent middle-class interests against the interests of poor and politically powerless communities. That betrayal is dealt with in depth by scholars situated in the areas of environmental justice studies and postcolonial ecocriticism. As Franklin's study also reflects, relatively recent notions of *wilderness* ignore the issue of indigenous people's coexistence with and custodianship of the Australian environment for tens of thousands of years before the discovery and takeover of this environment by newcomers. Franklin's study thus brings to mind Ursula K. Heise's study entitled *Sense of Place and Sense of Planet: The Environmental*

Imagination of the Global, a critique of localism in the context of nationalistic movements that meretriciously use "local" and "green" rhetoric to preserve and sustain insular xenophobic, racist, speciesist, and sexist political agendas.[4]

Carol Freeman, Elizabeth Leane, and Yvette Watt's edited anthology, *Considering Animals: Contemporary Studies in Human-Animal Relations*, is another important study for scholars of Australian literature who are interested in understanding and redressing the wrongs that humans have committed against members of other species as well as members of their own. In the chapter "Possum Magic, Possum Menace," author Kay Milton examines different attitudes toward the common brushtail possum (*Trichosurus vulpecular*), one of more than 26 native possum species in Australia. Protected and beloved in Australia, the brushtail possum is commonly regarded to be a pest in New Zealand, where the species has made a second home. In "The Speech of Dumb Beasts," another chapter in *Considering Animals*, Helen Tiffin begins by providing a short history of the fate of the flightless woodhen (*Tricholimnas sylvestris*), animals who were "clubbed to death" on Lord Howe Island when they came out to greet the human crew of the *Supply* of Australia's first fleet in 1788 (137). Tiffin goes on to examine literary texts that "deliberately breach" the "generic constraints" of giving agency (such as speaking parts) to animal characters and putative claims found under scientific theories that hold that animals are incapable of language, or "speech," and even the most rudimentary forms of communication are unavailable to animals other than humans (141). Her essay is particularly germane to the arguments in the last chapter of the present study, which focuses on language, translation, and communication across species and among members of species other than the human species.

In "Making Matter: Why the Art World Needs to Rethink the Representation of Animals," another chapter in Freeman, Leane, and Watt's edited *Considering Animals*, Yvette Watt argues that in the visual arts critical investigations of animals—animal language, animal communication, and cross-species communication between humans and other animals—have been "edging toward the mainstream," and the "mention of an animal-related research topic"—for example, trans-species communication—no longer "provoke[s] surprise and amusement" (Ritvo qtd. in Watt 119).[5] Nonetheless, there continues to be little interest in the subject of human–animal relationships in the mainstream art world (Watt 125). Even in the instances of exhibitions that are contributing to "the current rethinking" of those relationships, the exhibitions betray "simplistic or overly general curatorial agenda" (125). Often "nothing more than an animal's presence in an artwork" is required for a submission "to be deemed to fit within the curatorial premise" (125). Many of the exhibitions ultimately "[overwhelm]" animals under metaphors, trivialize animals, make use of animals "more for sake of amusement than for any serious investigation of the complexities of the animals themselves or of human-animal relationships," refuse "to take any clear ethical position regarding the way humans think about and treat nonhuman animals," and betray a "dearth of artists who are truly concerned with the issues surrounding animals as sentient, self-interested, identifiable individuals" (122–125).[6]

The criticism that Watt levies against the interest in animal representation in the visual arts is true to some extent of the interest in animal representation in literature and literary criticism. Literary studies are bringing more attention to the issues of rights of animals and so redrawing the boundaries of what constitutes literary studies. Nonetheless, literary studies remain anchored in anthropocentric critical and social harbors and underrepresent the issue of the rights of other species besides the human species. That said, literary studies have opened some of its doors to that issue. One those egresses refers to critical animal studies. At first a "smattering of work in various fields on human-animal relations and their representation" in the early 1990s (Wolfe, *What Is Posthumanism?* 99), animal studies coalesced into a "vibrant emergent field of interdisciplinary inquiry" at the end of the last century (99).[7] In its "full force," the discipline "fundamentally unsettles and reconfigures the question of the knowing subject" and calls for the re-evaluation of "the role and presence of nonhuman animals" in a wide range of disciples where those animals are "for the most part ignored" (Wolfe xxix; Twine 1). Although "no standard or widely accepted definition" of animal studies exists and while the "main terms and theoretical foci" of the discipline are "open-ended," its "main stakes" are clear: placing "questions concerning animals at the center of critical inquiry" (2).

In addition to the studies so far mentioned, work by scholars that straddles both animal studies and Australian literary studies includes the projects, initiatives, and publications of the Australasian Animal Studies Association (AASA), Animal Studies Research Network (ASRN), *Animal Studies Journal* (*ASJ*), and Human Animal Research Network (HARN). Members of AASA, ASRN, and HARN are among the most active in the area of animal studies in Australasia. Studies published by AASA and ASRN members include *Animal Welfare in Australia* by Peter Chen; *The Political Turn in Animal Ethics*, edited by Robert Garner and Siobhan O'Sullivan; *Foucault and Animals*, edited by Matthew Chrulew and Dinesh Wadiwel; *Extinction Studies: Stories of Time, Death, and Generations*, edited by Matthew Chrulew, Deborah Bird Rose, and Thom van Dooren; and *Animals in Australia: Use and Abuse* by Malcolm Caulfield. Two further studies are Deborah Bird Rose's *Wild Dog Dreaming: Love and Extinction* and Val Plumwood's *The Eye of the Crocodile*.

As the title of *Wild Dog Dreaming* reflects, Rose's study is inspired by Australia's dingoes (*Canus lupus dingo*), animals whose ancestors first migrated to Australia from South Asia about 5,000 years ago (62). Four of the twelve chapters of *Wild Dog Dreaming*, which is written from multi-disciplinary ethnographic perspectives, reflect Rose's background in philosophy as well as ecocriticism: "Singing Up the Others," "Job's Grief," "What If the Angel of History Were a Dog?," and "Ruined Faces." These and other chapters also reflect the author's extensive knowledge of the history of Aboriginal Australians' struggle for political recognition; they include discussions of dingo stories that have been passed down by the Yarralin and Lingara Aboriginal people in the north of Australia as well as analyses of white pastoralist "dogger" traditions. Rose thus documents the change in the status of the dingo from that of "protected species" to a "pest requiring eradication" in her discussion of racist attitudes toward Aboriginal Australian communities that share close bonds with dingoes and other "camp dogs" (mostly animals that are a genetic cross between dingoes and introduced European species) (1, 23). The ecocidal "war" that pastoralists wage on some of the oldest animal species in Australia, the site of "the highest rate of mammalian extinctions in the world today," goes hand in hand with acts of genocide against Australian people (56, 67).

Val Plumwood's *Environmental Culture: The Ecological Crisis of Reason* and *Feminism and the Mastery of Nature* are the author's most well-known works. They are complemented by a posthumous collection, *The Eye of the Crocodile*. In it, Plumwood brings together arguments forged out of ecophilosophy, ecofeminism, and ecocriticism. *The Eye of the Crocodile* also reflects the arguments of scholars situated in animal studies, which was a fledgling discipline at the time of the publication of the two earlier studies by Plumwood. Referring in *The Eye of the Crocodile* to the work of Jane Goodall, the ethologist, primatologist, and anthropologist, in her project of collapsing distinctions that encourage humans to distance themselves morally from the lives of other animals, Plumwood states that it is "no coincidence that the more revolutionary forms of ethology pioneered by women like Jane Goodall have given us new insights precisely because they have broken ... down" the "false choices" that humans make for themselves when they abide by such dyads as the nature/culture and human/nonhuman dichotomies (53). These "rule out the possibility of deep personal contact with animals except on...[anthropocentric] terms" (53).

The Eye of the Crocodile emphasizes that kind of contact with other than human beings, beings whom Plumwood calls "wild familiars" (53). Such relationships are forged on the basis of respect for and learning about those animals' terms of "contact and friendship" (53). One of the most powerful chapters in *The Eye of the Crocodile* that carries this argument is "A Wombat Wake: In Memoriam, Birubi." Plumwood writes about her many years of friendship with a wombat (named Birubi by Plumwood) (53). When he first came to Plumwood, the young animal was a "malnourished and very sick orphan" (49). Plumwood helped him to recover his health, he remained close to her, and he was one of her most frequent house guests until his death.

In another evocative chapter of *The Eye of the Crocodile*, Plumwood writes about the terrifying experience of being "rolled" by a salt water crocodile. She critiques the nature/culture boundary that is "so constitutive of our civilization" yet riddled with inconsistencies (53–54) by sorting through and explaining legislation that protects some native animal species, such as the salt water crocodile (*Crocodylus porosus*) but not others; programs to eradicate animals that were introduced into Australia in the eighteenth and nineteenth centuries and subsequently became unwanted; and cultural representations of animals that both belie and draw attention to the moral dilemmas of animal slaughter. Cultural representations include the children's film *Babe*, directed by Chris Noonan (and based on Dick King-Smith's novel *The Sheep-Pig*), a "work of art which takes a group of the most oppressed subjects and makes an effective and transformative representation of their situation" (55). It was filmed on a location not far from Plumwood's home in Australia, at the time Plumwood was in North Carolina in the United States learning about the lives of the porcine species in that part of the world, "the second highest US state for intensive hog production" (57).

Equally important texts that are responses to the call for more equal relations between human beings and other beings, and so to the call for "nonmodern onto-epistemologies" and "alternative, countermodern way[s] of framing, anticipating, and responding to eco-catastrophe" in the present century (Rigby, *Dancing with Disaster* 4), include "The Ecological Humanities Corner" of *The Australian Humanities Journal*; *AJE: Australasian Journal for Ecocriticism and Cultural Ecology*, the distinguished former outlet journal of the Association for the Study of Literature, Environment, and Culture-Australia and New Zealand (ASLEC-ANZ); *Swamphen*, the present journal outlet for ASLEC-ANZ; and *Plumwood Mountain: An Australian Journal of Ecopoetry and Ecopoetics*, which was founded not long after the death of Plumwood in honor of her inestimable contribution to the environmental humanities in Australia. Other key figures in the history of these journals include Libby Robin, author of "The Eco-humanities as literature: a new genre?"; Freya Mathews, a leading environmental philosopher and the author of, among many studies, *Without Animals Life Is Not Worth Living*; Ruth Blair, who taught environmental literature courses in the 1990s at the University of Tasmania; and Judith Wright, author of, among many books of poetry and prose, *The Coral Battleground*, a vivid account of the environmental struggle in the 1960s and 1970s to save the Great Barrier Reef. Eric Rolls's *A Million Wild Acres*, Bruce Bennett's *Australian Compass: Essays on Place and Direction in Australian Literature*, Veronica Brady's biography of Wright, and John

Kinsella's *Disclosed Poetics: Beyond Landscape and Lyricism* also represent major scholarly contributions to the field.

Two further important studies that are germane to and inspire the arguments of this study make little or no reference to Australian literature. They are Cary Wolfe's *What Is Posthumanism?* and Neil Badmington's edited collection of essays, *Posthumanism*. I single out Wolfe's book because it is one of the most eloquent, intellectually stimulating, and academically rigorous introductions to the disciplinary area of inquiry of posthumanism, which closely intersects with the disciplines of ecocriticism, animal studies, and plant studies. Badmington's anthology also merits attention, for it draws attention to now-classic essays in literary and cultural studies that put pressure on understandings of "the humanities" and "humanist" inquiries well before posthumanism emerges as a discipline in its own right in literary studies. Thus, I will briefly comment on Wolfe's study here (and in the final chapter) and also on some of the essays represented in Badmington's edited collection, which highlights how some brilliant humanist critiques of taken-for-granted definitions of the human, definitions that in effect marginalized certain human populations, helped pave the way for critical interrogations of even more deeply engrained, seemingly universal, sets of distinctions, those morally separating humans from other beings.

Posthumanism I

In *What Is Posthumanism?*, Wolfe identifies the two main paths that posthumanism takes after it makes its debut in the 1950s in the area of artificial intelligence. The first is the "intensification" of humanism and identifies with what Wolfe calls the transhumanist direction of posthumanist inquiry (Wolfe, *What Is Posthumanism* xv). The second, far outstripped by the first, is the recoil from speciesist frameworks of humanism. Wolfe rather inelegantly calls the second trajectory "posthumanist posthumanism" (125).

Humanism traces back to the Renaissance, when philosophers and other thinkers challenged ideas about the essential baseness and corruption of the human body. Subsequent thinkers, those who identify with the Enlightenment and the birth of the natural sciences, continued this challenge. These thinkers praised the human body, and other earthly bodies, for being, indeed, marvelous mechanisms, wondrous instruments, ingenious machineries, and intricate works (and testimonies to a divine creator). One of those same thinkers, Carol Linnaeus, the "founder of modern scientific taxonomy," catapulted the human species to the top of the species hierarchy with the publication of *Systema naturae* (Agamben 29). It accelerated the "anthropological machine of humanism," although Linnaeus did not intend that (29). In fact, Linnaeus omitted "any specific identifying characteristic" of the human animal species and resolutely placed *Homo sapiens* among the primate animal species (25). He was "not ready to concede easily" to the theological notion that animals were essentially different from man, or "lacked a soul" (23). "[S]urely," he says in one of his writings, "Descartes never saw an ape" (qtd. in Agamben 23). In another writing, a letter addressed to a hostile critic, Linnaeus writes, "I ask you and the entire world to show me a generic difference between ape and man which is consistent with the principles of natural history. I most certainly do not know of any" (qtd. in Agamben 26). In *Menniskans Cousiner* ("Man's Cousins"), he writes, "as a naturalist I hardly know a single distinguishing mark which separates man from the apes, save for the fact that the latter have an empty space between their canines and their other teeth" (qtd. in Agamben 24). Nonetheless, Linnaeus's *Systema naturae* became the standard reference for the argument that humans occupy the highest position on the ladder of moral consideration.

In the following century, under the impact of Charles Darwin's theory of evolution, Sigmund Freud's psychoanalytic theory of the unconscious, and Karl Marx and Friedrich Engels' historical materialist challenge to theological and other transcendentalist defenses of the so-called natural order of things, the scientific establishment was somewhat less optimistic about humans' moral superiority. In the twentieth century, that optimism was further shaken by the cataclysm of World War I. Nonetheless, the momentum of human exceptionalism that was set in motion several centuries before continued to gain political and cultural velocity and mass.

A brief recapitulation of the foregoing is that humanist beliefs and faith in the ability of humans to solve their and other species' problems, or what Wolfe calls transhumanist posthumanism (*What Is Posthumanism?* xiii), derive "directly from ideals of human perfectibility, rationality, and agency that trace back to the Renaissance and the Enlightenment" (xiii). The transhumanist posthumanism direction thus is, according to this same account of posthumanism, both a mere extension and a guise of humanism. Transhumanist posthumanism is analogous to an oppressive emperor or empress who wears new clothes to persuade his or her people that he or she is a new or reformed ruler. Transhumanist posthumanism is an iteration of humanism, which stands for or sides with beliefs that the human species is a superior species, that the interests of humans are absolutely paramount to those of other species, and that the human in its most perfected forms can be "achieved by escaping or repressing not just its animal origins in nature, the biological, and the evolutionary, but more generally by transcending the bonds of materiality and embodiment altogether" (xiii, xv).

At the same time, and somewhat confusingly so, transhumanist posthumanism shares with posthumanist posthumanism suspicion of the claim that the human is ontologically distinguishable from the nonhuman. Similar to posthumanist posthumanism, transhumanist posthumanism is an area of inquiry that points to the wealth of evidence for the claim that it is impossible to determine exactly where the human parts of a human body begin and where the nonhuman parts end, not the least so because of the prosthetics that we have devised for ourselves—for example, eyewear, hearing aids, artificial limbs, pacemakers, and computers which are like external memories or extensions of our brains. However, the transhumanist thinker is more willing than the posthumanist posthumanist thinker is to rationalize uses of animals and plants (and entire ecosystems) to enhance the human. The posthumanist posthumanist thinker points out that many of those uses are in fact abuses. They reflect the hubris of humans and their capitalizing "fantasies of disembodiment and autonomy" (Wolfe, *What Is Posthumanism?* xv). The posthumanist posthumanist thinker, one whom Wolfe represents, speaks for considering the rights of the natural world inclusive of species beside the human species. This same thinker does not merely identify posthumanism with "a historical moment in which the decentering of the human by its imbrication in technical, medial, informatic, and economic networks" is "increasingly impossible to ignore" and with "a historical development that points toward the necessity of new theoretical paradigms" (xv–xvi). This same thinker challenges long-standing "anthropological universals" of humanism, or the speciesist norms under which humans have assessed and judged other beings and things (Foucault qtd. in Wolfe, *What Is Posthumanism?* xvi). She or he redefines "the human" as something that is morally and ethically attached to, and morally and ethically comes after, the world, as well as something that is, "at its core and in its very constitution, radically ahuman and constitutively prosthetic" (xxvi).

Paradoxically, the new ecocentric paradigms called for by posthumanist posthumanist thinkers are challenging the most successful animal rights arguments, namely those formulated by Peter Singer and Tom Regan, thinkers whom Wolfe characterizes under the term of "humanist posthumanists" (*What Is Posthumanism?* 125). Their posthumanist thinking constitutes what Donna Haraway calls the "clear-sighted recognition of connections across the discredited breach of nature and culture" as opposed to the "irrational denials of human uniqueness" (72). This thinking has done more to advance animal rights than any other animal advocacy work to date; however, it betrays a speciesist bias in the sense that the worth of a nonhuman animal is fought for according to how much that animal shares in common with human beings. The nonhuman animal is measured against "a core humanity or common essential feature in terms of which human beings can be defined and understood" (Soper 9). In emphasizing similarities as opposed to differences between human animals and nonhuman animals in the effort to garner political recognition for the latter, humanist posthumanist animal rights thinkers thus reinforce the speciesist barriers that they are intent on bringing down. Yet, these thinkers cannot be dismissed. They have saved more animals from dying horrific deaths than the thinkers who associate with the more radical form of posthumanism of posthumanist posthumanism.

Ecofeminist scholars point out another failing of mainstream animal rights discourse, or of what Wolfe calls humanist posthumanist animal rights discourse. These scholars argue that classical animal rights arguments betray "masculinist" biases, or privilege so-called masculinist principles of rationality, universality, and autonomy over so-called feminist principles of affect and nonrationality (or emotionalism, relation, and dependence (Kheel 3).[8] Their argument coheres with Jacques Derrida's famous deconstruction of "the subject" under the neologism, *carnophallogocentrism.* For one to be recognized and given rights as a "subject" throughout much of recent history, one had to have a phallus ("phallo") as well as possess speech ("logo") (an attribute denied to animals in the modern period, from the fifteenth century onward). In addition, as animal studies scholar Matthew Calarco points out in his critical unpacking of Derrida's neologism, for one to be given the rights of "the subject," one must eat meat (132). "[B]eing a carnivore is at the very heart of becoming a full subject in contemporary society," and "[p]articipating, whether directly or indirectly, in the processes and rituals of killing and eating animal flesh is almost a necessary prerequisite of being a subject" (132). Derrida's own words in explanation of his neologism are that in order for one, typically a male, to be able to attain social, political, and cultural status, or in order for one to be able to be deemed to be a legitimate subject, she or he "accepts sacrifice and eats flesh" (" 'Eating Well,' Or the Calculation of the Subject" 114).

"[C]arnivorous sacrifice is essential to the structure of subjectivity, which is also to say to the founding of the intentional subject," Derrida states elsewhere ("Force of Law. The 'Mystical foundation of Authority'") (953). "Who would stand any chance of becoming a chef d'Etat [a head of State], and of thereby acceding 'to the head,' by publicly, and therefore exemplarily, declaring him- or herself to be a vegetarian?," Derrida rhetorically asks ("'Eating Well,' Or the Calculation of the Subject" 119). He reiterates, "The chef must be an eater of flesh" (119).[9]

Posthumanism II

Badmington's edited collection of essays *Posthumanism* is the identifying and highlighting of nascent posthumanist statements in literary theory and criticism. These statements appear before, in some cases long before, posthumanism emerges as a distinct area of disciplinary inquiry in literary theory and criticism. Although they hardly can be called defenses of other beings beside human beings—they are defenses only of certain groups of human beings—their exposure of the gender, race, and class biases of humanism opens it to further attack, one led by a later generation of thinkers, namely posthumanist posthumanist thinkers. The statements (essays) that Badmington singles out for reprinting in his anthology include feminist poststructuralist thinker Donna Haraway's "A Cyborg Manifesto"; postcolonialist Franz Fanon's "The Wretched of the Earth"; and Louis Althusser's "Marxism and Humanism."

In "A Cyborg Manifesto: Science, Technology, and Socialist-Feminism in the Late Twentieth Century," Haraway confronts the androcentric bases of humanism in her defense of the cyborg. The term "cyborg" traces to the Macy conferences on cybernetics, which were held between 1946 and 1953 (Wolfe, *What Is Posthumanism?* xii). Literary critics began to take notice of and use the trope following the publication of Haraway's essay (first published in 1985). In it, Haraway points out the similarities between chauvinistic ideas about women, a historically marginalized class of humans—a class the members of which are understood to be only half human or incompletely human because they are female not male humans—and ideas about cyborgs (hybrid human–machine being-things). Like the figure of the cyborg, the figure of the female human—as with the figure of the disabled human, the black human, the queer human, and so forth—is "a creature of social reality as well as a creature of fiction," a creature "simultaneously animal and machine," and a creature who "populate[s] worlds ambiguously natural and crafted" (Haraway 70).[10] Haraway and other nascent posthumanist thinkers lead the way to what Wolfe calls posthumanist posthumanism when they point out that "the human" is in fact a descriptive that only certain privileged human populations fully enjoy. Other human populations, populations that include women, share with nonhuman populations the status of something not quite human.

In "The Wretched of the Earth," Fanon argues that the entire concept and notion of "humanity" is an imperial, racist, and Eurocentric euphemism for Western European colonial enterprises. "Come, then, comrades," Fanon exhorts,

> We must shake off the heavy darkness in which we were plunged, and leave it behind ... Leave this Europe where they are never done talking of Man, yet murder men everywhere they find them, at the corner of every one of their own streets, in all the corners of the globe ... So, comrades, let us not pay tribute to Europe by creating states, institutions and societies which draw their inspiration from her ... Humanity is waiting for something other from us than such an imitation, which would be almost an obscene caricature. (25)

Fanon's explosively powerful postcolonial critique of humanism anticipates the arguments of posthumanist posthumanist thinkers, who question the privileged and exclusive traits ("higher" thinking) that humans give to their own species and refuse to all nonhuman species. Similarly, in "Marxism and Humanism" where the author, Althusser, argues that Marx "[breaks] radically with every theory that based history and politics on an essence of man" and where Althusser argues that Marx, as early as 1845, was producing a "theoretical anti-humanism," or "recognition and knowledge" that "humanism" was in fact an "idealist" and "bourgeois" philosophy, Althusser is forging a path for future thinkers inclusive of posthumanist posthumanism thinkers, who attack biases even more rigid and invisible than class biases—namely those that betray speciesism (30, 32).

Introducing Althusser's essay in the opening pages of his anthology, Badmington compares the nascent posthumanist arguments in Althusser's essay to aspects of Sigmund Freud's theory of the unconscious. Freud's theory, too, as Badmington astutely observes, carries the seeds of posthumanist interrogations of the human long before posthumanism emerges as a distinct disciplinary area of inquiry. Freud unintentionally challenged humanism by "proposing that human activity is governed in part by unconscious motives," or by a realm that escapes humans' conscious efforts to control it. In other words, Freud's theory of the unconscious "problematized the Cartesian model, in which the critical determinant of being is rational, fully-conscious thought" (Badmington 5). Psychoanalytic theory "requires that the words of Descartes be reformulated as follows: 'I think where I am not, therefore I am where I do not think…I am not wherever I am the plaything of my thought'" (Lacan qtd. in Badmington 5–6).

Since the publication of Badmington's *Posthumanism*, work in the area of biosemiotics has added to the understanding that human agency is in part fueled by the unconscious (or by decisions of which humans are not consciously aware). However, biosemiotics scholars disagree with Freud's theory of the unconscious insofar as they do not belittle (and sensationalize) it by associating it mainly with all that is irrational; their main point is that the unconscious mechanisms of human action (thoughts and deeds) are closely related to and indeed are made up of the same biological matter that is found in other species beside the human species and leads those species to do what they do, and, in more cases than not, these mechanisms suggest rationality or purpose. In other words, contrary to Freudian beliefs that nature "is meaningless and random," biosemioticians argue that natural processes operate or proceed according to a logic and this reasoning is as complex and sophisticated as the kinds of reasoning that we associate with human intelligence, conscious or unconscious (Wheeler "Natural Play, Natural Metaphor, Natural Stories" 70). Nature is more than "a passive substratum"; it is "a *meaning-bearing* field of agency," and, if meaning (information, semiosis) is "carried by matter," then it is "not reducible to it" (70). I recapitulate this biosemiotics argument in the fifth chapter of this study in my reading of several works of Australian literature. That argument is especially useful in the ongoing work of interrogating the anthropocentric biases that drive definitions of selectivity, creativity, agency, will, desire, language, and so forth.

Marvelous forms of language and thinking are found in species other than the human species; they are functions, interactions, and processes that humans share with millions of other planetary beings (Wheeler, *The Whole Creature* 17). Such beings, in Australia and its literature, are the primordial subjects of the chapters that follow. What follows is a brief introduction to them.

Chapter Summaries

Chapter 2 focuses on the figures of unwanted vermin animal and feral animal species in Nugi Garimara's autobiographical novel *Follow the Rabbit-Proof Fence* and film director Nicolas Roeg's adaptation of James Vance Marshall's novel *Walkabout*. Garimara makes an implicit postcolonial ecocritical argument about attempts to eradicate Australia's oldest people and Australia's rabbits, an imported "newcomer" animal species that subsequently acquired phenomenal status as a vermin species and was subject to extermination under more or less ineffective ecocidal policies. *Follow the Rabbit-Proof Fence*, in the many references it makes to pre-1788 flora, also draws attention to critical plant studies arguments about the massive ecocide of plants in Australia after 1788. I refer to those arguments as they are found in John Ryan's *Green Sense: The Aesthetics of Plants, Place and Language*; Ryan's *Posthuman Plants: Rethinking the Vegetal through Culture, Art, and Poetry*; Jessica White's "Georgiana Molloy, Botanical Networks and Naming in 19th Century Western Australia"; and Tony Hughes-d'Aeth's "Salt Scars: John Kinsella's Wheatbelt." I also draw on a much older study, *Dryandra*, by the environmental conservationist Vincent Serventy, in my discussion of the ties between Australia's intertwined histories of ecocide and genocide.

Roeg's film *Walkabout* has been justifiably criticized for representing Aboriginal Australian identity in offensively simplistic and reductive terms. On the other hand, as a film that some critics situate in the New Australian Cinema (Rattigan 309), *Walkabout* was ahead of its time in focusing on the Australian environment as much as on the Australian human and in calling attention to debates, which are ongoing, over culling practices involving the slaughter of macropod species.

Chapter 3 is about the cows and sheep of Australian pastoral and post-pastoral literature and the Australian cows and sheep who inspire those figures. The chapter also includes discussion of the porcine species, a highly consumed and an intensively farmed animal species if one that does not conjure Australian pastoral and post-pastoral. In my focus on the animals of Australian pastoral and post-pastoral, I discuss Evie

Wyld's novel *All the Birds, Singing*, Francesca Rendle-Short's fiction *Bite Your Tongue*, and *Cow*, a collection of poetry by Susan Hawthorne. *Cow* is a discernibly feminist text and a winsome and witty exploration of the cows of the literary and cultural fields and paddocks of etymology, comparative literature, philosophy, Sanskrit culture, and Ancient Greek myth. With the exception of the introductory poems, the collection makes no references to the cows of Australian pastoral or post-pastoral; yet, by these inaugural poems, if not by the collection in its entirety, Hawthorne reminds us of the millions of animals that have defined Australian life and literature since 1788. Rendle-Short's novel is a post-pastoral text in the sense that the main events of the narrative associate with the literature of suburbia and with the phenomenon of the suburbs, which mushroomed in the post–World War II decades, the timeframe of the events of *Bite Your Tongue*. These new environments encroached upon and overtook rural environments as many people moved away from either the city or the bush onto suburban tracts of land. Also accompanying the birth and growth of the suburbs is the disappearance of two of Australia's most farmed animal species, cows and sheep (as well as chickens, goats, and pigs), from the sight of many Australians except in the form of meat.

Bite Your Tongue provokes ecocritical engagement with a related issue of visibility and presence, that of current proposed agricultural gag laws, so-called ag-gag laws. They are aimed at deterring animal advocacy activists from accessing industrial farming facilities, investigating the operations of these facilities, and disseminating the surveillance to the public. The laws, if passed, will decrease the lack of transparency in meat production, or decrease it further. Not only will the animals who are used up in this production continue to remain out of sight and out of mind for most Australians; also, animal advocates who do want to see those animals and have a say in how they are born, bred, raised, and killed will be denied access to sites where those animals expire after truncated existences. Reading *Bite Your Tongue* against the proposed laws elicits analogies in particular between Rendle-Short's account of attempts by moral right activists in Queensland in the 1970s to censor the "tongue" of politically left-leaning writers and communist party members and attempts today by industrial pastoral interests to "cut out the tongue" of animal advocacy groups that disseminate information about industrially farmed animals, animals who are denied speech altogether.

The main subject of investigation of Wyld's novel *All the Birds, Singing* is content that ties to one of the novel's major themes, a country haunted by racism and struggling to come to terms with it. This same content identifies the novel with the robust tradition of post-pastoral literature as well as postcolonial ecocritical literature. Post-pastoral literature, as I mostly refer to it in this study, is a body of literature that engages with the darker and sadder aspects of Australian pastoral traditions. Thus, I focus on the allusions that Wyld makes to the violence to which people subject sheep in intensive wool and meat production as well as to the violence committed against the descendants of Australia's oldest people.

Chapter 3 concludes by referring to Val Plumwood's critique of industrial animal farming in a study entitled *The Eye of the Crocodile.* In it Plumwood admonishes vegan and vegetarian consumers under her "ecological animalism" versus "ontological veganism" argument (79). In responding to and taking issue with some of that argument, I critically tie it to Eric Yoshiaki Dando's novel *Oink, Oink, Oink*, a surreally real narrative about humans' dependence on porcine flesh in the areas of food production and biotechnology, namely the transhumanist projects of xenotransplantation and transgenic experiments on pigs.

Chapter 4 focuses mostly on Merlinda Bobis's cli-fi novel *Locust Girl*, a thinly disguised account and critique of climate change in Australia after 1788, the year that colonizer and settler people from England and other parts of Europe first began to immigrate in large numbers to Australia and pursue activities that resulted in widespread environmental degradation. The novel also is an implicit rebuke to the notion that Australia before 1788 was an environment uncultivated and undermanaged by humans. In this reading of Bobis's fiction, I rely mostly on Gammage's *The Biggest Estate on Earth: How Aborigines Made Australia*; Bruce Pascoe's *Dark Emu. Black Seeds: Agriculture or Accident?*; and Kate Rigby's *Dancing with Disaster: Environmental Histories, Narratives, and Ethics for Perilous Times.* Describing a drought-stricken, denuded, and burnt country where thousands of people struggle to live after their local "countries" are deliberately or carelessly destroyed by the rulers of the "Five Kingdoms," *Locust Girl* resonates with the arguments that those authors forward about Australia's environmental and human history since 1788. Those arguments fly in the face of mainstream popular foundation narratives, which gloss over the dark side of colonization and settlement of Australia.

Chapter 5 addresses the problem of translating and speaking for *the other*, where the other is *an other than human* being; it utilizes arguments generated out of biosemiotics, specifically arguments by biosemiotics and ecocriticism scholar Wendy Wheeler, and current summary statements about translation by translation studies scholars. As Wheeler cogently represents, language, communication, and translation extend far beyond the kinds of communication that occur between humans; yet, in modern times our governments have consistently underrepresented, underestimated, and underrated the linguistic realms of plants and animals. Translation studies, similarly to biosemiotics, also offers extraordinarily useful insights to ecocritics in the context of the effort to garner more respect for and understanding of natural languages in addition to human languages, and so to the work of translating nature in terms that speak as much for the interests of nature as for the interests of its human translators, who too often are employed by companies to extract as much information from plants and animals primarily to benefit the human. Two works of Australian literature that I address in this chapter, as they engage with the subject of natural languages and the subject of the translation of the natural world, are Peter Goldsworthy's novel *Wish*, about a sign-language instructor, John James ("J. J."), and his relationship with "Wish," a young female gorilla who becomes a hybrid hominoid, a human-gorilla, after she is biologically modified by (human) animal scientists; and Robyn Davidson's travel narrative *Tracks*, about Davidson's travel in the 1970s with camels from Alice Springs in the Northern Territory of Australia to the coastal inlet of Hamelin Pool in Western Australia. Efforts to define and assumptions about the speech of the nonhuman other typically are based on human language models, and mostly on one area of human language, so-called articulate language (Wheeler, *The Whole Creature*); they blind us, as they blind *Wish's* animal activist Clive F. Kennear, to the panoply of languages, affects, and communications that other than human beings engage in and use.

Chapter 5 also draws on the work of ecofeminist scholar Greta Gaard. In *Critical Ecofeminism*, Gaard comments on the fact that humans have tended to talk at and over the nonhuman other more than they have communicated with and listened to other than human beings. In other words, when our species speaks for the other, we often do that in order to deny, suppress, or abuse the other's own language and expression of self. More often than not, we have effectively dismissed, denied, and stripped agencies from the others of animals and plants. Those agencies include communicative agencies. When we listen to the nonhuman other in the attempt to serve its interests as much as our own, we give up our own mainstream "masculinist" notions a little, and submit a little to the nonhuman other according to our "feminist" principles.

Mainstream "masculinist" notions about language also tie to what Simon C. Estok theorizes under the term "ecophobia." I elaborate more on Estok's theorization of ecophobia in the final, sixth, chapter of this study. Estok compellingly argues that indifference to, disregard for, fear of, and contempt for the natural world critically tie to other prejudices inclusive of misogyny, and racism and homophobia, and without addressing ecophobia we cannot fully address those prejudices. In Chapter 6, I also draw on Timothy Morton's work in the area of Object-Oriented-Ontology (OOO) theory. The theory seeks in effect to reappraise certain so-called objects, or certain beings or things that are denied so-called subject-hood. In Morton's engagement with the theory, he draws attention to how plants, nonhuman animals, and the environment typically have the secondary status of objects. I relate Morton's ecocritical deployments of OOO to the arguments that Theodor Adorno, the Frankfurt School critic and historical materialist thinker, makes in an essay entitled "Subject and Object." Just as OOO carries or is useful to ecocritics, Adorno's essay, a defense and reappraisal of "the object," beckons an ecocritical reading. I offer such a reading here in Chapter 6 and illustrate it in my discussion of Patrick White's novel *Riders in the Chariot*. Long regarded as being an author who identifies with Romanticism, subjectivity, and the metaphysical imagination, White was nonetheless keenly aware and critical of transcendentalist forms of thinking that effectively sacrifice the environment by giving it the status of an object, or an identity that signifies all that is limited, jejune, passive, and unfulfilled.

The final pages of Chapter 6 comprise the recapitulation of an argument that Cary Wolfe makes in defense of disciplinarity and, paradoxically, in defense of kinds of studies such as this study that bring into literary studies knowledge generated out of other disciplines. That kind of scholarship is hardly new; however, it has been confined largely to anthropocentric kinds of inquiry. Wolfe draws attention to that form of speciesism in his explanation of systems theory and a key concept of systems theory, "openness from closure." His discussion is useful for literary studies scholars who write about literature from critical animal studies perspectives (or from any critical perspective, for that matter), for it effectively highlights the importance of transdisciplinary approaches even as it warns scholars about overloading or burying their arguments when they do not respect the protocols of their own discipline. Literary studies benefit mightily from more sustained address of the floral and faunal figures in addition to the human figures that abound in literature. The strongest kinds of that address are those that open literary studies to other disciplines by assiduously attending to the critical tenets of literary studies.

This book is written with the intent to add to, complement, and push in new directions the arguments that appear in such publications as those mentioned so far and in publications cited in later chapters. *Packing Death in Australian Literature: Ecocides and Eco-sides* is part of the ongoing call to bring species other than our own species into our ethical frameworks and practices, or more so than we have done, and to give more material and discursive room to species other than our own species, room that is on terms that are fashioned as nearly as much by those species as by our own.

Notes

1 The term *speciesism*, coined in 1970 by Richard Ryder, an animal laboratory scientist turned animal rights activist who spoke out against experiments on animals (Singer iv, 3), refers to the widespread and unexamined, "institutionally taken for granted" belief that "the subject is always already human" and corollary conviction that it is "all right to systematically exploit and kill nonhuman animals simply because of their species" (Wolfe, *Animal Rites* 1, 8).

2 The environmental humanities is an interdisciplinary area that brings together the social sciences, the humanities, and the natural sciences. It engages

with "old and new environmental challenges, values, environmental justice issues, and theoretical conceptions of the human and non-human natures" and addresses "the complexities of material networks that cross through local and global cultures, economic and social practices, and political discourses" (Oppermann and Iovino 1).

The phrase *the question of the animal* is often used by animal studies scholars. It traces to interest in a late essay by Jacques Derrida, "The Animal That Therefore I Am (More to Follow)." In it, Derrida addresses "the anthropocentric dimensions of ontotheological humanism," a set of prejudices and biases that he had been "keenly aware of and intent on problematizing" from the time of his earliest work (Calarco 104).

3 See Flannery 390.

4 For a related argument, see Peter I-min Huang's essay "Canon Formation in the Study of the Environment in China and Taiwan."

5 See Harriett Ritvo's essay, "Animal Planet" 205.

6 In her own work as a visual artist, Watt tries to avoid using animals merely as a "stand in for other thematic concerns" but nonetheless finds herself constantly balancing on a tightrope between making "overtly polemical" animal advocacy statements and acquiescing to subtler animal rights rhetoric, or between alienating her audience through shocking images of abuses of animals and winning gallery goers by downplaying the abysses of human-animal relations (124, 130).

For a discussion of other visual artists who engage with a range of animal advocacy positions, see Steve Baker's *The Postmodern Animal.* Like Watt, Baker singles out the postmodern "animal artist" Sue Coe, for she represents the small number of artists who engage in earnest and often disturbing problematizations of *the animal.* Similar artists include Mark Dion, Olly and Suzi, Joseph Beuys, Emily Mayer, Mike Kelley, Britta Jaschinski, and John Isaacs.

Philip Armstrong's *What Animals Mean in the Fiction of Modernity*, is an early important animal studies publication for literary studies scholars. It looks at representations of animals in literature between the eighteenth and twentieth centuries—the work of writers who include Jonathan Swift, Daniel Defoe, Mary Shelley, Herman Melville, H. G. Wells, Ernest Hemingway, Upton Sinclair, and D. H. Lawrence.

7 As Twine makes clear, animal studies, or critical animal studies, as the discipline also is called, is not to be confused with "animal research" and "mostly emerges from the humanities and social sciences" (1).

8 See, also, *Critical Ecofeminism*, by Greta Gaard; *International Perspectives in Feminist Ecocriticism*, edited by Gaard, Simon C. Estok, and Serpil Oppermann; and *Ecofeminism: Women, Animals, Nature*, edited by Gaard.

9 Two (among many) notable exceptions to the de facto, masculinist and carnophallogocentric, rule that one had better eat meat if she or he wishes to run for political office are Jeremy Corbyn, the leader of the Labour Party in the United Kingdom between 2015 and 2019; and Al Gore, the 45th vice president of the United States.

10 Wolfe places Haraway in his list of "posthumanist posthumanist" thinkers along with Bruno Latour, Niklas Luhrmann, Jacques Derrida, and Humberto Maturana and Francisco Varela (*What Is Posthumanism?* 125).

2 Genocide and Ecocide

Follow the Rabbit-Proof Fence

In Joan London's novel *The Golden Age*, the main events of which take place in the post–World War II decades in Western Australia's capital city of Perth, Meyer Gold knocks off work one balmy evening and makes his way home by foot through the streets of the city that he has come to call home. A delivery driver for a beverage company and a recent arrival to Australia from Hungary, Gold remembers the fall of Budapest at the end of the war. "Nobody here," he thinks,

> could imagine the waters of the Swan [River] running red. The Causeway bombed, tanks rolling up St. Georges Terrace. Block after block of empty buildings, blackened and broken like ruined teeth. Shots ringing out. The hunted running through King Park. Bodies piled ten high on the steps of Parliament House. (87)

Gold is unaware of a conflagration in Australia that was more protracted but no less horrifying than that which broke apart Europe and not widely understood, let alone debated, among Australians in the 1950s. He surmises that apart from the refugees who have recently arrived in Australia from war-torn Europe no-one in Perth can imagine the hatred and indifference that targeted him, his wife Ida, their young son Frank, and millions of other Jewish people when Adolf Hitler rose to power in Germany. His character speaks for the widespread ignorance in Australia of attempts to eradicate Aboriginal Australians under genocidal policies and practices in the same period of time.

Follow the Rabbit-Proof Fence by Nugi Garimara (Doris Pilkington) foregrounds those policies and practices; it also elicits comparisons between genocide and ecocide. The narrative does that in the specific context of three Aboriginal children who escape from an institution near Perth, the Moore River Settlement, and walk back to their country in the East Pilbara by following a rabbit-proof fence. A second text examined in this chapter, director Nicolas Roeg's film *Walkabout*, more or less persuasively addresses the connections between genocide and ecocide in the context of a lost-in-the-bush narrative. Its scenes of feral animal slaughter constitute, as *Follow the Rabbit-Proof Fence*'s allusions to white people's attempts to eradicate native and non-native fauna and flora comprise, notice of a carnage that most Australians are unaware of or underestimate.

Garimara's semi-autobiographical *Follow the Rabbit-Proof Fence* is inspired by the story of the author's mother Molly Craig, a Mardudjara (also known as Mardu or Martu) and Budidjara woman who spent much of her life trying to reunite with country against the government's efforts to tear her from it. In 1931, under the orders of the Chief Protector of Aborigines, A. O. Neville, Craig was abducted from her country in the Pilbara region in Western Australia, near Jigalong, the site of a depot established for the purpose of erecting one of three long, so-called rabbit-proof, fences. Molly, her sister Daisy Kadibil, and their cousin Gracie Cross were taken by force to the Moore River Native Settlement, also known as the Mogumber Native Mission, a detention center for Aboriginal children, located about 1,600 km^2 southwest of Jigalong.[1] The girls escaped from the institution and walked back to their country, heading north and west through "strange" country in the southwest corner of Western Australia and then along a north-south-running rabbit-proof fence (Garimara 82).[2]

The position of Chief Protector of Aborigines evokes the infamous figure of Auber Octavius Neville (1875–1954), a chief architect of the Stolen Generations (Huggan and Tiffin 97). He had joined the public service in Western Australia as a records clerk in the Department of Works, where he earned "a reputation for efficiency" (Haebich and Reece). In 1902, he was promoted to registrar of the Colonial Secretary's Department (Haebich and Reece). In 1906, he became an immigration officer. In 1910, he was appointed "head of the new sub-department of tourism and immigration" (Haebich and Reece). He became secretary of the Patriotic Relief Fund in 1914. Thereafter, he continued as chairman of the Fund's permanent relief committee.

Neville first "came to the public eye" when he was appointed to the position of Chief Protector of Aborigines (Haebich and Reece). He held that position until 1926, when Aboriginal affairs were placed under the control of the Aborigines Department. From 1915 until his retirement in 1940, he significantly "shaped official policy towards Aborigines" (Haebich and Reece). He advocated a "three-step approach" consisting of overseeing the "forced removal of 'half-caste' children from their mothers, control of marriage among 'half-castes,' and encouragement of intermarriage with the white community" (Huggan and Tiffin 97). In his positions of Chief Protector of Aborigines and Commissioner for Native Affairs, the latter position of which he held between 1936 and 1940, Neville extended the Aborigines Department's "legal authority, particularly over people of part descent" (Haebich and Reece). That extension was his "main interest" (Haebich and Reece). He "aggregated" power throughout this time in his effort "to assimilate Aborigines of part descent through economic and social (genetic) absorption" and acceleration of "the pauperization and segregation" of Aborigines, which had begun in the 1900s (Haebich and Reece). He actively enforced rules under legislation that included the 1905 Aborigines Act and the Aborigines Protection (Amendment) Act of 1936. The latter act gave to the Aborigines Department even more power than before, "particularly over children" (Haebich and Reece). Under the Aborigines Protection (Amendment) Act of 1936, Neville advocated for

> permanent segregation of Aborigines of full descent, who were believed to be near extinction; and temporary segregation and training of those of part descent who would re-enter society as domestics and farm-workers, eventually blending with the white population through intermarriage. (Haebich and Reece)

The Moore River Native Settlement was established in 1918 by the government of Western Australia. It closed in 1951. Government authorities forcibly sent children classified as Aboriginal under the Aborigines Act of 1905 to the settlement. "Over-crowding, disease and 'grossly inadequate health and sanitary facilities'" were among its failures (Rosser). They "persisted ... throughout its existence" (Rosser). Of the 374 fatalities, most of these were children who died of "treatable respiratory and infectious diseases" (Rosser). Many children tried to escape, especially those "trying to get back to family" (Rosser). One method used to punish captured runaways was to put them in an iron cage, known as "the Boob" (Rosser). When the settlement was finally closed down, the Department of Native Affairs handed the premises over to the Methodist Overseas Mission. It reopened the site as Mogumber. Mogumber closed in 1974 (Rosser).

Differently from London's novel *The Golden Age*, which centers on Meyer and Ida Gold's young son Frank and The Golden Age Children's Polio Convalescent Hospital in Perth—Frank's home for much of his boyhood and the place he comes to love as he undergoes painful treatment for polio—Garimara's book is about three Aboriginal children forcibly taken from their home in the East Pilbara and placed in an institution in Perth against their interests and parents' will. The three children represent Australia's Stolen Generations, the official term for the Aboriginal families torn apart under assimilationist legislation between 1869 and 1969 (Heiss and Minter 246).

The Stolen Generations represent a betrayal in two senses: ecocide and genocide. When the local, state, and federal authorities split apart Aboriginal families, they also destroyed "country." This word and concept as it is used in Australia owes to specifically Aboriginal inflections of the English word. It is a proper noun as well as a common noun and refers to both people and place. It represents "the interconnected matrix of entities, living and deceased, biotic and abiotic, human and otherwise that sustains the life of those whose forbears dwelt in the territory to which they remain bound by ancestral kinship ties" (Rigby, *Dancing with Disaster* 161). People "talk about country in the same way they … talk about a person; they speak to country, sing to country, visit county, worry about country, feel sorry for country, and long for country. People say that country knows, hears, smells, takes notice, takes care, is sorry or happy" (Rose qtd. in Rigby 162). According to this belief in Australia, "Country is a living entity with a yesterday, today and tomorrow, with a consciousness, and will to life" (Rose qtd. in Rigby 162).[3]

To read Garimara's book and other Australian literature for what it says about country and the destruction of it is to read this literature for what it says about nonhuman beings as well as human beings. In *Follow the Rabbit-Proof Fence*, in addition to the narrative's three diminutive, frail, yet powerful human figures, there are such compatriot figures as these: "tightly bunched swamp paperbarks" in the vicinity of Moore River, "giant marri gums" in more open areas of country, and forests of "banksia, prickly bark and Christmas trees" that populate the dry areas of sand dunes (Garimara 82–83). "[B]eautiful" kangaroo paw flowers, "from the smallest" variety, the "yellow and orange cat's paw," to the larger varieties of "yellow and green and black" kangaroo paw (83), also count among those figures, as do the "zamia palms" that once were interspersed among the "clumps of grass trees" north of the Moore River (89). "[S]cattered here and there" in the same area of country are "wandoo and mallee gums" (89). Further north, after a week's walking for Molly, Gracie, and Daisy, there are acacia trees and mallee gums (106). They give way, further north still, to "red soil, tall, thick mulgas, gidgies and the beautiful bright green kurrajong trees that [stand] out against the grey-green colours of the other vegetation" (106). A "green carpet of everlasting flowers," soon to become a "blaze of pink, white and yellow papery flowers," mantles the ground (106).

Critical plant studies and postcolonial ecocriticism studies as well as the older discipline of natural history studies offer insights into Garimara's record of country as it refers to Australia's understudied biota. The publications include Vincent Serventy's *Dryandra*; John Ryan's *Green Sense: The Aesthetics of Plants, Place and Language*; Ryan's *Posthuman Plants* and *Rethinking the Vegetal through Culture, Art, and Poetry*; Jessica White's "Georgiana Molloy, Botanical Networks and Naming in 19th Century Western Australia"; and Tony Hughes-d'Aeth's "Salt Scars: John Kinsella's Wheatbelt." Ryan's and White's studies refer to and cite Noongar people's knowledge of country as well as what newcomers were saying about it in the time between 1788 and today. The latter people mainly were learning about country through critical lenses grinded and polished to accommodate Western European values and beliefs. In countless instances, newcomers destroyed country out of a mixture of fear, distaste, and sheer ignorance. Some of those newcomers consciously and aggressively carried out this destruction; others did so without fully realizing what they were doing. The latter newcomers include Georgiana Molloy (1805–1843), a botanist "unwittingly embedded" in the destruction of country even as she respected and sought to preserve the language of its people. Molloy wrote down the Noongar names for local flora alongside names based on Carl Linnaeus's taxonomy and "Western naming system" (White 8).[4] Her notebooks are one of countless newcomers' records of a country that today is "haunted by extinction" (8).

In the nineteenth and twentieth centuries, pastoral enterprises rapidly replaced Australia's older animal and plant ecologies. Those activities brought prosperity to many Australians and impoverished many others, people who were more willing to accommodate, make room for, and coexist with the environment. In 1826, in the southwest corner of Western Australia, the traditional country of Noongar people, English newcomers set up a military post at Albany, then called King George Sound. Three years later, newcomers established the first civilian settlement, the Swan River Colony, in what is now Freemantle, south of Perth. What followed after 1826 was ecocide on a massive scale, as more new arrivals claimed vast acreages of "Arcadian" country for the farming of cattle, sheep, and wheat (Garimara 11, 18).[5] Between 1900 and 1930, pastoralists cleared 17 million acres (approximately 70,000 km^2) for wheat (Graham). In the 20 years between 1950 and 1970, wheat growers cleared another 20 million acres (approximately 81,000 km^2) (Graham). Seventeen indigenous groups of Australians lost their country in the same period of time (Graham). In 1973, three years after Serventy's study was published, a survey of a mere 50 m^2 of "remnant bushland" near the northern wheat belt town of Eneabba (about 270 km north of Perth) yielded a finding of 13,000 individual plants (Hughes-d'Aeth, "Salt Scars" 19). This surviving ecosystem is one of the most "botanically diverse Mediterranean ecosystems in the world" (Ryan, *Green Sense* 3). It is part of a region whose "geographical isolation by ocean and desert, coupled with a temperate yet oscillating climate," allows for a speciation "rivalled only by canopies of tropical rainforests" (Hughes-d'Aeth, "Salt Scars" 18). What survives of it, the old country, also includes what is now called the Dryandra State Forest, 27,000 ha of "discontinuous blocks" of bushland at the western edge of the "Central Southern Wheatbelt" ("Dryandra Forest"), and an area of bushland in the Busselton-Augusta area, where Georgiana Molloy and her husband once lived. The latter area was given official recognition in 2003 for being one of Australia's 15 national diversity hotspots (Jessica White 8). Thirty-five percent of the plants that make their home there are endemic, or "occur in uncultivated conditions only within that region's geo-geographical boundaries" (Ryan, *Green Sense* 3).

Banksias and zamia palms, plants that make a prominent appearance in Garimara's book, have life spans of up to 500 years (Ryan, *Green Sense* 200; *Posthuman Plants* 2). Both species held great value for the Noongar (Ryan, *Green Sense* 312). They used the flower heads of banksias to make a nectar drink, the cones of the *Banksia grandis* to make fighting clubs, and the bracts of the cones, which have smoldering properties when lit, as portable fire. They carried the lit cones in fire resistant paperbark (melaleuca bark) containers and after using the cones to light fires at campsites recycled the cones and turned them into water bottles (*Green Sense* 312). They also relied on the banksia flower, which "spikes on the warm north face first in the southern hemisphere in an arc following the sun," as a travel guide (312). In other areas of Australia, Aboriginal Australians burned the cones of banksia (*Banksia dentata*) as a cure for diarrhea (312).

Zamia palms were equally valued. Australia's oldest people "relished" its farinaceous cyad fruit (which has a flavor similar to that of chestnuts) (Serventy 97–98). They called the fruit *by-yu* (Serventy 98; Ryan, *Green Sense* 76). Before eating it, they first dried it and either steeped it in water or buried it in moist earth (*Green Sense* 76). Colonial-settler people were mostly indifferent toward or disliked zamias because of the experience of indigestion and vomiting after eating zamia fruit; they called that condition the "zamia staggers" (286). (Ryan writes about that in a poem entitled "Sunday Zamia Swagger" [286].) Other newcomers appreciated the zamias, and not the least for their astonishingly lithic, geological character. Serventy quotes these lines from a poem by Judith Wright about one of the zamia cyad species: "Among the complicated birds and flowers, / They seem a generation carved in stone" (96).

As Serventy writes about the Christmas trees (*Nuytsia floribunda*), another plant that makes an appearance in *Follow the Rabbit-Proof Fence* (Garimara 83), when the trees flower in the winter month of June, they are "black trunk[s] alight with the blazing golden torch set against the bleached blue of an Australian sky" (Serventy 106). Grass trees or balga trees (*Xanthorrhoea preissii*) also appear in Garimara's book (89). White Australians called them "blackboys," a colonial-era description reflecting the putative resemblance between the dark black trunks of the trees and "the distant appearance of Nyoongar" (Ryan, *Green Sense* 140). Like the zamia palms, balgas are a "primordial and profoundly slow-growing" tree species that have lifespans of more than 500 years (Ryan, *Posthuman Plants* xi, 16). Serventy describes them as they appear in the hot month of January as "Black spearmen on a cloth of gold" when seen from a distance and "tall, twisted grass trees, not brandishing spears but waving long brown flowering spikes" when seen close up (15). Noongar people used the leaves of the trees for thatching or for torches, the dead flower stems for spears, the living flower stalks for a fermented drink, and the sticky resin for construction of implements (Ryan, *Green Sense* 140).

Garimara also mentions the Mangles Kangaroo Paw (*Anigozanthos manglesi*), or Red and Green Kangaroo Paw (83), a plant that is endemic to southwest Australia and has been the floral emblem of Western Australia since 1960. She mentions in addition wandoo (*Eucalyptus wandoo*) and marri trees (*Corymbia calophylla*) (83). White settlers appreciated the wandoo, a eucalypt tree species, mainly for its usefulness as a construction material. They used it in "bridge [building], wharf planking, wheelwright's and millwright's work, knees of boats and shipbuilding generally" (Serventy 67). When it was used in the construction of "undercarriages of trucks," the wood lasted "twenty years" (Serventy 67). Marri takes its name from a Noongar word that denotes flesh, meat, and sustenance (Ryan, *Green Sense* 220). It is also known as redgum, a reference to the tree's dark red resin or *kino*. Noongar people used marri trees to make an antiseptic and both white and black people used it to make a tonic for alleviating diarrhea (Ryan, *Green Sense* 220; Serventy 52).[6]

Ryan is foremost a critical plant studies scholar, but where he cites Noongar oral histories and conducts interviews with Noongar elders about country he frequently crosses over into the terrain of postcolonial ecocritical studies. In one of these interviews, Noel Nannup, a Noongar elder, recalls "the destruction of indigenous vegetation near the coastal town of Geraldton" (about 415 km north of Perth) (Ryan, *Green Sense* 200).[7] As a child growing up in the 1960s and 1970s, he "watched [that vegetation] get smashed to smithereens" (qtd. in Ryan, *Green Sense* 200). A million acres of bush were being cleared annually at that time. "That's heartbreaking," Nannup continues,

> And my father would say "This is Australia's greatest asset, its natural vegetation and look what we're doing to it" as we followed the bulldozers along around places like Dalwallinu, Wongan Hills, Ballidu, Talingeri ... We were sad to watch it ... How do you cope, when your dad's telling you that these [plants] are our totems and yet we're watching them get smashed to bits. (qtd. in Ryan, *Green Sense* 200)

In another interview, Noongar elder Robert Bropho compares white settlers' felling of trees to genocidal policies. Noongar people were "felled" alongside the trees (Ryan, *Green Sense* 78). Looking at some old photographs of timber—"the logs laying there with no limbs on them"—Bropho compares the logs to the "body of a Blackman ... from the neck down to his ankles and everything's been trimmed ... that hurts me" (qtd. in Ryan, *Green Sense* 78).

Such oral histories join with Garimara's *Follow the Rabbit-Proof Fence*, and Kim Scott's novel *Benang*, recipient of the prestigious Miles Franklin Literary Award. In *Benang*, the young protagonist Harley slowly and painfully reconstructs his Noongar family history after discovering a genealogy of his family written down by his white assimilationist grandfather, Ernest Scat Solomon, a devotee of A. O. Neville. In the first decades of the twentieth century, Harley's Aboriginal great-great-grandfather, Sandy "One" Mason, deliberately passes as a white man in order to protect his children from being abducted by white authorities under Stolen Generation policies. Affectionately called "almost-a-white-man" by his family (Scott 319), Sandy follows the first telegraph line that was constructed in Western Australia to a town where he and his wife, Fanny Benang (categorized as a *full-blood* under the current racist legislative language) (195), seek to register the birth of their daughter Harriette and so protect her from the fate of becoming one of the thousands of Stolen Generations children. He describes the felled trees that now are "straight and upright posts" of telegraph poles stretching across country. They are still "raw and red, the life smell still clinging to them" (178).

Lucy Treloar's *Salt Creek*, shortlisted for the 2016 Miles Franklin Literary Award, is another novel that functions as a record of the twin histories of ecocide and genocide. *Salt Creek* traces the fortunes of the Jane Eyre-ish figure of Hester Finch and Finch's family, who have settled in the Younghusband Peninsula along South Australia's southeast coast in the 1850s. The young protagonist describes the felling of a great tree by her father and brothers. Hester, an unusual newcomer in the sense that she has glimmerings of awareness that her people's notions of progress are terribly flawed, watches her father "directing the angles of the cuts" of the two-handed saw wielded by her brothers and "chopping in at the corners" of the tree with his own axe (173). She watches her brothers "worrying away" at the tree, too, with the saw (173). As the tree trembles, Hester remembers a picture that she once saw of "a bear being baited by bulldogs" (173). Then, in a weak concession to her father and brothers' claims of superior wisdom, she says that she may simply be imagining that the tree is a suffering being not unlike suffering human and nonhuman animal beings (175).

Follow the Rabbit-Proof Fence is about attempts by newcomers to weed out, remove, and eradicate many animal and plant species that populated Australia either before or after 1788 as well as the people of 1788—among them, Garimara's people in western Australia's Pilbara country, Scott's Noongar people in the southwest of Western Australia, and the Ngarrindjeri people in country in the southeast of South Australia, in what is now called the Younghusband Peninsula, the setting of Treloar's historical fiction. Foremost among the animal and plant species that newcomers came to intensely dislike and attempt to eliminate was the European rabbit (*Oryctolagus cuniculus*). Newcomers introduced these animals to Australia in 1788. Six hundred years earlier, in 1176, people in the British Isles introduced rabbits into that region of Europe, "presumably to improve the protein diet of the peasantry" (Neil White 19). In Australia, the animals thrived, quickly overrunning the Australian continent to the consternation of pastoralists (Rolls 21).

The first five rabbits arrived in New South Wales aboard one of the ships of the First Fleet. A second consignment of rabbits, from Capetown, South Africa, arrived in 1791. By the mid-1820s rabbits were breeding around houses in Sydney. In the early 1820s, newcomers released wild rabbits into Tasmania. By 1824, workers in a firm in the capital city of Hobart were making felt hats from a seeming inexhaustible supply of rabbit skins. In 1829, on the mainland, rabbits were imported to Swan River, Western Australia, and in 1834 they were imported to Portland, Victoria. By 1837, rabbits had migrated to the capital city of Adelaide in South Australia. In 1839, they were populating the city of Ballarat in the northwest of Victoria. In 1859, the grazier Thomas Austin introduced wild rabbits to his property in Barwin, Victoria. This introduction was a so-called "harmless addition to the activity of hunting animals for sport" (Agricultural Protection Board). Within eight years, descendants of Austin's rabbits had made homes for themselves at Barwon Heads, on the Bellarine Peninsula in Victoria. By the early 1890s, they were "in plague proportions" in western Victoria (around Colac, Hamilton, Portland, and Warrnambool) and in South Australia around Mount Gambier (Eather and Cottle). In New South Wales, in the 1860s, the pastoralist Thomas Holt bred rabbits at his Marrickville property on the Cook's River. By the 1880s, the descendants of those lapin residents had moved west to Camden and south to Bulli. By 1894, they had advanced across the Nullarbor Plain and reached Western Australia's border.[8]

Rabbits thrived. They also died in large numbers because of overpopulation. In "It's Grand," composed in upbeat, jaunty iambic tri-meter verse by one of Australia's most popular newcomer poets (Andrew Barton) "Banjo" Paterson (1864–1941), the speaker jests,

> It's grand to be a rabbit
> And breed till all is blue
> And then to die in heaps because
> There's nothing left to chew.[9]

Rabbits died "in heaps" also from human consumption of rabbits, in industries that included the trade in rabbit meat as well as rabbit fur, such as the felt hat trade in Hobart that started up in the early 1820s. A hundred years later, in the 1920s, the rabbit fur and meat industry in southeastern Australia (in southern Queensland, New South Wales, Victoria, Tasmania, and eastern South Australia) was the largest employer of labor in the country (Eather and Cottle). Over 20,000 trappers worked full-time, trapping and poisoning rabbits for their carcasses and skins. Thousands more workers were employed in numerous freezer works, grading, sorting, packing, skinning, and transporting rabbit carcasses by the "tens of millions" (Eather and Cottle). Thousands more people were employed in skin-buying firms located throughout rural areas and in capital cities. Hundreds of people sold rabbits in the streets in cities or worked in small goods shops that retailed rabbits. Nearly 10,000 workers made felt hats out of rabbit skins, gelatin from rabbit skin scraps, fertilizer and animal feed from the remains of rabbits deemed unfit for human consumption, and packing boxes (made from pinewood) for the rabbit export trade (Eather and Cottle).

The so-called rabbit-proof fences number among the many attempts by newcomers to curb rabbit populations. The title of Garimara's book refers to the first of three long fences constructed to stop the invasion of rabbits from eastern Australia into pastoralist properties in the west of Australia. It was the fence that enabled Garimara's mother, sister, and cousin to find their way home. Construction on the first fence, also known as the State Barrier Fence, State Vermin Fence, and Emu Fence, began in 1901. The fence covered a distance of 1,834 km, running from south to north, from near the port of Esperance (on the Southern Ocean) to the Eighty Mile Beach above Port Hedland (Garimara 31).[10] Two more fences were constructed in 1904 and 1906. The town of Jigalong was one of the depots for workers hired to construct the first rabbit-proof fence; it was where Molly's mother Maude was born and where Thomas Craig, Molly's white father, worked as a government inspector (32, 109). Many of Molly and Maude's people, the Mardu and the Budidjara, moved to the Jigalong depot from their country further north, as attacks on them by white settlers became more frequent. Garimara describes the fence at Jigalong as a beacon of "love, home and, security" for her people as well as "typical response to a problem of [newcomers'] own making" and their "futile attempt" to marginalize an unwanted fellow creature (Garimara 109). Harley, the protagonist in Scott's novel *Benang*, compares the rabbit barriers to the Great Southern Railway that "first fenced off the [southwest] corner" of the Australian continent (322). The constructions reflect ambitions that were utterly devoid of any moral consideration whatsoever of either the people of 1788 or the flora and fauna that apparently stood in the way of those aims.

The building of the rabbit-proof fences in Australia was a relatively benign attempt to keep out an unwanted animal species. A later practice, the infection of rabbits with the mosquito-borne viral disease myxomatosis, a method akin to the poisoned bait that farmers use today to kill dingoes, was not. The Commonwealth Science and Industrial Research Organization (CSIRO) first released the myxomatosis virus in Australia in 1951. Farmers and "diligent rabbit inspectors, aided and abetted by their employers, the Pastures Protection Boards," accelerated the spread of the virus by inoculating rabbits directly and mixing the infected animals with healthy ones (Eather and Cottle). By mid-1953, as much as four-fifths of rabbits in southeast Australia had died from the virus. The infection causes painful swelling and discharge from the eyes, nose, and anogenital regions. Death from it is slow and agonizing.

Deliberate infection of rabbits with myxomatosis significantly declined after 1972, the date of publication of *Watership Down*, a novel by the English author Richard Adams. Journalist Christopher Hitchens writes about the enormous influence that Adams's "lapine masterpiece" had in bringing public attention in the United Kingdom to the "horrible laboratory-confected disease" of myxomatosis (360). The novel was remarkable not only because it evoked better than any book before it the world of "hedgerows and chalk-downs and streams and spinneys" of Kenneth Grahame's beloved work of children's literature, *The Wind in the Willows*, but also because it succeeded in doing what no scientific paper had been able to achieve (360). Similar to Rachael Carson's *Silent Spring*, a narrative that was instrumental in halting farmers' widespread use of the pesticide DDT on agricultural crops in the United States, Adams's *Watership Down* mobilized the British public to protest the "gassing and massacre" of and "organized cruelty" against rabbits (360–361).

The central trope of the rabbit-proof fence in *Follow the Rabbit-Proof Fence* elicits connections between attempts by the Department of Native Affairs to weed out so-called pure or full-blood Aboriginal Australians and efforts by the Australian wheat and livestock industry to halt the western spread of rabbits in the early decades of the twentieth century. Today, a century later, comparisons between the suffering of nonhuman animals and that of human animals no longer are routinely overlooked or regularly met with acrimony and ridicule among literary and cultural studies scholars. Yet, many of these scholars still hold that art and literature are provinces under which the lives of humans should be given far more moral consideration than others' lives. A "particularly pertinent example" of the hostile response to comparisons between the suffering of nonhuman animals and suffering of human animals concerns a 1988 study by Marjorie Spiegel, *The Dreaded Comparison: Human and Animal Slavery*; Spiegel was severely criticized for making analogies between the enslavement of African people and the enslavement of animals (Huggan and Tiffin 136). Another example is found in J. M. Coetzee's novel *Elizabeth Costello*. The eponymous heroine, a university professor, causes a furor among her peers when she delivers a lecture in which she compares the Holocaust—the murder of more than six million Jewish people under Adolf Hitler's Nazi government—to the fates of industrially farmed animals.

Coetzee also compares the fates of enslaved and incarcerated nonhuman animals to those of humans in a work of nonfiction, in an essay entitled "The Lives of Animals." It appears in a collection of essays (edited by animal studies scholar Amy Gutman) that engages with the moral and ethical dilemmas surrounding humans' many uses of animals and with questions of why and under what particular conditions do humans reduce both human and nonhuman animals to a thing or being without rights.

In mainstream society, "any direct or metaphorical connection" between the abuse of the human and other animal species continues to be "a politically dangerous one to argue, whatever the obvious analogies," and many literary and cultural studies continue to close doors in their disciplines to scholars who are interested in pursuing those connections (Huggan and Tiffin 136). While these scholars can no longer use with predictable professional impunity the word "animal" to denote something or someone that is base, primitive, insensitive, and stupid, then that use of the word continues to abound in literary and cultural studies.

Walkabout

Ironically, the escalation after the nineteenth century of "massive, industrialized, and intensive modes of violence against animals" aided the emergence of the "counterforce of animal protection" in the twentieth century (Calarco 113). "Unequal" and "protracted" as it is, the fight over "the question of violence and compassion toward animals" is a significant struggle and informs a "broad spectrum of movements, activist engagements, and theoretical articulations" (113). This work includes the areas of critical inquiry of postcolonial ecocriticism, animal studies, and plant studies, and it appears also in aesthetic production, in such texts as Garimara's *Follow the Rabbit-Proof Fence*, Scott's *Benang*, and Lucy Treloar's *Salt Creek*. Director Nicolas Roeg's film *Walkabout* is another one of those texts.

The film opens with unglamorous shots of the anthropogenic environments that replaced ecogenic environments along much of the east coast of Australia by the middle of the twentieth century. Vehicular traffic, bitumen roads, concrete curbs, high rise buildings, and other urban-industrial infrastructure and anthropogenic things of a city are shot in drab, muted, monochromatic hues. People hurry along the streets, step off trams, alight from other vehicles, and enter and exit buildings hardly aware of where they are exactly or what they are doing. One of these city dwellers comes home to a high-rise apartment. It is modern, even luxurious, but Roeg films it in such a way that the exterior appears hard and alien and the interior cramped and confined. The man is battling some kind of crisis, possibly to do with his work for, as viewers later find out, a mining company. A stiff drink in hand, he leans out over a small balcony above a concrete swimming pool where two children frolic. Side by side with the pool is the sea, blocked off from the pool and the urban environs of the apartment building as a whole by a formidable mass of concrete slab.

A woman, about the same age as the man, slices pieces of melon in the small and confined space of the kitchen. Her expression is one of boredom, resignation, and distantness. Like her male partner, she appears fatigued. A lit cigarette dangles from a sideboard near her, almost touching the shiny skinned fruit that she slices. The fruit has an artificially lacquered or cosmetic look. The polychromatic colors remind one of acrylic paints. The faintly repulsive, disturbing images of the commercially packaged and produced fruit—it seems too ripe, too fleshy, too exposed, naked, or pornographic—manifestly contrast with the representations of native flora and fruit that appear later in the film, in the scenes where a white boy and girl, about nine and fourteen years of age, respectively, walk in the bush with a black boy, who is perhaps one or two years older. The wild berries that the black boy finds for the white children seem understated, modest, and hardy in comparison with the lascivious, louche, and adulterated fruit that the white children's mother prepares for them days before. Roeg depicts the commercially produced packaged fruit in pornographic visual language. That eroticization contrasts with his filmic depictions of the naturally produced wild fruit. The obvious message is that something possessing great integrity was ransacked, cheapened, debased, and defiled after 1788, as successive governments transformed country from integrated human–environment spaces into hyper-controlled, -commodified, and -segregated human–environment spaces.

In subsequent images of a city playground and botanical garden, Roeg films the playground in hard, un-giving, and graceless language, just as he films the city streets and buildings in earlier scenes in the film, and he films the botanical garden such that it appears as drab and lifeless as its concrete surrounds. One feels sorry for the plants. Neatly labeled, evenly spaced, separated from one another by wire and walking paths, each flora specimen appears isolated, alone, cut off, resigned, and eerily quiet. Here again, the film prompts viewers to ask what has been lost in replacing older so-called natural environments with urban-industrial environments. It implicitly argues that under that takeover Australians prostitute, parade, sequester, and pimp country.

In another scene in *Walkabout*, the man drives a black Volkswagen bug out to the bush. The two children sit in the back of the car's hot stifling interior. The car lurches unceremoniously across untarmacked and unmarked roads. At one point, the children's father stops the car and makes notations on a piece of paper, a list of mineral and other geological deposits. With his spare hand, he ineffectively drives away the flies that collect about his draggle of hair and flushed face. He makes a second stop and all three figures alight from the car. It seems that he has taken the children out for a picnic lunch, but as the girl begins to set out food some distance from the car, her father, who is standing by the car, takes out a firearm and shoots at his two children. The children take cover behind some flora. Their father then sets fire to the car with a container of petrol and kills himself with the gun that he aimed at his children moments before.

Stranded in the bush, the two children are rescued by an Aboriginal boy. Not long before he brings the white children into a town, the boy dies. The film does not make explicit the cause of his death; however, the suggestion is that he committed suicide by hanging himself because he could no longer bear seeing and experiencing the destruction of country by a people who seem to be mostly intent on exploiting the Australian continent and hardly interested in it according to the belief that country should be shared by people and other beings alike.

In addition to the scene of the Aboriginal boy's death, *Walkabout* carries scenes of men armed with rifles and shooting native animal species—kangaroos and wallabies—in legalized commercial culls. Roeg depicts the violence in chaotic, uncontrolled, and even frenzied visual language. In contrast, in the scenes depicting the black boy killing animals for food for himself and his two young companions, the violence is represented as being hardly gratuitous. The legalized commercial animal culling scenes evoke "the spree." In the media today, a spree refers to mass shootings. Older meanings refer to the sexual exploitation of Aboriginal Australian women by male newcomers. In colonial times, they preyed on, abducted, and raped black women, often on breaks from their work in remote areas of Australia. Treloar's *Salt Creek* refers to that largely unaddressed and unacknowledged version of spree. Hester Finch's brothers go on a spree not far from where they have settled on the Younghusband Peninsula in South Australia in the mid-nineteenth century (Treloar 238–244). Scott's *Benang* also alludes to this kind of spree as it took place in remote areas of Western Australia in the same time period. The protagonist Harley's great-great-uncle, Sandy "Two" Mason, the son of Sandy "One" Mason and Fanny Benang, recalls one of those sprees in particular. It involved Sandy Two's sister, Dinah. She is sexually exploited by several white men and has given birth to a child during one of the sprees that regularly take place at the time of "that combination of things called Christmas" (Scott 221). The men who have sexual relations with Dinah and then abandon her when she becomes pregnant are hunting kangaroos. When Sandy Two and his father (Sandy One) come across Dinah alone with her baby, she and the newborn infant are close to death—"Mother and child lay among blood, shit, the stale mess of birth" (219)—and surrounded by the carcasses and "smell—well, call it a stench—" of dead kangaroos (219). Sandy and his father see in the distance a boat heaving in and out of the sea. The boat is piled with kangaroo skins and carries (two of the three of) the men who sexually exploited and then abandoned Dinah:

> two blood-spattered men were lifted into the stormy sky. The men were laughing and, having waved a little goodbye, randomly fired into the sea, and into the birds and kangaroo hides dancing around them in an ever upward spiral. It was the ending of a spree. The men's crotches bulged, thinking of the mother. (220)

In his neo-western crime-thriller film, *Mystery Road*, Ivan Sen refers to this same kind of spree as it is taking place in the present century. In the film, *roo* hunters sexually prey on and murder Aboriginal women in Winton, a remote rural town in Queensland. Roeg's film explicitly alludes neither to that kind of neo-colonial spree nor to the older colonial form to which Treloar and Scott refer. However, the film's sexualized, quasi-pornographic representation of commercial animal killing and commercial food production evokes the nefarious colonial and postcolonial spree. It is one that is hardly mentioned by the popular media.

Prior to 1788, Australian people relied on kangaroo meat as "an important food source," not a for-profit commodity (Boom et al. 20). The animals "provided up to 91% of energy intake" during some time of the year and 84% of energy intake at other times in the year (20). Aboriginal people killed the animals using different strategies inclusive of "pursuit by dogs, spearing and clubbing, ambush, battues and encirclement, stockages, pit-fall traps, and flushing out with fire" (20). The animals "were killed only as immediately needed" (21).

Since 1788, Australians have hunted kangaroos mostly for gratuitous reasons. Among newcomers, the meat of the animals initially "provided an occasional supplement to imported rations and was traded with Aboriginal people or sold privately and then through the public market from 1793" (Boom et al. 21). The meat was also a "low-cost meat relative to that from introduced livestock" (21). However, when newcomers "were in a position to import and raise sufficient livestock to meet their protein needs," they began to kill kangaroos "primarily for recreational reasons" (22). Landholders hunted kangaroos for sport using dogs, "mimicking the fox hunting parties of the British upper classes" (22). Kangaroo killing also functioned as "a rite of passage for ambitious young men to … establish their colonial credentials" (Gelder and Weaver, "The Australian Kangaroo Hunt Novel (1830–1858) as *Bildungsroman*").[11]

Kangaroos are classified under the *Macropus* genus and are its "large and intermediate" animals (Boom et al. 18). Wallabies make up the smaller animals in that genus (18). The *Macropodoidea* (superfamily) under which kangaroos are classified according to modern taxonomy evolved around 20 or 25 million years ago. Approximately ten million years ago, the modern large kangaroos emerged. Those animals include the red, eastern grey, and western grey kangaroo and the common, Antilopine, and black wallaroo. Adult male red kangaroos now are Australia's largest terrestrial mammalian wildlife, weighing up to 92 kg. In the nineteenth century, as claims on country by pastoralists increased, newcomers sought to eradicate as many kangaroos and wallabies as possible. They argued that the animals were pests and competed with their livestock for feed. They further contended that the kangaroo numbers were much higher than they were before 1788 because of the decline in both Aboriginal populations and dingo populations (22). Despite limited evidence for this argument, it was widely accepted. In the 1880s, the states in eastern Australia introduced legislation "for the destruction of macropods" (23). Kangaroos and wallabies were declared to be vermin in New South Wales. In 1884, in one district alone (Tamworth), 260, 780 animals were killed (23). In Queensland, between 1877 and 1907, eight million kangaroos were killed under one of the bounty programs established in Australia's eastern states (23). Between 1877 and 1987, 65 million kangaroos were killed. The main reason given for "this mass killing" was the need to protect the pastoral industry (23). Key stakeholders argued that the industry played a necessary "economic role" in Australia, and especially so "in terms of exports" (23).[12]

The establishment in 1888 of the Committee for the Protection of Native Birds and Mammals represents one of the first efforts to legally protect kangaroos and wallabies. Nonetheless, "systematic killing" and "massive exploitation" of the animals continued, shaping the present century and twentieth century as much as it shaped colonial Australia (Boom et al. 25). Organized and systematic kangaroo culls are comparable to industrial slaughters of sheep and cows.

When the kangaroo meat industry first emerged in the 1950s, kangaroo meat was mostly sold for pet food domestically and exported abroad for human consumption (Boom et al. 25). Twenty years later, public opposition succeeded in persuading state governments to enact legislation "to protect wildlife in general and to manage kangaroo populations" (Boom et al. 27). Most of the state governments also "placed a ban on the sale of kangaroo meat for human consumption" (27). Roeg's film *Walkabout* is set against this 1970s background—the growing public awareness of the kangaroo meat industry—a well as against the slightly early historical backdrop of Aboriginal land rights, which took place in the mid-1960s (Heiss and Minter 4). However, the success of animal rights groups in persuading the government to ban kangaroo killing was short-lived. By 1975, the Commonwealth Government had disposed of the ban and once again legalized the export of kangaroo meat (Senate Select Committee on Animal Welfare, qtd. in Boom et al. 27). Approximately a decade after this, the Senate Select Committee on Animal Welfare reported that cruelty to kangaroos had become institutionalized under the legislated management of them (27). The government ignored these findings and instead "supported the continuation of the industry" on the basis that "regular killing reduces the number of kangaroos [and] … reduces the pressure on farmers" (Senate Select Committee on Animal Welfare, qtd. in Boom et al. 28).

In 1998, ten years after the findings report of the Senate Select Committee on Animal Welfare, the Senate Rural and Regional Affairs and Transport References Committee produced a report that endorsed continuing the commercial exploitation of kangaroos (Boom et al. 28). In addition, the committee called for changing mainstream public perception of kangaroos from "pests" to a valuable "resource" (Senate Rural and Regional Affairs and Transport Committee, qtd. in Boom et al. 28). Kangaroo killing now was euphemistically referred to as "a land management tool" (Boom et al. 30). At the same time, in the popular imagination, particularly in rural Australia (Pople and Grigg, qtd. in Boom et al. 30), kangaroos continued to be regarded as "pests."

In the intervening 30 years, the view that kangaroos are vermin has hardly changed. The two most frequently cited rationales for killing kangaroos among pastoralists and kangaroo industry stakeholders are that the animals "compete with livestock for resources in the rangelands" and kangaroo numbers "have increased because of the installation of artificial waterholes" (Boom et al. 30). "[M]inimal evidence" accompanies these claims (30). There is more evidence to support the argument that kangaroos have a "relatively low monetary impact" on the agricultural sector (30).

Today, the commercial killing of kangaroos in Australia for meat and leather takes place in five states: Queensland, New South Wales, South Australia, Western Australia, and Tasmania. Four kangaroo species are commercially killed on the mainland: red kangaroos (*Macropus rufus*), eastern grey kangaroos (*M. giganteus*), western grey kangaroos (*M. fuliginosus*), and common wallaroos (*M. robustus*). In Tasmania, two non-kangaroo species, Bennett's wallabies (*M. robustus*) and Tasmanian pademelons (*Thylogale billardierii*), are killed primarily for their skins. The industry in Australia under which this commercial killing takes place is "the largest consumptive mammalian wildlife industry in the world" (Boom et al. 18).[13]

Twenty years after the release of *Walkabout*, in *Images of Australia: 100 Films of the New Australian Cinema*, film scholar Neil Rattigan situated the film in the New Australia Cinema, a movement that blossomed in the pivotal decade of the 1970s, which profiled more Australian producers, directors, and actors than any other film movement had done since the birth of the technology of film itself (309). Few or no other critics before Rattigan so identified the film. The apparent reason for not including the film in the New Australia Cinema movement was that the director, Nicolas Roeg, and script writer, Edward Bond, were British nationals, and Donald Gordon Payne, the author of the children's novel that inspired the film, was a "London-born" author (308–309).[14]

A second reason for the omission, one that is less understandable in hindsight, as Rattigan argues, relates to the film's "obsession with the Australian landscape" (309). The film was the only Australian film released between the 1950s and 1990s that gave the Australian landscape a central role. It "is more than a character, more than a visual expression of the film's themes; the landscape *is* the film" (309). Other film critics and film studies scholars have since made that same observation. Roeg's film (along with Canadian film director Ted Kotcheff's 1971 film *Wake in Fright*) was a response to "the beauty and poetry in a landscape [that] many Australians took for granted as cruel and ugly"; it "lovingly captured [the environment's] rich colours and textures" and is a "classic [example] of how foreign eyes can see and understand local issues with a clarity unimagined at home" (Scott Murray 72). *Walkabout* "destroyed the cliché of the Dead Heart, and made us Australians see it from a unique perspective, as something wondrous, mysterious and sensuous. It took a stranger … to reveal it to us" (Nowra qtd. in Alexis Wright 23). That cynosure was taken to be "so completely an outsider's response to Australia" (Rattigan 309) that *Walkabout* was not included in Australian film canons up through the 1980s.[15]

Aided by the film script of Edward Bond, "the British heir to Antonin Artaud's 'theatre of cruelty,'" Roeg took Payne's children's novel—an etiolate, sentimental "parable" about lost innocence (Siegel 34)—and transformed it into a postcolonial ecocritical indictment of the governance of Australia after 1788. "[Verging] on travesty," the film flouts the rules of decorum dictated by a political class that effectively had ruled Australia since 1949. That class was toppled, albeit incompletely and inconclusively, between 1972 and 1975 and 1983 and 1996 by the Whitlam (1972–1975), Hawke (1983–1991), and Keating (1991–1996) governments. Roeg's film reflects some of the political and social inequities that those governments tried to overhaul with more or less amounts of lasting success. Those inequities include ecophobic attitudes toward Australia's pre-1788 environments.

In the opening pages of *The Fatal Shore: A History of the Transportation of Convicts to Australia between 1787–1868*, Robert Hughes writes about the English, Irish, Welsh, and Scottish convicts who were sentenced to be transported to the penal colonies in Australia. The human transports were certain they were being sent to a place of no return, a vast unchartered underworld comparable to a Spenserian "filthy maw" (Hughes 787).[16] The guards and the administrators who accompanied the convict transports had similar misgivings about the remote antipodean realm that awaited them. Australia "remained as obscure and unimaginable after [the English explorer] Captain James Cook's death [in 1799] as it had been before his birth, and as monstrous: an oceanic hell" (43). Hughes thus describes the arrival of the First Fleet in 1788: "their sails like stained clouds, [the boats] moved up the harbor to Sydney Cove, and the anchors splashed, and the outcasts of Mother England were disgorged upon this ancestral territory to build their own prison" (18).

In "Strange Lands: The Lexicon of Settler-Colonial Landscapes in Charles Fletcher Lummis's and Arthur Groom's Portrayals of the American West and the Australian Outback," Tom Lynch, writes about the Anglophone cultural heritages that were "maladaptive in the spacious arid and semi-arid regions" of both "the (American) West and the Australian) Outback" (701).[17] Those heritages constituted "a key element of the settler-colonial condition of both the West and the Outback," playing a critical role in the all but relentless ecophobic processes of "accumulation in both the United States and Australia of dust bowls, massive species extinctions, and other ecological catastrophe" (702). Colonial-settler people "subliminally and consciously produced" testimonies and accounts of "the arid landscapes of Australia" that portray those environments as being "flawed" or "deficient" (if also "exotic, surprising, and in any number of ways, *strange*") (702).

In his comparative colonial-settler analysis of the literature of two former British colonies, Australia and the United States, Lynch also discusses the English language that newcomers used to represent their colonial-settler experiences. Citing a study by Jay Arthur, *The Settler-Colonial Default Country: A Lexical Cartography of Twentieth-Century Australia*, Lynch notes that this language, which had "evolved on a small, green, reliably rainy, and very foggy island," is "poorly suited for representing the landscapes of much of Australia, especially the large, dry, clear, rocky, and multihued landscapes of the arid and semi-arid bioregions that constitute more than 70% of the continent" (702). Alexis Wright lays blame at the feet of the wielders of that language and not on the language itself. It was one of the "weapons of a modern state in a war against memory, deployed in propaganda, camouflaged by upbringing, instruction and popular culture in order to deny the entry of memory—or what should be remembered" (Wright).

Alexis Wright's postcolonial argument appears in her review of Roeg's film. As an "Aboriginal writer reading this fable of English sensibilities," she writes, she is "angered by the film's portrayal of the Aboriginal character, reductively 'Aboriginal boy,' who conveniently commits suicide at the end of the film because he fails to gain the affection of Mary, the white girl he saved." Apart from rudimentary forms of communication, there are no exchanges between the Aboriginal boy and white Australians. "He is in fact muted, silenced" (Wright). This apparently "was not a problem for the purposes of the story," Wright ironically says. The Aboriginal boy is in the film only to provide a

> backdrop, an offering from Indigenous Australia ... The male Aboriginal character in *Walkabout* [is] in fact choked—an idiosyncratic choice—hanging himself from a tree at the end of the film, after leading the girl and her brother to safety. With his silence complete, the film totally succeeds in enforcing an invisibility of the

racial reality of the times, strengthening the dire consequences of a distorted history for Aboriginal people today. (Wright)[18]

Wright's criticism of *Walkabout* alerts critics to how apparently earnest attempts, that is to say attempts that are apparently earnest in the eyes of mainstream white audiences to represent Aboriginal Australian history, consistently fall short of what they purport to accomplish. They reflect the thinnest of understandings of the walkabout itself, or "travel embarked upon by Aboriginal people for the purpose of death and funeral ceremonies, cultural ceremonies, bartering, food, water and so on" (Minter and Heiss 246). For some critics, the film indeed does capture a moment in history, the 1970s, when a majority white Australian population was becoming more aware of country, and the decimation of it. Nonetheless, such awareness does not make a debut in literary and cultural studies, which is dominated by white Australians, colonial-settler people of mostly Anglo-European descent, until the 1990s and establishment of the critical area of inquiry of postcolonial ecocriticism.

In "Teaching the Postcolonial/Ecocritical Dialogue," Erin James asks what kinds of texts should teachers use to teach "ecocritical English" (66). She answers that question by pointing out that "ecocritical English" is not only about reading literary texts "for *environment*," or about reading texts that are or appear to be "mimetic or realistic depictions of nature"; it also is about reading texts "for *environmentality*," or about reading texts for evidence of the ways in which texts are always embedded in and are produced and shaped by people's "ecological homes" (66).

In the "Afterword" of Bonnie Roos and Alex Hunt's co-edited *Postcolonial Green: Environmental Politics and World Narratives*, Ursula Heise addresses postcolonial ecocriticism in the context of doubts about and affirmations of the usefulness that aesthetic production plays in shaping political consciousness.

> Postcolonial as well as ecocritical analyses have often tended to assess creative works most centrally in terms of whether they portray the realities of social oppression and environmental devastation accurately, and what ideological perspectives they imply Such an assessment is undoubtedly necessary, but just as surely if factual accuracy, interesting political analysis, or wide public appeal is what we look for, there are better and more straightforward places to find them than novels and poems ... If we believe—as I assume that most ecocritical and postcolonial critics do—that the aesthetic transformation of the real has a particular potential for reshaping the individual and collective ecosocial imaginary, then the way in which the aesthetic forms relate to cultural as well as biological structures deserves our particular attention. (258)[19]

In the last scenes of *Walkabout*, the white girl Mary now is in her mid- or late 20s. She is standing in a kitchen, preparing food. These scenes and the figure of the young, thirtyish something man who stands behind Mary mirror the time approximately ten years earlier, captured in the opening scenes of the film. Mary, in these last scenes, resembles her mother in the opening scenes; she has a slightly slumped posture, and an air of resignation and defeat cling to her. A memory of her youth then comes to her. She recalls when she and her brother and the black boy were together in the outback, eating, hunting, playing, and swimming together. The film flashes back to that time. Accompanying the flashback is a voice-over recording of lines from a poem ("XL") from *A Shropshire Lad* by A. E. Housman: "Into my heart an air that kills / From yon far country blows: / What are those blue remembered hills, / What spires, what farms are those?...That is the land of lost content, / I see it shining plain, / the happy highways where I went / And cannot come again." Housman's poem nostalgically evokes a past Edenic English rural landscape. As many critics point out, Housman in fact knew that such a landscape had never been.[20] Roeg captures that understanding of Housman in *Walkabout*, a film that dispels the romanticized contours of Australian pastoral. Garimara's *Follow the Rabbit-Proof Fence* also is a record of the dark side of Australian agriculture after 1788.

Les Murray's poem "On the Present Slaughter of Feral Animals" (*Subhuman Redneck Poems*, 37–38) is another such text. It is about Australians' efforts to exterminate, in addition to kangaroos and rabbits, brumbies (feral horses), and feral water buffalos and Asian cattle. The speaker surmises that the planet will not end ecologically. Post-pastoral, as we will see in the next chapter, reflects the effort, as meager as this has been, to choose another route besides the terminal route forecast in Murray's poem.

Notes

1 Molly Craig (later Molly Kelly) died in 2004; Gracie Cross died in 1983; Daisy Kadibil died in 2018 (Williams).
2 Molly subsequently married Toby Kelly, an Aboriginal stockman. She was abducted again, in 1940, along with her two daughters, and taken to Moore River. She escaped a year later, carrying her 18-month-old daughter, Annabelle, and leaving Doris at Moore River, with instructions for a relative to look out for Doris. Doris and her mother were reunited 21 years later (*The Sydney Morning Herald*). (Molly, and Daisy Kadibil and Gracie Cross, elderly women at the time of the release of director Phillip Noyce's film adaptation, *Rabbit-Proof Fence*, appear in the final scenes of this film.)
3 See Rose, *Nourishing Terrains: Australian Aboriginal Views of Landscape and Wilderness* 7.
4 Today, efforts to save the Noongar language include The Wirlomin Noongar Language and Stories Project. Initiated by Kim Scott, the aim of the project is to give back to the project participants the stories of Noongar people that

were collected in the 1930s (preserved in the archives of the American linguist, Gerhardt Laves) (Jessica White 8).

5 Today, the wheat belt extends for approximately 160,000 km^2, an area larger than the size of many European countries (Hughes-d'Aeth, "Salt Scars" 18). In Australian literature, John Kinsella, who grew up in Western Australia's wheat country, is "undoubtedly the key laureate" of that new country and obliteration of Noongar country (Day 174). Other writers who write about the wheat belt include the poet Dorothy Hewett; Elizabeth Jolly, author of the novel *The Well*; and Tom Flood, author of *Oceana Fine*, the "Great Australian Wheatbelt Novel" (Hughes-d'Aeth, *Like Nothing on this Earth* 500). For more on these writers and the wheat belt, see Hughes-d'Aeth's *Like Nothing on this Earth: A Literary History of the Wheatbelt* and Gregory Day's review of Kinsella's collection of poetry ("Review of John Kinsella's *Drowning in Wheat*").

6 Early settlers and explorers mistook the resin of the marri for gum and so called the trees "red gums." The resin, a kino, not a gum, is an astringent that is packed with tannins (Serventy 51).

7 Nannup served as a National Parks ranger and was the first Aboriginal head ranger in Australia (Ryan, *Green Sense* 200).

8 This information is taken directly from Warwick Eather and Drew Cottle's "The Rabbit Industry in Australia, 1870–1970" and the Agricultural Protection Board's "State Barrier Fence of Western Australia, 1901–2001."

9 See Paterson 374.

10 Much of the original fence was still being used and maintained up through the end of the last century. A newer fence was also constructed east of the older fence. It runs southeasterly from Kalbarri in the north to Jerdacuttup in the south and covers 1,170 km (Agricultural Protection Board).

11 Ken Gelder and Rachael Weaver make this argument in their article, "The Australian Kangaroo Hunt Novel (1830–1858) as *Bildungsroman*," in their reading of three works of literature: Sarah Porter's *Alfred Dudley; or, The Australian Settlers* (1830); Sarah Bowdich Lee's *Adventures in Australia; or, the Wanderings of Captain Spencer in the Bush and the Wilds* (1851); and Anne Bowman's *The Kangaroo Hunters; or, Adventures in the Bush* (1858).

12 The legalization of kangaroo killing also spawned a lucrative trade in kangaroo and wallaby skins (Boom et al. 23–24).

13 For more on the ongoing eradication of kangaroo populations, see Gelder and Weaver's "Killing and Sentiment in the Colonial Australian Kangaroo Hunt Narrative."

14 Payne published his novel under the pseudonym of James Vance Marshall. The novel was first published in 1959 under the title of *The Children* and afterward, in 1961, under the title of *Walkabout*.

15 See, for example, Tom Moran and Tom O'Regan's *The Australian Screen* and Graeme Turner's *National Fictions: Literature, Film and the Construction of Australian Narrative*, which do not include mention of *Walkabout*.

16 See Spenser, *The Faerie Queene*, Canto I, Stanza XX.

17 Lummis was a newspaperman (Lynch 703). He first encountered "the strange southwestern corner" of the United States on an "epic walk from Cincinnati to Los Angeles in 1884 and 1885" (703). After working for "several years as a reporter for the *Los Angeles Times*," Lummis "suffered a debilitating stroke that parlay[z]ed his left side" (703). He returned to the southwest to recuperate and traveled throughout the region. The many articles that he wrote about the region, published in magazines and newspapers, form the basis of *Some Strange Corners of Our Country*. Many national parks and

other conservation areas owe their existence in part to Lummis's writings (704). These protected areas include the Grand Canyon, the Petrified Forest, Montezuma's Well, Tonto Natural Bridge, El Morro, and the El Malpais lava flows (704).

Groom was born in Victoria, Australia, in 1904. He was later raised on a cattle station near Longreach in Queensland, where his family relocated when Groom was still a child (Lynch 704). As a young man, he worked as a jackaroo at Lake Nash Station on the border of the Northern Territory. In 1926, he moved to Brisbane to work as a journalist. There, he "became concerned about the protection of nature and in 1930 ... joined with R. M. Collins and Romeo Lahey to create the National Parks Association of Queensland, Australia's first such organization." In 1933, along with Lahey, Groom established Binna Burra Lodge on the edge of the Lamington National Park in southeast Queensland (Lynch 704).

18 For more on Wright in the context of her contribution to Australian literature, most notably the novel *Carpentaria* (winner of the Miles Franklin Award in 2007), and in the context of ecofeminist and postcolonial ecocritical analyses of this novel, see Rigby's essay, "The Poetics of Decolonization: Reading *Carpentaria* in a Feminist Ecocritical Frame." In it, Rigby describes the novel as being an articulation of hope for the dismantling of "alien law" of Australian "masculinist culture" and of, more broadly, the dismantling of "eurowestern patriarchal and 'anthroparchal' thought and social relations" (123, 128). (The term "anthroparchal" is Cudworth's [63–65].) Under the law, Aboriginal Australian women have been among the most oppressed human minority populations.

19 For other seminal postcolonial ecocritical studies, see DeLoughrey, Didur, and Carrigan; DeLoughrey and Handley; and Roos and Hunt.

20 See, for example, Blake Morrison's recent review of Peter Parker's book, *Housman Country*.

3 (Post-)pastoral

Cows and sheep are centripetal tropes in Francesca Rendle-Short's novel *Bite Your Tongue*; Susan Hawthorne's poetry collection *Cow*; and Evie Wyld's eco-gothic fiction *All the Birds, Singing*. Rendle-Short's enlistment of the trope of cow tongue to portray formidable efforts by right-wing groups in Queensland to cut out the tongue, metaphorically speaking, of writers who were shedding light on socially and politically taboo subject matter in the 1970s provokes critical comparison with efforts today by stakeholders in the meat industry to silence animal advocacy speech. Hawthorne's *Cow*, a discernibly feminist text and a winsome, witty, and erudite collection of paeans to the cows of the literary and cultural paddocks of etymology, comparative literature, philosophy, Sanskrit culture, and Ancient Greek myth, makes few references to the cows that are intensively farmed in Australia and are a staple of its economy.[1] The given dearth stands out for ecocritics and animal studies scholars and inspires the discussion here. *All the Birds, Singing* is a superlative post-pastoral text. That is to say, Wyld's novel confronts and grapples with the darker, sadder, venal aspects of the modern pastoral enterprises of sheep and cow farming. Eric Yoshiaki Dando's novel *Oink, Oink, Oink* confronts another animal species that humans heavily depend upon and exploit, the porcine species. Although pigs do not distinguish Australian pastoral and post-pastoral practices or the Australian pastoral and post-pastoral literary landscape, Australians consume pig flesh in large amounts, as do people elsewhere on the planet. Porcine production in Australia has declined in recent decades, but there continues to be a high demand for pork, which is met by importing pig flesh from overseas. Pigs, similarly to cows, are among the world's most intensively farmed animal species; they also are a staple of the biotechnological and biomedical research industries. That subject forms the basis of my discussion of Dando's novel, a surrealistic narrative of the ties between pork production and transgenic experiments on pigs.

Bite Your Tongue

Philomela and Theseus, aka Animal Advocates and the Meat Industry

Bite Your Tongue is a fictionalized account of the battle over works of literature taught in schools in Queensland in the post–World War II decades, when an arch-conservative government controlled the state. The novel represents that historic battle mostly through the eyes of a young girl, Gloria ("Glory") Solider, growing up in the quiet "leafy, university suburb of St Lucia" under the watchful eye of her mother, MotherJoy Solider (Rendle-Short 29). MotherJoy is an active member of the "Moral Right" (43), an allusion to socially and politically conservative groups that were active in Queensland in the 1950s—when Brisbane was not much more than a "big, fat, country town ... in the south-east corner of Queensland" and "everybody did go to church in hats ... and [wear] gloves" (29)—and in the next two decades, for Queensland remained obstinately conservative when "the swinging sixties took a hold in the rest of Australia" (29). As Rendle-Short represents in her narrative, and as it occurred in reality, a powerful right-wing majority in Australia's north-eastern state "dug its heels in" (29) in the 1960s, voted for the Country Party (later renamed the National Party), and brought to the helm one of Australia's most infamous politicians, Joh Bjelke-Petersen, State Premier from 1968 to 1987.

The "Moral Right" in *Bite Your Tongue* alludes specifically to two actual conservative groups: STOP (Society to Outlaw Pornography) and CARE (Campaign Against Regressive Education). Founded by Rona Joyner in 1971 and 1972, respectively, STOP and CARE launched campaigns to remove works of literature from school reading lists on the grounds that the content was immoral (Rendle-Short, "Permissions" 242).[2] The targeted literature included, among hundreds of other books, Ernest Hemingway's *The Sun Also Rises*, J. D. Salinger's *The Catcher in the Rye*, Gunther Grass's *The Tin Drum*, Harper Lee's *To Kill a Mockingbird*, D. H. Lawrence's *The Rainbow* and *Sons and Lovers*, John Steinbeck's *Grapes of Wrath*, Virginia Woolf's *To the Lighthouse*, Arthur Miller's *Death of a Salesman*, Truman Capote's *Breakfast at Tiffany's*, Samuel Beckett's *Waiting for Godot*, Henrik Ibsen's *The Doll's House*, Anton Chekov's *Three Sisters*, and William Golding's *The Lord of the Flies* (Rendle-Short, "Permissions" 240, 242).[3]

In Rendle-Short's fiction, MotherJoy is a major mouthpiece for STOP and CARE. She and other of the groups' members confiscate and burn hundreds of books that affront their political and social sensibilities. In addition to hurling such epithets as "filthy," "[d]irty," "[s]mut," and "garbage" at the books and their authors, MotherJoy "rails against ... permissive educationalists, teachers who [promote] alternative lifestyles, unabashed sex education ... moral corruption, homosexual marriage and lesbianism" (57). Little Gloria does not question her mother's beliefs and behavior. She dutifully follows at the heels of MotherJoy or otherwise stays close to her mother's protective flanks. However, she does have misgivings, jejune as they are, about the values that her mother publicly and privately zealously touts.

In the opening pages of *Bite Your Tongue*, the middle-aged Gloria (who moved away from her mother, politically as well as geographically, many years before) flies up to Queensland to visit and care for MotherJoy, now in her 80s and terminally ill. The reunion between mother and daughter brings back vivid memories of a quarter of a century earlier. Gloria's love for her mother has neither soured nor abated. Nonetheless, she recalls, with more discernment than she had many years before, her childhood years in the house on Durham Street in St. Lucia. "[T]he going" seemed "pineapple-sweet" then; now, in the older Gloria's recollection of it, it appears in a darker light (Rendle-Short 29). The principal metaphor by which Rendle-Short describes the change in Gloria's remembrance of that past is the trope of cow tongue. Gloria remembers MotherJoy often cooking the dish of cow tongue for her, her five sisters (Elsie, Mary, Ruthy, Eve, and Gracie), and their father, the quiet, patient, and forbearing "Onward Solider." Gloria remembers: "[T]ongues and the eating of tongues" then were "ticklish and innocent" (5). They no longer are. Rendle-Short foregrounds the sinister associations of cow tongue in the opening pages of the novel, in the section entitled "It's a Sin." There, the first description of cow tongue—one of many in the novel—begins invitingly—little Glory's "very first taste of tongue" is like her "very first kiss"—and ends in unmistakably off-putting tones:

> Glory wishes she could remember her very first taste of tongue, the first mouthful, that first bite. It is like trying to remember her very first kiss.
>
> You see tongue was Little Glory's favourite food. She asked for it as a special treat on her birthday, even though the Solider family had it served up to them by MotherJoy at least once a week ... they ate pressed tongue and boiled potatoes with the smoothest of white sauces served with the mushiest of pale-green peas from a tin. (9)

Something not quite Edenic lurks in these descriptions of little Glory's love of "pressed tongue ... [served] with 'the smoothest of white sauces' and 'the mushiest of pale-green peas'" (9). The sense of something being not quite right or suspect, or something being *too* perfect, continues and intensifies as the narrative progresses. When Gloria and her younger sister Grace accompany MotherJoy into Brisbane on a Sunday to attend an "anti-Communist march through Queen Street," their mother gives her daughters placards to hold up that bear the slogans, "The Communists

Want Your Children" and "Burn a Book a Day for Jesus" (46). She tells her daughters that "the Communists behind the bamboo curtain" in China "cut out the tongues of 'brave Christians'" (86). Afterward, when she and the "Little Girls" return home, MotherJoy serves them and the other members of the family a supper of cooked cow tongue. It symbolizes, she says, "the punishment for Communists ... 'A tongue for a tongue' ... The price of [the Communists'] sin [is] this precious organ of speech" (86). Naively but not completely acceptingly, little Glory "reckon[s]" that "if MotherJoy really had her way with her morals campaign, her anti-smut ways, she'd not only burn all the books in the world, but she'd cut out the tongues of all the writers of all the wicked books in all the world" (86).

Little Glory's doubts and vague misgivings about MotherJoy's convictions are nurtured by the recruitment of Gloria and her siblings by their mother in her moral crusades. Gloria's nascent awareness of alternative views of the world also is catalyzed by her friendship with Lisa, a slightly older girl enrolled in the same school that Gloria attends. Gloria looks up to Lisa, so when Lisa rebukes her for her consumption of cow tongue, Gloria reluctantly renounces her favorite dish. A tiny but irreparable crack appears in the armor of Gloria's loyalty and devotion to MotherJoy.

> At home, Glory could eat more tongue than her fair share, if none of the others around the table wanted their portion. But at school, at big lunch with all the other school girls, when Lisa told her to stop scoffing the leftover tongue that sat between slices of white bread, she did, she threw it into the scraps bin. From then on Glory had a crunchy peanut paste and homemade marmalade sandwich for lunch. (Rendle-Short 52)

As slight as it is, there is the suggestion that Lisa's family practices veganism or vegetarianism. Admittedly threadbare, the given finding critically ties to other content in that novel that for animal studies and ecocriticism scholars is extraordinarily provocative: the enlistment of cow tongue in a coming-of-age story that focuses on efforts by conservative social and political groups to curb freedom of speech in Queensland in the 1970s.

The trope of severed cow tongue and the particular deployment of it in Rendle-Short's novel evokes a current controversial freedom-of-speech issue, a recent slate of proposed agricultural laws, so-called ag-gag laws. The proposed laws are intended to silence the "tongues" of animal rights groups who seek to publicly disseminate relatively little known facts about the meat industry. Under the proposed ag-gag laws, an individual or group of individuals can be prosecuted for acts such as "accepting work on farms without disclosing links to animal groups," "capturing images without permission," and "distributing those images via the media" (O'Sullivan). Undercover investigators, whistle-blowers, and journalists are chief targets under the proposed laws. They include "criminalising undercover or covert surveillance of commercial animal facilities," "requiring that any obtained footage of animal cruelty...be turned over to enforcement agencies immediately," and "requiring potential employees of commercial animal facilities to disclose current or past ties to animal protection groups" ("Ag-Gag").

As animal studies scholar Siobhan O'Sullivan states, "[t]he age of agricultural innocence [that] extended well into the 1980s ... is over," Australia's "political landscape" is very different from what it was 30 years ago, and Australia's "urban elite" are better informed about animals who are "intensely reared" for human consumption. Yet, the proposed ag-gag laws ominously reflect that any animal advocacy gains in recent decades are not sure footholds. One of the staunchest defenders of the proposed ag-gag laws is Katrina Hodgkinson, Federal Vice President of the National Party of Australia, who in 2014 infamously compared animal activists to "terrorists" when she was the Minister for Primary Industries in New South Wales ("Animal rights activists 'akin to terrorists,' says NSW minister Katrina Hodgkinson"). Western Australian Senators Chris Back (Liberal) and Glenn Sterle (Labor) both also supported the proposed laws (O'Sullivan). If they do come into effect, ethical choices about animal food products will depend more than ever on "the work of a trespassing animal advocate ... not the work of farmers who ... would prefer as few people as possible to know how Babe came to bacon" (O'Sullivan).[4]

The publisher of *Bite Your Tongue*, Spinifex Press, an independent feminist press founded in 1991 by Susan Hawthorne and Renate Klein, supports work that focuses on GLBTQ, indigenous, and environmental rights in addition to women's rights. Their publications include *Ngarrindjeri Wurruwarrin: A World That Is, Was, and Will Be*, by Diane Bell, feminist scholar, anthropologist, and Aboriginal land rights and law reform scholar; *The Coral Battleground*, by the late Judith Wright, one of Australia's most distinguished and celebrated environmental writers, poets, and activists; and *The World According to Monsanto: Pollution, Politics and Power*, by Marie-Monique Robin, winner of the 2010 Rachel Carson Prize.[5] Recently, Spinifex also published Lindsay Simpson's *Adani: Following Its Dirty Footsteps*, about the Adani Group's interest in the Carmichael coal mine in the Galilee Basin and expansion of the port at the Abbot Point coal terminal in Queensland. As the publishers describe the fight to prevent Adani from going ahead with its plans, the battle over the coal mine is "the biggest since [the fight] to prevent the construction of Tasmania's Franklin Dam in the 1980s" (Spinifex Press). Rendle-Short's *Bite Your Tongue* engages with another rights issue, specifically that of embattled freedom of speech acts in defense of humans in Queensland in the post–World War II decades. Rendle-Short's use of the central trope of severed cow tongue to address that issue elicits, in addition, questions about freedom of speech in defense of other kinds of beings—namely nonhuman animals.

Susan Hawthorne's *Cow*, also published by Spinifex Press, ostensibly addresses neither animal advocacy related freedom of speech issues nor human advocacy related issues of free speech. Nonetheless, *Cow*, similarly to *Bite Your Tongue*, is a provocative text for scholars interested in animal advocacy issues in the specific context of the cows of Australia's agro-industries. Hawthorne's oblique and all but absent notice of those animals in *Cow*, a collection mainly devoted to cow figures in ancient European and Asian myth, is part of that provocation.

Cow

In Susan Hawthorne's poetry collection *Cow*, the notable absence of almost any mention of Australia's historically farmed cows immediately brings to mind Carol J. Adams's famous term, "the absent referent," in a study entitled *The Sexual Politics of Meat*, a seminal text for ecofeminists and animal studies scholars. It addresses cows and other industrially farmed animals who are mostly only visible, and deathly present, in the form of meat at the supermarket, milk and mozzarella in the fridge, and steak and sausage on the grill. *Cow* is a disarming and whimsical celebration of feminist and queer identity as well as a text inspired by philology and ancient myth. The title of the collection and its principal bovine avatar, "Queenie," carry respective allusions to a common pejorative term for women, "cows," and male homosexuals, "queens." Hawthorne co-opts both terms, reprising them in her celebration of feminist identity and queer identity as well as the bovine myths of Ancient Greek and the bovine narratives preserved in the subcontinental Indian languages of Gandhari, Prakrit, Sanskrit, Tami, and Pali. The cows in these narratives include Meena, the Vedic goddess of dawn (Hawthorne 12); Sita, the daughter of the earth goddess Bhudevi, married to Rama (characters in the epic Ramayana) (22); Demeter, the Greek goddess of agriculture (cereal crops) (27); Sarasvati, the Indian goddess of writing, knowledge, and music (31); Lakshmi, the Indian goddess of wealth and good fortune (36); Durga, the ten-armed Indian goddess (43); Hera, a pre-Homeric Greek goddess (39); Iphigeneia, the sacrificed daughter of Clytemnestra and Agamemnon (58); and Sappho (ca. 630–570 BCE), the poet from the island of Lesbos (138).

Although *Cow* makes almost no references to the cows that were brought to Australia in 1788 or to the descendants of those fairly recent ancestral creatures, some references do make an appearance, and they inaugurate the collection, as if Hawthorne is saying to her readers that if one wishes to write about cows as an Australian writer, then one will be hard-pressed to do so without paying some modicum of respect to the cows close to home. Four of the first six poems in the collection, the poems that make up the first of the collection's four sections ("strings"), explicitly or implicitly reference the cows that mostly associate with Australian realities. The setting of the debut poem is the milking yard of a dairy farm (Hawthorne 1). Similarly, the setting of the third poem is a cowshed (4). The fourth and fifth poems are about the cattle breeds that Anglo-European colonizer and settler people brought to Australia both before and after Federation.

There "were no emancipations for good behaviour" for the cows who "came to Australia / with convicts," the narrator of the fourth poem in *Cow* (Hawthorne 5) utters in prosaic tones. The subtle comparison of these animal transports and the human transports who were sentenced to death or servitude for life in the antipodean realm of Australia throws into relief the plight of the thousands of nonhuman animals who made the forced migration to Australia with human beings in 1788. In the past, the nonhuman animal transports were not greatly noticed by literary scholars. Today, aided by work situated in one or more of the disciplines of critical animal studies, postcolonial ecocriticism, and posthumanism, literary scholars are challenging and extending the anthropocentric contours of literary studies. Alfred W. Crosby's *Ecological Imperialism: The Biological Expansion of Europe, 900–1900*, is a study that is particularly useful to these scholars. Crosby documents the cows and other nonhuman animals transported to Australia in the early days of colonization and settlement of the continent by European newcomers.

The first "discomforting number" of cows were picked up from Cape Town, South Africa, and shipped to Sidney in the holds of Governor Phillip's First Fleet (Crosby 180). Within "the first few months" of their arrival, some of the stock, two bulls and six cows, disappeared. When they were next "spotted" in 1795, grazing in an area known as "Cowpastures," their numbers had increased to "sixty-one head" (180). By 1804, the "feral herds" numbered between 3,000 and 5,000 (181). The colonial government had left the cattle alone, welcoming their increase in numbers and anticipating that the animals might "become hereafter a very great Advantage and Resource to this Colony" (181). However, as the bulls and cows thrived in their wide new world, the colonial government "reversed its policy toward the wild cattle" (181). In 1824, "convinced that humans, not cattle, had been ordained to be the dominant species in New South Wales," the government "ordered the last wild descendants of the strays of 1788 destroyed" (181).

Other cows, mostly animals of European, rather than South African, ancestry, continued to be brought to Australia (Crosby 181). In 1820, those cows numbered 54,103 in New South Wales; in 1830, they numbered 371,699 (182); in "another human generation," they numbered in the millions (182). Between 2017 and 2018, cows in Australia numbered

26.4 million (Meat and Livestock Australia, "Fast Facts: Australia's Beef Industry"). Approximately three quarters (72%) of these cows, in the form of beef products, were exported to 70 countries (Meat and Livestock Australia, "Fast Facts: Australia's Beef Industry"). Almost half of the 26.4 million cows (approximately 12 million), came from cattle stations in Queensland (Meat and Livestock Australia, "Fast Facts: Australia's Beef Industry"). Australia was the world's third largest exporter of beef in 2018 (behind Brazil and India) (Meat and Livestock Australia, "The Red Meat Industry"). Australia also is the fourth-largest exporter of dairy products (Department of Agriculture, "Dairy").

Cow does not evidently celebrate the cows who have been a backbone of the Australian economy since 1788. Yet, in giving first place to the poems that do reference those animals, Hawthorne seems to be saying that one cannot as an Australian writer do justice to the cows of far-flung pastures without making a bow, as brief as that may be, to the cows of Australia. A celebration of the beautiful cow figures of European and Asian literature and art, *Cow* nonetheless invites consideration of Australia's cows, animals who have largely disappeared from society except in the form of meat at the butcher shop or the supermarket, meat on the kitchen table, and meat on the grill in the back garden.

All the Birds, Singing

Post-Pastoral, the Black Sheep of Pastoral

Evie Wyld's post-pastoral, eco-gothic novel, *All the Birds, Singing*, shortlisted for the 2014 Man Booker Prize and winner of the 2014 Miles Franklin Literary Award, is about sheep, animals who share with cows the condition of being among the most farmed animals in Australia and elsewhere on the planet. The novel alludes to the venal aspects of the pastoral practice of sheep farming in its portrait of a character named Otto and the attempt to both escape from and redeem the violence of the pastoral tradition of sheep farming in the character of Jake Whyte, the protagonist of the novel, and two minor characters, Don and Lloyd. Whyte's character, representing the critical confrontation of the pastoral tradition of sheep farming and the desire to salvage from that tradition what is worth saving on ethically and environmentally sustainable moral grounds, epitomizes the post-pastoral imagination.

All the Birds, Singing opens when Jake is living on an island in the United Kingdom and farms sheep on a small holding. She is close to a point in her life that beckons reconciliation with and release from a terrible past event, which has extraordinarily debilitated her psychologically up to this time. The novel's ending does not make clear that Jake will be able to move forward emotionally, but there is some hope that that will occur. On a deeper level, that hope is that Australian pastoral might also be able to move forward and so take a different path than that which it has mostly taken in the last quarter of a millennium.

The events that are recounted in the odd-numbered chapters go forward in time and take place in the United Kingdom. The events that constitute the even-numbered chapters go backward chronologically and transpire on Australian dirt. In the final even-numbered chapter, readers learn about the event that triggers Jake to choose the life that she leads for much of her young adult life. In the first odd-numbered chapters of *All the Birds, Singing*, the older Jake assiduously avoids contact with the people in a town, especially its men, on a remote island in the British Isles where she farms sheep. Gradually, however, she forms a friendship with Don, a neighbor and fellow small-hold sheep farmer. She also befriends and forges an emotional bond with a drifter, Lloyd. His and Don's support and companionship help Jake to come to terms with the act that many years before caused the death of two teenagers. Jake was infatuated with one of those teenagers, Denver Cobby, because he was kind to her when many other kids made fun of her, calling her a lesbian, "Jake the Flake the Dyke," in homophobic and pejorative language (Wyld 222). Jake also is jealous of and angry with Denver because he is in love with another white girl, Flo Carter. When Denver meets Jake and confides in her his plans to run away with Flo, whose father will not allow her near Denver, a "black bloke," Jake, hurt and angry at this betrayal (as it seems to her), drops a lit "joint" in dry grass and ignites a bush fire (221, 224). Denver runs directly into the fire, toward Flo's house, which is on the other side of and in the direct line of the fire. He is unable to save Flo, who dies almost immediately. Denver will die of third-degree burns in a hospital ward shortly afterward.

Traumatized but not confessing, or not yet confessing to, the arson (and potential charge of second-degree murder), Jake goes to see Denver in hospital to beg forgiveness from the only real friend she ever had. She slips through the police guard around the boy, for the white townspeople, who have long scapegoated Denver, "the half-Aboriginal kid" who has lived on the outskirts of town and is its pariah, pin the fire and death of Flo on Denver (Wyld 215). He is barely alive. He has "no eyelids, no lips. Not enough skin to see him through the grafts" (203). The smell of his burnt body is that of a "deep-fat fryer" (203). "A machine pumps air into the body inside the plastic" wrapped around his burnt body (203). He seems to have "no arms or legs to use" (203). He is "just flesh, cooking while he sits inside it and stares at the ceiling" through an opening in the plastic (203). The "smallest sound ... like a squeal, the noise of fat spitting in a pan" comes from him. Unsure whether or not Denver can hear or see her but knowing that he—the "wet wound of meat" and the "thing under the plastic" still "lives"—Jake tells Denver she is sorry and will tell "them" (her family and the other townspeople) the truth about the fire (203–204). It is unclear whether or not she does confess her guilt to others. Sometime after this, Jake runs away, drifts into prostitution in Darwin in the Northern Territory and Port Hedland in Western Australia. Sometime after this, she finds casual employment on sheep stations in remote rural towns. Compounding her guilt and horror at what she has done is her debilitating and almost psychotic fear of Otto, a man with whom she lived for some months when she was a teenager and prostitute and whom she believes is following her. She finally moves to the United Kingdom, to a remote island, and does what she has learned to do well, farm sheep. There, she also comes close to a complete psychological breakdown as she sees or imagines the bloody and mangled carcasses of sheep on her property.

On an immediate narrative level, *All the Birds, Singing* is about a woman haunted by guilt for a wrong committed as a youth that led to a devastating bush fire and the deaths of two innocent kids. On a deeper representational level, Jake is a figure for a country haunted by an ecocidal as well as genocidal past, one marked by newcomers' pastoral violence against Australia's oldest environments as well as the country's oldest people. On that same representational level, Jake is a metaphor for, on the one hand, Australians' attempts to run from or ignore the dark side of pastoral, and, on the other hand, Australians' potential openness to revising pastoral and practicing it more ethically and on an environmentally sustainable scale.

When Jake leaves Australia, moving to the United Kingdom to take refuge on a remote island there, her past clings to her. Farming sheep on a small holding, she comes across carcasses of sheep, or imagines those bloody figures. The sheep's bodies are strewn about her property. They have been "mangled and bled out, [their] innards not yet crusting and the vapours rising from [them] like steamed pudding" (Wyld 1). For ecocritics and animal studies scholars, the piles of bodies conjure Australia's exponential trade in wool and sheep meat at the expense of sheep and the environment. In 2018, Australia supplied approximately 25% of the world's wool (Department of Agriculture, "Wool"); between 2018 and 2019, it exported 66% of the world's "total ... lamb production" and 96% of its "total ... mutton production"; it is the world's "largest exporter of sheep meat" and "fourth largest live sheep exporter" (Meat and Livestock Australia, "The Red Meat Industry"). Whyte does not manifestly indict Australia for literally living off of billions of sheep, but her novel opens readers to questioning that road to wealth.

The recent practices of exporting live sheep (and other farmed animals) is a particularly gruesome aspect of Australian sheep farming. The animals endure horrific conditions in the holds of transport carriers; they drown in their own urine and feces, die of heat exhaustion, and literally cook to death in their own skins below deck on transport carriers in the summer months. Closer to home, undercover surveillance film of sheep shearing in Australia reflects the violence that accompanies intensive sheep shearing work. Male workers routinely "violently [punch] and [beat] sheep with metal tools," "kicking them," and "leaving them unconscious" (Salemme). This violence was found in four shearing sheds in New South Wales and Victoria (the top two wool-producing states in Australia) in 2017 (Salemme).

Sheep are "gentle animals who are petrified of even being held down" (Salemme). They suffer the same fear and terror as many humans do when they are punched in the face, kicked and stamped, and slammed by their heads onto the floor. The figure of Otto in *All the Birds, Singing* especially evokes the violence in Australia's sheep industry, in sheep meat as well as wool production.

Not long after Jake runs away from home, turns to prostitution, and meets Otto, a so-called client, he convinces her to live and work for him on his sheep farm. Otto brutalizes the sheep, and he takes pleasure in that and making Jake watch him as he tortures the animals, for he is a misogynist as well as well as a pedophile and sheep hater. Their cries "rattle [Jake's] bones" (Wyld 93). On one particular occasion, when Otto forces Jake to watch him as he slaughters an ewe, Jakes is torn between protesting the killing and protecting her own body from Otto. He "swings [the ewe] up the ramp in front of him, and she gives out a terrible sound" (93). Jake "[stands] … outside the woolshed, mute, [tackling] the urge to kick down the fence and tell [the other sheep] to flee" (93). When Otto orders Jake to kill a second ewe, "the [one] with the black spots … whipping about underneath Otto," and rolling her eyes in fear, Jake complies (95). Otto "is enjoying seeing [her] scared" and "has a hard-on through his shorts" (95). She feels her "strong arms [float] from [her] shoulders, as weak as feathers" (95). She kills the ewe to show Otto that she is "stronger than he thinks" but cannot forgive herself for this act of self-interest and punishes herself for it afterward (95). When Otto demands to have sex with her, she "[lets] him do what he wants with [her], which is everything" (96).

Otto's character is one of the many dark pastoral figures that stamp Australian pastoral literature. Famous antecedents include Phonce Wallace-Pimble in Bruce Pascoe's short story "The Slaughters of the Bulumwaal Butcher." It is about a group of respectable townsmen who secretly steal, slaughter, and sell the flesh of sheep. Clive Glossop, the town drunk, witnesses some of the thefts. Wallace-Pimble, one of the group of respectable citizens and the local chemist, murders Clive (poisoning him) to prevent him from telling anyone. A more recent dark pastoral figure is Mal Deacon in Jane Harper's detective fiction, *The Dry*. Aaron Falk, the protagonist and a financial fraud investigator from Melbourne, returns to the (fictional) town of Kiewarra in Victoria's wheat belt country in the northwest of the state to attend the funeral of his boyhood friend, Luke Hadler. Soon after he arrives, he becomes caught up in the police investigation of the death of Hadler and Hadler's wife and son. In the course of the inquiry, Falk and another detective find out that Mal Deacon, a sheep farmer whose daughter Ellie was murdered many years before, is the murderer of Ellie. Falk, who had been in love with Ellie when they were teenagers and whose father was driven out of town many years before because Mal Deacon had spread a rumor that Falk's father had killed Ellie, slowly pieces together the little known details about Ellie's death as he meets people around town and at the local town pub, "the Fleece." In doing that, he remembers Mal Deacon abusing sheep.

> When Aaron Falk was eleven he'd seen Mal Deacon turn his own flock into a staggering, bleeding mess using shearing clippers and a brutal hand. Aaron had felt an ache swell in his chest as he, Luke and Ellie had watched one sheep after another brawled to the ground of the Deacons' shed with a sharp twist and sliced too close to the skin ... [there was] A pitiful cry from the smallest ewe. (Harper 67)

Harper gives her readers clues about Deacon and other morally suspect characters according to their degree of insensitivity toward animals. Mal Deacon, who murders his daughter, is vicious to sheep. Gretchen Shoner and Luke Hadler are not entirely unscrupulous but betray some questionable moral turpitude, for they had an affair and lied about it to Luke's wife; and they shoot rabbits for the reason not only that the animals interfere with the pastoral economy but also for sport. Aaron, who has long given up the pastime activity of shooting rabbits, is the least morally suspect of the characters in *The Dry*.

Australian pastoral is synonymous with the farming of sheep and cows; it both parallels and veers away from its European counterparts, referring mainly to "the work of raising sheep or cattle—as opposed to crops—on the land" (Tredinnick 125).[6]

For many people, and in particular those who have lived hard lives in the struggle to turn bush into paddock, pastoral is "where one will find the fiercest love for and the deepest wisdom about the land" (126). For many others, pastoral represents a mighty "[contribution] to the wreck ... of country" (126). The first group of Australians celebrates pastoral largely for economic reasons. They are reflected in the popular expression, "[Australia] rode to prosperity and nationhood on the sheep's [and cow's] back" (123). The second group of Australians associates pastoral with betrayal and loss as well as gain. Pastoral literature that confronts both these sides of pastoral, literature that includes Wyld's *All the Birds, Singing*, reflects the post-pastoral imagination. Ecocritic Mark Tredinnick, writing about post-pastoral in the context of the poet Robert Gray, describes post-pastoral as being expression that

> picks up the frequencies of Australian pastoral landscapes, where, more than anywhere else, the business of reconciliation with

> country and with Indigenous people is being played out; where the experiment in large-scale Western land use is being tested and found wanting; and where the price for all that tree-felling, for all that overstocking and all that plundering of the rivers and aquifers is being paid. (126)

Ruth Blair, a founding figure of Australian ecocriticism, comments on the Australian post-pastoral imagination in the context of nineteenth-century and early twentieth-century newcomers who turned against pastoral when they saw how it was betraying the environment. Those newcomers included Robert Martin Collins, Romeo Lahey, and members of the O'Reilly family (Blair 180–181). In the late 1890s, Collins set out to establish a national park in the McPherson Range on the Queensland–New South Wales border. Lahey continued the work begun by Collins and succeeded in bringing to fruition his vision for a national park (Blair 180). In 1915, the Lamington National Park (approximately 47,000 acres of country) was established. Between 1915 and 1935, managers expanded the park (181). In 1911, eight members of the O'Reilly family took up blocks of land on what is now named the Lamington Plateau in the McPherson Range (181). After the area became a national park, several members of the O'Reilly family were given the title of honorary rangers in recognition of their work in combating crude, short-sighted, and reductive instrumentalist uses of country (181). Collins, Lahey, and members of the O'Reilly represent some of the earliest post-pastoral attempts to mitigate pastoral.

In its latest fictional articulations, the post-pastoral awareness of the uglier aspects of pastoral and post-pastoral effort to come to grips with those aspects appear in Wyld's *Bite Your Tongue*. The main character, Jake Whyte, leaves Australian pastoral behind her, for as she has experienced and witnessed it, it has little to do with innocence, nature, and gentle swain. She now raises sheep on a small holding in the United Kingdom. In her character, and in the novel as a whole, there is a subtle indictment of Australian pastoral. Yet, at the same time, the novel articulates the post-pastoral reluctance to abandon altogether the raising of sheep and cattle and the post-pastoral desire for pastoral engagements that are more fair to the animals themselves, the land on which those animals are farmed, and the traditional custodians of that land.

Without actively searching for information about Australia's industrial wool, lamb, and mutton production, consumers may not learn much about the sentience and suffering of the animals who are used up in pastoral production. What consumers are learning about without having to undertake a great deal of research is the major role that modern pastoral is playing in climate change. This aspect of industrial animal farming receives far more attention in the media than does the issue of animal suffering; it is welcome, nonetheless. Mainstream news media now are reporting more frequently and regularly on the links between deforestation and beef production and greenhouse gases and beef production. Ninety-one percent of land cleared in Queensland is for the raising of cattle for beef products, a direct consequence of the weakening of environmental laws protecting remnant bushland (AnimalsAustralia). Almost a million native animals die per year there as result of the clearing of that land for beef production (Robertson). Every year throughout Australia, 34 million animals are "burnt" alive, "minced alive," or die of stress where deforestation occurs (AnimalsAustralia). In Queensland, between 2015 and 2017, there was a "33% rise in clearing to almost 400,000 hectares" (Robertson). The annual rate of deforestation in the state now equals two-thirds "of the rate of deforestation in the Brazilian Amazon" (Robertson). Today, Australia is "one of the deforestation hotspots in the world" and "the only advanced economy to be named in the 12 deforestation hotspots in the world" (Robertson).

One of Australia's most distinguished contemporary poets, John Kinsella, a "pacifist/anarchist/vegan" Australian (Taylor 11), writes about Australian pastoral in a collection of essays entitled *Contrary Rhetoric: Lectures on Landscape and Language*. In the chapter "Is There an Australian Pastoral?" (131–162), he admits how strong the pull of Australian pastoral continues to be even for him and other Australians who actively address the ecocidal and genocidal policies and practices that adumbrate pastoral. In his discussion of sheep farming and the well-known and beloved anonymous nineteenth-century Australian sheep ballad "Click Go the Shears," he writes, "I am always going to be at odds with what I see as the exploitation of sheep … and yet in many ways shearers are the country people I feel most akin to. They are the singers of the rural spaces" (152–153).

Similar to the poetry of Robert Gray and Evie Wyld's novel, Kinsella's literary output shapes and defines post-pastoral, or "the inability to celebrate [pastoral] without negativity" and the understanding that the traditional "pastoral arcadia—a golden age of plenty, and ideal social interactions based on a hierarchy of class"—is "unacceptable outside its historical context" (Kinsella 152). Even in this given context, pastoral is "hard to accept" (152). At its worst, pastoral reflects ecocidal policies and practices. At its best, it is post-pastoral, or work that confronts and gives up those policies and practices, an engagement that Kinsella calls "confrontation, recognition, conversation, and … reconciliation" (133).

Oink, Oink, Oink

Transgenic Matter on a Porcine Platter

In Australia, as elsewhere on the planet, pigs are prolific, yet very little is known about them outside of the facilities where they are industrially slaughtered for processing as food and experimented on to enhance humans in transgenic research (the "exchange of genetic material between different species" [Twine 54]). Billions of anthropogenic pigs are farrowed annually in these facilities. The unspoken *raison d'être* for that birthing is akin to the tectonic plates that comprise the earth's lithosphere; it floats the food and biomedical industries but is mostly concealed from everyday view. This reason is that pigs (along with most chickens on the planet as well as cows and goats) have almost no value whatsoever beyond that of commercial viability.

Global corporate capital livestock genetics companies piggyback particularly heavily on swine and stash in their piggybanks substantial profits from riding "high on the hog." The material reduction and moral debasement of pigs by those companies have intensified as pig populations have exploded throughout the world. Eric Yoshiaki Dando's novel *Oink, Oink, Oink* represents the dark, cannibalistic, and eco-phagic side of the bedfellow industries of industrial pork production and porcine genome research. One in a long line of porcine texts, *Oink, Oink, Oink* joins, in the twenty-first century, Bong Joon-ho's film *Okja* and Mark Brozel's film adaptation of Shakespeare's *Macbeth*.[7] One of the most memorable scenes in the latter film is the scene where Joe (Macbeth), a master meat chef whose totem is a wild boar and a butcher of humans as well as hogs, meets his untimely death shortly after a police helicopter lands near or on the roof top of the premises of the restaurant that Joe takes over after he murders his boss (Duncan), the former owner of the business; so, the prophesy that Joe heard from the lips of three garbage men [Shakespeare's witches] is fulfilled: "Pigs will fly." Brozel capitalizes here on a common pejorative for the police, "pigs."

Oink, Oink, Oink is a novel in which pigs and humans change places and merge identities to the extent that they become indistinguishable species. The novel explicitly addresses the controversial issue of xenotransplantation and other genome research experiments on pigs. The first-person "porcine-hominoid" narrator, Squirly Fern, has grown up in Tokyo, where his mother, the daughter of a poor Okinawa pig farmer, is employed at a fish cannery. In the late 1970s, the 16-year-old Squirly moves to Melbourne after receiving "a letter and plane ticket from his estranged Australian father, urging him to come and stay" (Clancy). He learns that his father "is a rich and famous scientist" who "dabbl[es] in cloning" (Clancy). "[T]hat's when the book gets weird," reviewer Laurie Clancy says, "people become pigs, pigs become people and S[quirly] F[ern] must battle with [a transgenic pig] Pauline, the mother of all genetically enhanced hogs."

If transgenic research (and genome research, more broadly) has brought "into relief the porosity of previously cherished species boundaries ... underlining similarity between ourselves and other species," then it has been guided from its inception virtually solely by the desire "to establish a fixed and special 'human'" relative to other species (Twine 31). Pigs are used to enhance and prolong human lives under a broad range of biomedical and biotechnological experiments because these animals share close genetic ties with humans (Kim Baker 67; Carr 84). These experiments include proposals to use pigs in xenotransplantation, which involves partially humanizing pigs, or transgenically "enhancing" them, so as to prevent the rejection by the human recipients of the donor pigs' organs (Twine 53–54, 69, 80). *Oink, Oink, Oink* raises questions about those proposals as they concern human–pig ratios, or the extent to which humans who incorporate pig flesh are more porcine than human. The novel is a dark romp down the brightly lit, labyrinthine (and increasingly publicly inaccessible) halls of transgenic research involving pigs.

Oink, Oink, Oink also is about "enhancement" as this term also refers to meat production. Livestock genetics companies disingenuously use this term in their transhumanist posthumanist projects of anthropogenically producing tailor-made breeds of pigs (and other animal species).[8] A cheap substitution is taking place here. The "enhancement" of pigs refers to their moral and material debasement. If one is to be honest about the kinds of augmentation seen in livestock genetics companies, then one ought to use the term to refer to the spectacular growth of those companies at the expense of pigs. Other terms that livestock genetics companies use in the business of putatively improving pigs include "SuperMom" pigs and "Meidam DL GP" pigs (Twine 110, 112). The latter is used in advertising a pig breed that also is called the "mother of all mothers" breed (110). These pigs are genetically designed to have a high number of teats, a high number of offspring, and a docile disposition (112). Another pig breed, the "PIC410" (110), a "hybrid boar," is advertised for "combin[ing] high primal yields, leanness and robustness with the excellent growth rate, feed conversion, carcass leanness and meat quality of the ... leading terminal boar[s]" (the "PIC337") (110).

The governments that we elect have been complacent or resistant in addressing moral questions relating to intensive genomic interferences in pigs' lives, from the artificial insemination of the animals at a young age, to the separation of piglets from their young mothers immediately after birth, to the termination of young pigs in a slaughterhouse or biomedical laboratory (Twine 54). *Oink, Oink, Oink* represents and satirizes that nonchalance and refusal in such memorable characters as Squirly Fern, Squirly's father, Pauline, and Dr. Akiyoshi.

Squirly's father works for the corporate capitalist industrial behemoth "MonsantoTM" (Dando 11). In the 1960s, MonsantoTM sends him to an "American military think-tank in Okinawa" (11). There, he meets the poor daughter of a pig farmer and, on "a dirty weekend to Mt Fuji," impregnates her (16). Soon thereafter, he abandons her, a woman whom he pejoratively calls "[t]he pig girl" (29). He returns to Australia and begins to experiment on pigs in the back garden of his home in the quintessential, middle-class, staid, and affluent Melbourne suburb of Ashburton. Since his work for MonsantoTM in Australia and the military think-tank in Japan, he has become interested in the porcine species, the "most convenient human-like test subjects for the benefit of human research" (59). His work leads him and a longtime associate, Dr. Akiyoshi, on a "gene-splicing" quest "for the most human pig" (58).

Squirly's father is especially obsessed with one pig, "P-42," whom he later renames "Pauline," a seductive dominatrix with "fluttering ... long lashes" (Dando 61). Pauline leads other transgenic pigs in the laboratories in the back garden of Squirly's father's home to revolt against the human scientists who fiddle with their lives. Secretly "educat[ing] themselves" (61), they overpower the scientists employed by Squirly's father, "[fatten] them up in solitary metal enclosures," feed them what they have been fed, and eat some of them (62). Squirly's father negotiates with the pigs and a treaty of sorts is signed. However, it is unclear now who is a pig and who is a human, for in the course of the experiments that the humans have performed on the pigs (and those the pigs have performed on the humans) everyone involved has become "part pig" (63).

Squirly also will become "part-pig" when he undergoes a xenotransplantation operation (Dando 63). Indeed, his father already is a transgenic porcine-hominoid, having undergone "a [porcine] liver transplant in the late 1980s" (108). Scientists "grew a custom designed liver for him in one of his transgenic pigs and [he has] been using it ever since" (108). Pauline now is "pressuring him to have more vital [pigs'] organs installed in his body" (108). In the case of Squirly, Dr. Akiyoshi, the distinguished "protégé" of a scientist in Japan who worked on inventing and refining biological weapons during World War II (72), discovers and removes a malignant cyst in Squirly's thigh and "bog[s] up the hole in [Squirly's] leg with pieces of bone from a transgenic pig" (107).

Oink, Oink, Oink's "MonsantoTM" is a naked allusion to the actual company of Monsanto and the ethical questions that it and other biotechnology companies raise about merging human and nonhuman animal genetic material in the areas of medicine and agriculture (Twine 110).[9] Squirly's father's experiments on pigs to reduce the fat content of their flesh, manipulations that result in such pigs as the uncommonly "lean" and "skinny" Pauline (Dando 35, 78, 85), are a direct allusion to the controversial drug ractopamine hydrochloride, developed by the pharmaceutical global giant company Eli Lilly and subsequently used in pork production "to promote leanness in pigs" (Twine 110). Pauline's unusually high number of teats is an allusion to livestock genetics companies' intensive selective breeding of sows so as to increase the animals' reproductive capacities (which correlate with the number and size of the animals' teats). "I have never seen so many breasts," Squirly says of his stepmother (Dando 77). The hominoid-porcine offspring that

Squirly's father and Pauline produce, and their successful efforts in cloning Squirly, carry further allusions to current research in the areas of cloning and transgenic experiments on animals.

Squirly's father's ambitious plans to increase Australia's consumption of domestically produced pork (classified as a "red meat") is another marbling of the plot of *Oink, Oink, Oink* that ties to global pork production and consumption. Australians are "the largest consumers of meat in the world per capita, consuming almost twice the average of consumers in the United Kingdom," and their appetite for meat has continued to grow (Chen 41–42). However, in recent decades, Australians have moved "away from red meat and towards chickens" (41). Squirly's father's plans to increase Australians' consumption of pork allude to that actual shift as well as to Australia's modest amount of pork production relative to beef and sheep meat production, which far outstrip pork production. Australia is the third largest exporter of beef in the world (after Brazil and India) and the largest exporter of sheep meat (Meat and Livestock Australia, "The Red Meat Industry"). "This nation has been riding on the sheep's back for long enough … Time to ride into the new economy, ride piggy-back," Squirly's father says to his son (Dando 63). He "slaps [Squirly] really hard on the back, 'Ha! Piggy-back!'" (63). Squirly's back indeed is a "piggy-back." The xenotransplantation operation has made Squirly a transgenic porcine-hominoid animal.

Oink, Oink, Oink is a postmodern text, a pulp fiction, and a work of speculative fiction. The character of the voluble Pauline identifies the novel with another genre, that of the bestiary or beast fable, a minor but persistent literary form. Up through the end of the thirteenth century, beast fables were common throughout Western Europe. They became a marginal form of expression after that time. In England, the most celebrated beast fables that appear after the thirteenth century include Geoffrey Chaucer's "The Nun's Priest's Tale" in *The Canterbury Tales* and Robert Henryson's "The Cock and the Fox." Both texts were written for adult, highly literate, and culturally elite readers. More commonly, however, beast fables after the thirteenth century took the form of elementary texts for teaching Latin to school children (Greenblatt 299). Writers, under the spell of Renaissance humanism, perhaps did not consider beast fables to be eminently suitable for addressing serious subject matter. Today, bestiary texts continue to identify with children's literature. Humanist beliefs about the speech of animals persist. We tend to think of speech, language, and sophisticated forms of communication as being available only to humans and to distinguish humans from other species. *Oink, Oink, Oink* is a text that constitutes the testing of that humanist grip.

"Pigs" by Les Murray, a poem that appears in the collection, *Translations from the Natural World* (36), is another porcine bestiary text. In this poem, Murray implicitly questions the widespread, institutionalized denial of speech to the nonhuman world. The porcine narrator recounts the last moments of his life as he is dragged along a cement floor, hung upside down, and scalded by boiling water while still half-conscious. Delivered in the "pungent idiolect" of a hog (Chiasson 138), the poem commits the pathetic fallacy, as bestiary texts do. The fallacy reflects a presumptive knowledge of animals on our part but also the strong hold that animals have on us even as we seem fully intent on annihilating and oppressing them and meretriciously speaking for them. Animals speak to us despite our efforts to silence them and deny them language. They inspire such poems as "Pigs," other poems in *Translations from the Natural World*, Dando's novel, and myriad other narratives of "interdependence" and "unlooked-for-relation ... dispersing the human without disembodying" (Cohen 26). Such texts remind us to ask again why it is that we "suppose all things a resource for use, abuse, and transformation, and therefore blind ourselves to all matter's vibrancy" (26).

The principal moral costs of industrially producing pork and experimenting on the porcine species include denying pigs any right to existence on their own terms, material, social, linguistic, and so forth. The chief material costs are global warming (Cummins; Estok, *The Ecophobia Hypothesis* 92–93). Pork products from industrial facilities one day might carry warning signs, similar to those on tobacco products, that alert consumers to the negative impact that industrial animal farming is having on the planet's lungs (forests and wetlands) and circulatory systems (waterways, marine environments, etc.). Already, the health industry is advising consumers to reduce their intake of red meat. (That is a salutary step forward for pigs, cows, and sheep; unfortunately, that same step is a leap backward for chickens, for consumption of chickens has escalated as that of pigs has stabilized in some countries.) In the future, the health industry may join with climate change scientists in recommending that consumers back off on their consumption of industrially farmed animal flesh so as to protect and preserve the body at the planetary corporeal level.

In major pork producing and economically impoverished states in the United States, waterways are heavily polluted by facilities where pigs are industrially produced and slaughtered (McCorkie). In East Asia, the South China Seas now are among the most polluted waters on the planet because of the acceleration of the industrial farming of pigs (and chickens) in China and Vietnam (McCorkie). The United States gave birth to industrially farming animals in the second half of the twentieth century (McCorkie).[10] Subsequently, despite their awareness of the huge environmental costs and the equally mounting moral questions surrounding the massive incarceration of the porcine species, major stakeholders exported the industrial methods of procuring pork to East Asia. Australia has scaled down its pork production industries but imports many pork products from overseas. Pork consumption has played a significant role in the "'meatification' of global diets" in the last 50 years (Weiss qtd. in Estok, *The Ecophobia Hypothesis* 92).

On its website, the Melbourne-based bookseller Readings advertises *Oink, Oink, Oink* as "a surreal, black comedy, a seductively hip, hilariously funny satire of popular culture and consumerism" and a "savage modern fable about science, family, television, and love gone wrong." *Oink, Oink, Oink* also is about killing swine and the heavy investment in that killing by the global corporate capital food industry and the biomedical companies that converge with that industry.

In the preface to Val Plumwood's posthumous writing *The Eye of the Crocodile*, editor Lorraine Shannon notes that the crocodile, the animal that is central to Plumwood's speculative work in feminism, ecofeminism, and ecophilosophy, is famous for being, in both ancient Egyptian narratives and Indigenous Australian narratives, "a trickster figure" and "a deliverer of judgement on the errant human" (iv).[11] The species, as Shannon adds, also is "one of the last remaining major predators of human beings" (ix). In Australia, crocodiles are a protected species and thrive because of that classification status. The central animal figures of Wyld's *All the Birds, Singing*, Hawthorne's *Cow*, Rendle-Short's *Bite Your Tongue*, and Dando's *Oink, Oink, Oink* likewise exist in large numbers in Australia but for different reasons. They exist because they are a lucrative food commodity.

Plumwood writes about the excessive appetite for animal flesh in *The Eye of the Crocodile*, in the sixth chapter, entitled "Animals and Ecology: Towards a Better Integration" (77–90). However, she points out that consumers who practice the principle of "ecological animalism" when they kill and consume animals properly situate human life in ecological and ethical terms (79). Those consumers, who include Plumwood, are not opposed to the killing of animals, for they argue that humans are predatory animals and so ecologically designed to prey on other animals (80). Therefore, they call not for the cessation of animal killing but rather for "great reductions in first-world meat-eating" (79), "respectful use" of animals (80), and challenging of "disrespectful conceptions and treatments of animals, especially in factory [intensive] farming" (78).

In contrast, as Plumwood continues to argue, "ontological veganism" consumers, or consumers who abstain altogether from consuming the flesh of animals, misguidedly reinforce the "human/animal" dualism (78). These consumers anthropocentrically position humans outside of the food chain—"outside nature"—and thereby deny the ecological place of humans, a predatory animal species, on the planet (78). Thus, according to Plumwood, the "ontological veganism" position is problematic for "both theory and activism [relating to] animal equality and ecology" (78). Consumers who practice "ontological veganism," insisting that "neither humans nor animals should ever be conceived as edible or even as usable" not only re-enact a false "human/nature dualism" (78); in indiscriminately "proscribing all forms of animal use as having the same moral status," they also fail to provide "a philosophical guidance for animal activism that would prioritise action on factory farming over less abusive forms of farming" (78). The unquestioned "universalism" of the "ontological veganism" position also betrays a "highly ethnocentric" bias; it legitimates a privileged Western consumer's perspective, and it treats all other perspectives as "minor, deviant 'exceptions' to what it takes to be the ideal or norm" (78–79).

Plumwood's "ecological animalism" versus "ontological veganism" argument is intended less to defend meat eating and more to persuade meat eaters to rigorously question their consumption of and dependence upon the flesh and reproductive organs of animals that are bred, raised, and slaughtered in facilities identifying with intensive animal farming practices. However, this argument somewhat unfairly or disingenuously demonizes vegetarian and vegan consumers. Perhaps, such a term as "ecological veganism" would be a fairer one. As I coin and use it here, "ecological veganism" refers to people who abstain from consuming in copious amounts the flesh and other organs of animals *not* because they are fundamentally opposed to eating the bodies of their fellow creatures but rather because they cannot readily purchase the carcasses of animals that have *not* been killed in industrial agriculture facilities. Plumwood's "ontological veganism" characterization of vegans in effect reduces vegans to an essentialist, one-size-fits-all, group of consumers and her "ecological animalism" characterization of meat eaters implies that meat eaters are a more diverse group, or hold diverse positions about animal consumption.

Admittedly, the main difference between Plumwood's "ecological animalism" consumer and what I call the "ecological veganism" consumer lies mostly in the nominalizations themselves. As Plumwood characterizes the "ecological animalism" consumer, she or he is a "context-sensitive semi-vegetarian" who is opposed to industrial animal farming (78). Plumwood's "ecological animalism" consumer thus hardly differs from what I call the "ecological veganism" consumer, who avoids consuming industrially farmed animal products but is not fundamentally or philosophically opposed to eating the body of a fellow animal (or fellow plant). She or he becomes vegan by a sort of default or de facto route.[12] However, the argument that Plumwood makes under her term "ecological animalism" diverts attention away from the fact that intensive farming of animals is so entrenched and widespread that "ecological animalism" is all but impossible to practice for many people. Animal meat that is from animals who are allowed to live out their natural lives, who are not separated from family members, and who are treated with kindness up to the last moments of their life (before a human kills them), is a rare find. "Ecological veganism," similarly to "ecological animalism," might or might not push a meat eater in the direction of "ontological veganism," but "ecological veganism" stands for practices that do not tie to any absolute moral renunciation of flesh.

Rendle-Short's novel *Bite Your Tongue*, published in 2011, generates ecocritical notice of efforts by the meat industry in and after that year to cut out the tongues, metaphorically speaking, of animal rights advocates. In response to their efforts to reduce or ban some practices of industrial farming, practices that include the live animal export trade, the meat industry has been pushing for agricultural gag laws, so called ag-gag laws. Such laws, if they are enacted, will make it even more difficult than it already is for animal advocacy groups to access industrial animal operations and sites, conduct surveillance of the sites, and disseminate the surveillance to the public. The novel's central trope of severed cow tongue especially generates the given notice. Hawthorne's *Cow*, named after an animal species that is one of Australia's (and the world's) most intensively farmed species, celebrates the figural cows of ancient European and Asian myth. References to the cows of Australia—namely the cows of Australian pastoral—are few, yet they are there. Those and other bovine figures in Hawthorne's collection, similarly to the cow tongues in Rendle-Short's novel, garner ecocritical notice. Wyld's *All the Birds, Singing* is another work of Australian literature that beckons ecocritical attention, provoking questions about the terms on which sheep are allowed to exist. Those terms mostly are dictated by humans; sheep hardly have any say in their own lives. Dando's *Oink, Oink, Oink* likewise beckons that cynosure in the context of pigs; it asks readers to relate to pigs as fellow creatures more and to eat pigs less.

Notes

1 In this book, I mostly use the word "cows" in preference to "cattle."

2 Unless otherwise noted, all page numbers of *Bite Your Tongue* that I cite refer to the main pages, the fictional narrative, not to the pages that consist of factual information. The latter pages constitute the appendices and include the appendix entitled "Permissions."

3 In a memorable passage about the porcine text, Golding's *Lord of the Flies*, MotherJoy pulls Gloria out of a public school after its principal refuses to remove the novel from the list of required reading for the English classes, and she enrolls Gloria in a private Catholic school. She subsequently learns that the Catholic school also includes in its English-class reading lists books that are reprehensible to her, so she marches into the school and seizes copies of the books (with Gloria innocently helping her):

> Motherjoy must have picked up a book from every pile in the basement that afternoon, all of them now squashed against her body, many more than the number Glory needed for English. She looked like she was coming home from the butcher with an assortment of meats. (159)

4 O'Sullivan refers to the popular film *Babe*, directed by Chris Noonan. For an extensive discussion of this film, see Plumwood, "Babe: The Tale of the Speaking Meat," one of the chapters of *The Eye of the Crocodile* (55–74).

5 *Ngarrindjeri Wurruwarrin* is about the Hindmarsh Island Affair, one of the notorious and prolific dismissals of rights of Aboriginal Australian people. For a brief summary of the controversy, see Tindall.

The Coral Battleground, first published in 1997, and reissued by Spinifex Press in 2013, narrators the environmental fight to save Australia's Great Barrier Reef beginning in the 1970s and continuing today in the face of massive mining and port development projects. The threats of these projects are so intense that "the United Nations Educational and Scientific Organization (UNESCO) has warned the Australian and Queensland Governments that if they do not make real improvements to [its] deteriorating condition," it will be removed from the list of world heritage sites (Thorsborne xix).

The World According to Monsanto is an expose of the unethical practices of the corporation Monsanto inclusive of how it controls the production and distribution of a wide range of agricultural products, from genetically modified (GMO) grains, to pesticides, to a genetically engineered growth hormone, recombinant bovine growth hormone (rBGH), commonly known by the trade name of Posilac, a drug now widely used in the dairy industry.

6 For summations of the origins of literary and cultural pastoral in wider European ecocritical contexts, see Gifford; Casteel; Huggan and Tiffin ("Pastoral in Black and White" 85–95); and Pughe, Chorier-Fryd, and Holdefer. For more on pastoral in Australian literary contexts, see Lynch ("Pastoralism")

7 In the last century, porcine literature includes William Golding's *Lord of the Flies*, a post–World War II, ecophobic, and dystopic novel about a group of schoolboys stranded on an island among its resident wild pigs in the Pacific Ocean in the aftermath of nuclear war; E. B. White's children's fiction *Charlotte's Web*, about several farm animals who include the wise Wilbur, a livestock pig; the television series *Sesame Street*, starring the thespian Miss Piggy; Dick King-Smith's novel, *The Sheep-Pig*; director Chris Noonan's film *Babe* (an adaptation of King-Smith's novel); and Patrick McCabe's novel *The Butcher Boy*, shortlisted for the 1992 Booker Prize. For an ecocritical and animal studies analysis of the pig figures in Golding's novel, see Iris Ralph's essay "Ecophobia and the Porcelain Porcine Species."

8 For a concise summary of the area and direction of posthumanism known as transhumanism, see Wolfe (xiii–xiv, xx, xv); see, also, Chapter 1 of this study.

9 For a comprehensive account of Monsanto's controversial practices, see Robin's study *The World According to Monsanto: Pollution, Politics and Power.*

10 For more about the relationship between industrial pig farming and industrial capitalism, see Blanchette. Richard P. Horowitz's *Hog Ties: What Pigs Tell Us about America* is a less useful study about industrial pig farming.

11 The title of the collection alludes to Plumwood's encounters with crocodiles, including the traumatic, and morally and philosophically altering, experience of being "death-rolled" three times by an Australian Saltwater crocodile (Matthews, Rigby, and Rose 4).

12 For a related argument about Plumwood's "ontological vegetarianism" argument, see Gaard (*Critical Ecofeminism* xxiv). At an ecofeminist conference that took place in 1995, Plumwood "parted ways" with several other ecofeminists "on the topic of species justice" by perceiving arguments for vegetarianism articulated by Carol Adams, Dean Curtin, and others as calls for a "universal mandate" rather than a "contextual moral vegetarianism" (xxiv).

4 Veggie-Might

Locust Girl

Shirley Hazzard's pyric fiction *The Great Fire* narrates the lives of several Australian and British subjects who are caught up with hundreds of thousands of other people in the incendiary events of the Second World War. The novel foregrounds several of the most horrific of those events in its opening pages: the nuclear bombing of the cities of Hiroshima and Nagasaki and the firebombing of Tokyo, "the single most deadly bombing raid in history" (Carney).[1] It is "the spring of 1947," and Major Aldred Leith, a British soldier whose past and present are the main threads of Hazzard's plot, is pulling out of Tokyo by train. From his seat in the train carriage, he observes with a mixture of fatigue, resignation, detachment, and suspension of faith in his species, the city's "charred suburbs ... raising, even within the train, a spectral odour of cinders" (Hazzard 1, 5).

Another pyric novel, Merlinda Bobis's cli-fi novel, conjures a less well-known, studied, and understood conflagration, one that has decimated hundreds of thousands of other beings, animal and vegetal, in modern times: post-1788 bushfire in Australia.[2] The term, post-1788 bushfire, as it is used here, refers to arguments by environmental historians that fire in Australia changed phenomenally after 1788, and became less controllable and more unpredictable, because of ignorance, misunderstanding, and misuse of its agencies, many of which are distinctly Australian native agencies. Bobis's novel also evokes arguments by those same scholars that much of the current conditions of drought, salinization of soils, and loss of water catchments in Australia are due to mismanagement and overexploitation of the environment by newcomers since 1788. Much of the action in the novel takes place in a drought-stricken, denuded, and burnt-out land where thousands of people struggle to live sustainably after their countries are deliberately or carelessly destroyed by fire by the rulers of the "Five Kingdoms." The setting evokes post-1788 bushfire in Australia. Whereas before 1788 people in Australia recognized fire as a powerful ally and worked closely with it, after that fateful year people, mainly newcomers, feared or hardly understood or bothered to understand bushfire, or wielded it one-sidedly, as a weapon of destruction more than a tool for regeneration. Tokyo, Hiroshima, and Nagasaki, and countless other cities were horrifically erased by human-made pyric forces in Asia and Europe during the Second World War. Between 1788 and today, large tracts of country in Australia were obliterated by fire magnified by human agencies. While many of those agencies point to facts of ignorance as opposed to those of intentionality, the loss of country was stupendous. The purpose of this chapter is to bring notice to relatively more anthropogenic, than ecogenic, fire in Australian literary contexts and so to discernibly and consequentially add to and support eco-centric critical readings of Australian literature.

In "Locust Girl," the first of the three parts of *Locust Girl*, its protagonist, nine-year-old Amedea, lives with her father and mother and fellow country people in one of hundreds of camps, "Missions" (Bobis, *Locust Girl* 152), in a vast arid region. The people survive by feeding on "[s]and porridge and locust" (3). The authorities who control the missions are the rulers of the Five Kingdoms. Every person subjected to their rule is identified by a number and letter inscribed in "blue ink" under his or her ear (3). She or he wears a uniform-like blue garb and receives orders from the rulers through a "blue box" (3). Amedea, the daughter of Alkesta and Abarama, is "425a" (3). Amedea has never seen the stars, blue sky, the color green, trees, or large bodies of water. Not long before the rulers of the Five Kingdoms destroy her country by setting fire to it, she asks her father, Abarama, what the word "tree" means.

> "But what's trees, Father?"
> "Tall things with leaves."
> "What's leaves?"
> "Green things."
> "What's green?"
> My father frowned deeply to squeeze from his brow the apparition of trees for me. "Green was tall and proud." (4)

Abarama also tells Amedea about a time when their people's country, now desiccated, had "big, big waters, sometimes as big as this desert and coloured blue" (6).

When the Rulers of the Five Kingdoms destroy her country by fire, Amedea, the sole survivor of her people, hibernates below the surface of the earth. During this time, another lone survivor, a locust, buries itself in Amedea's forehead. "Trapped" and "confused," it mistakes Amedea for a stone that is "blocking its way" and so "nibble[s]" at the "burnt crust" of Amedea's skin (Bobis, *Locust Girl* 9). When it becomes tired of that, it attaches itself to the young woman's forehead. Ten years later, the merged creature, the hybrid-insect "Locust Girl," is discovered by Beenabe, a 16-year-old girl from a neighboring country, Beenabe is lost and trying to find her way back home. Similar to Amedea's country, her country has been seized by the Five Kingdoms rulers, who deliver orders to Beenabe's people through an "orange box" and identify the people by orange identification letters, numbers, and uniforms (10).

The two young women make their way through the parched and denuded region in search of Beenabe's country. Along the way, they desperately search for water and grain ("barley") (Bobis, *Locust Girl* 12). They meet other displaced people, characters who appear in the novel in alphabetical order of the first letter of their names (an arresting device by Bobis that evokes Gertrude Stein's modernist "cubist" experiments with prose). After Amedea and Beenabe (whom Amedea calls "Beena" [33]), there are Cho-choli, Daninen, Espra, Fau-us, Gurimar, Hara-haran, Inige, Just-me-uhm, Karitase, Lumi, and so forth. They are from countries that the rulers of the Five Kingdoms have destroyed or mismanaged or are the illegitimate offspring of Five Kingdoms rulers—minor or major officials of the kingdoms—who exploit the women of those countries. In order to keep alive their history, language, and culture, the people sing stories. They refer to this as "trading in rumours" so as to avoid punishment by the rulers of the Five Kingdoms, who prohibit the circulation of anything that contradicts their own official accounts of the past (61).

Except for the monotonous brown color of the environment, the blue and orange color of such things as the boxes through which the Five Kingdoms rulers issued orders, and the uniforms that Amedea's and Beenabe's people were forced to wear, the two young women have no or only distant memories of color. When Beenabe asks Amedea about the color green, Amedea has difficulty in explaining what it:

> I knotted my brow until it hurt, to remember. Nothing. Even my locust did not stir. We slept dreaming of green. We invented it. It became everything that was good once upon a time ... Green was anything we wanted it to be. Like dry cheeks and dry eyes ... or hot barley soup, or barley sprouting on blessed earth ... or sleeping with sisters, or drinking not salty water, or walking past the horizon then home. (Bobis, *Locust Girl* 44)

They and the many other displaced people speak about the color green with the greatest sense of loss. "Green," when they hear that word, overcomes them with silence:

> "Red," the first mouth whispered to the second ear, who
> whispered back, "Red flowers," and then passed on the next
> colour to the third in line: "Orange."
> "Orange birds," the third mouth whispered back and, to the
> fourth, passed on: "Blue."

"Blue sky," the fourth mouth whispered back and, to the fifth,
passed on: "Yellow."
"Yellow fields," the fifth mouth whispered back and, to the
last, whispered: "Green."
All grew silent. (64)

In the second section of *Locust Girl*, "Singing," Amedea loses her close friend and companion soon after they reach Beenabe's country. The rulers of the Five Kingdoms burn it to the ground and the two young friends (and possibly lovers) are separated in the chaos. For three years after this, Amedea takes refuge in a cave (Cho-choli's sanctuary). When she regains her strength, she begins to walk again, this time in search of the famed central territories of the Five Kingdoms. She meets "Just-me-uhm," "a bastard of the Five Kingdoms" (Bobis, *Locust Girl* 77). His mother had been, as had Amedea's mother, "a 'green tree' favoured by" a Five Kingdoms ruler. His father is Wilidimus, the Minister of Mouths (77). He abandoned Just-me-uhm and his mother when Just-me-uhm was six years old, or no longer "an uncomplicated joy" (77). Now, Just-me-uhm works for his father, supervising "rationing outside the border"; in addition, he makes a living by illegally smuggling green trees into the central territories of the Five Kingdoms (78).

In "Love," the third and final section of *Locust Girl*, Amedea reaches the border of the central territories of the Five Kingdoms. She is carried across the border by a man named Verompe. He leaves her unconscious under a tree. When she wakes up, she is overcome by the sight of blue sky and a green tree:

> Blue fire assaulted my eyes. I had to shut them tight. Had I not seen that brilliant blue before? But not this close ... When I opened my eyes again, I felt as if they were just being born. They opened wider and wider to this thing above me that seemed to open even my chest, so my heart could share the feast. I started crying with my first vision of a green tree. (117)

Amedea also sees for the first time guri, one of the few or the only surviving large animal species in the time of the rule of the Five Kingdoms. The rulers use the species as a major food commodity, for policies and practices of the Five Kingdoms have resulted in the precipitous decline in and extinction of most of the countries' other species, vegetal as well as faunal. Women (from countries now controlled by the Five Kingdoms) slaughter the animals in organized culling operations under the close watch of Five Kingdoms officials and other government administrators.

Amedea also sees birds, oils, and flowers for the first time. They are found in plenty within the borders of the central territories (or cities) of the Five Kingdoms and are tightly controlled by the government.

Amedea also finds and is reunited with Beenabe, now a sex slave of one or more of the rulers of the Five Kingdoms. She and other young women have been taken by force into the central territories or have come to the central territories of the Five Kingdoms in desperate search of family members, water, grain, and so forth. The rulers call them "green trees" because they are "fresh and supple" and have "sweet smelling skin" (Bobis, *Locust Girl* 139). Young men whose parents came from countries outside of the Five Kingdoms also are exploited. So, too, are many other people who have lost their countries to the Five Kingdoms government. It trades in their flesh, both condoning and colluding in the lucrative trade in body parts—legs, arms, eyes, and so forth.

Amedea, who has been hiding in Beenabe's room, is discovered by one of the officials who buys and sells arms, Xuqik, the Minister of Arms. Wilidimus, the Minister of Mouths, Ycasa, the Minister of Legs, Zacarem, the Honorable Head, and Xuqik drug and interrogate Amedea. They have heard the rumors of an insect-girl who can sing, have found this being, and want to punish it. In the meantime, Zacarem lectures Amedea about the improvements that the Five Kingdoms government has made since it took over the countries of Amedea's people, Beenabe's people, Cho-choli's people, and other people's countries. He tells Amedea that the Five Kingdoms' control of what is left of "the water, the oils and the grains, the trees and the grass, and the few animals" is "*For symmetry. For equality. For justice.* So the Kingdoms are more equal now" (Bobis, *Locust Girl* 150). Amedea "desperately [wants] to believe him" but cannot (150). She is aided by the "whirring" locust in her head, who "admonish[es]" her for countenancing betraying her people and encourages her to ask the Honorable Head, "'Tell me, please, why can't us strays be equal too—with you?'" (150). Amedea "choke[s] on [her] last words, afraid [that Zacarem will strike her] for saying them" (150). He rebukes her, telling her that she and other people whose countries have been usurped by the Five Kingdoms are lazy ("wasters") and do not deserve an equal share of what wealth remains (149). He further justifies the Five Kingdoms government in words that echo arguments that Amedea heard many years before, when she and her family lived on one of the Five Kingdoms' missions: "*We will protect you*—the Book of Borders. *We will care for you*—the Book of Rations. *We will act for you*—the Book of Fires. *We will think for you*—the Book of Songs" (152).

Zacarem shows Amedea a room (hollowed out from a tree) full of "boxes of all shapes and sizes, walls of them" (Bobis, *Locust Girl* 151). It is an archive for the remains of Five Kingdoms people ("Kingdom builders"), "victims" of stray fires (153). "They're all here," Zacarem says, "lest we forget them" (152). As Amedea examines the boxes, the walls of the room turn "black and begin to move" and the ghosts of people begin to appear (153). "Silently they began milling about, walking towards me" (153). Amedea looks among them for members of her family and other people from her country, for she does not know that the room only houses the histories and bodily remains of Five Kingdoms people. "Are you number 425? Or 500?," she asks several of the silent figures (153). Later, when she asks Beenabe about the human skulls, boxes, and moving walls (film projections), Beenabe explains to her that the Five Kingdoms rulers have decreed that "[a]ll other stories and devastation must be forgotten, like they never happened" and so celebrate and preserve only "*their* stories, *their* own devastation" (158).

Following three days of solitary confinement, Amedea and Beenabe stand trial. They are charged with crimes that include "walking to the border," "singing," "feasting in the wrong season," "spreading ill-rumours," "inspiring revolt," "sleeping in the impure rooms," "bringing in the plague," and "contaminating the Kingdoms" (Bobis, *Locust Girl* 163). During the trial, they and everyone else in the courtroom hear singing. It comes from Amedea's friends eking a living outside the borders of the central territories of the Five Kingdoms. Amedea also begins to sing. "I could not help it. I had to sing" (173). The crowd is "relieved," for it now has a "culprit," "a body, a host," to scapegoat (173). As Amedea "[gathers] all the unseen voices in [her] throat," her body "swell[s] with many more voices" until it can no longer "bear the strain" (173). She "burst[s] and [catches] fire" (173). Everyone in the courtroom scatters. Amedea feels the wind lifting up "bits of [her] remains" as she is transformed fully into a winged insect (174): "My back quivered. Fluttered. Then slowly it opened, spread itself, and suddenly I was airborne, risen from my charred flesh and bones" (174). Amedea flies over the central territories of the Five Kingdoms; "I went from one tree to another. I visited the fruit and the flowers and the biggest water. I hovered over the fields of grain, afraid to land. I memorized the colours, afraid I'd forget them" (174).

Past the outskirts of the central territories of the Five Kingdoms, Amedea finds the remains of her "beloved Beenabe," guarded by Karitase and Lumi, two people from the old countries (Bobis, *Locust Girl* 178). She flies further from the borders of the central territories, to her country. There, she is astonished to see "green stubble as far as the eyes can see" (178). She then remembers that Beenabe had planted the earth there with barley seeds three years before. "I know our nature, I know our history," Amedea says, "How we plague, how we love. How frail the heart, yet how enduring" (179).

Australia after 1788: The New *terra nullius*

In the context of its identity as a work of Australian fiction, *Locust Girl* provokes a powerful comparison with arguments by environmental historians, ecocritics, and indigenous studies scholars about the loss of trees and water, loss of extensive grain belts and other arable land, intensive farming of several animal species, increasing centralization of human populations, and attempts by humans to dominate the environment in Australia after 1788. Above all, the theme of fire that the rulers of the Five Kingdoms misuse and abuse carries allusions to Australia's post-1788 pyric phenomena.

Newcomers to Australia who arrived in and not long after 1788 compared their new country to a landed estate, a vast "gentleman's park" (Gammage 5). The descriptive, "gentleman's park," as well as the word "park," frequently appears in their letters, journals, and other records (5–17). After the word "bush," which derives from southern Africa, "park" is the most frequent word in their descriptions of Australia. That is because parks "chequered" the continent (15). "Where else but in Australia," one newcomer writes,

> could I find such a park-like Acady?—mile after mile of the smoothest greensward, unbroken by any kind of fence; a sweet undulating land of knoll and slope and glen studded over, not too thickly, but in a most picturesque manner, with she-oaks, trees of the softest and richest character imaginable. (qtd. in Gammage 266)

Most people in Australia today think of parks as the green spaces that are public parks in cities or the larger state and national public parks. According to the association of parks with the latter kinds of green spaces, "park" also means "wilderness" and "untouched forest" (Gammage 15). People in Europe in the eighteenth century did not associate parks with nature, and not until "national park" was coined in the United States did the word "park" mean a public space (15). Few public parks existed in Europe in 1799. Rather, the word "park" in Europe in the eighteenth century almost always meant "tastefully arranged private estates financed by people comfortably untroubled by a need to subsist" (15). Yet, newcomers, observing trees that appeared to have been planted "as if for ornament" and woodland alternating with grassland akin to "a gentleman's park," wrote in their notebooks, diaries, letters, and so forth that Australia was just that, "an inhabited and improved country, a civilised land" (14).

Such records constitute evidence for the argument, one hardly entertained by many Australians up through and continuing until today, that before 1788 humans successfully managed the environment. A second related argument is that management ensured the flourishing of both humans and the environment. People and the environment coexisted on remarkably bounteous terms, notwithstanding the inevitability of killing on both sides, for that was modest in scale in comparison to that of today. The argument that Australia was once a vast managed estate rarely appears in Australian literature—either its histories or works of fiction—until recently. Studies such as Gammage's superb tome are crucial in the reappraisal of Australia's history and significantly support readings of literature from critical positions—namely, ecocriticism, critical plant studies, and critical animal studies stances—that are quite recent in literary studies.

Gammage's study instantly bring to mind another novel, Kim Scott's, *Benang*, and its references to Australia's vast pre-1788 parks, as well as a collection of poetry, *in the garden*, by South Australian poet Miriel Lenore. The main events of *Benang* span the years between 1880 and 1980 and center on the family of Fanny Benang, a Nyoongar woman whose story is brought to light by her great-great-grandson, Harley. He learns about Fanny and Fanny's husband, Sandy "One" Mason, by piecing together stories told to him by his Nyoongar uncles and racist white grandfather. One of the stories told to him by his uncles is about an area of parkland that was still extant in southeastern Western Australia at the turn of the nineteenth century. The young Fanny Benang and Sandy Mason are making their way home across some "grassy plains" (Scott 179). There, they see

> flowers spread across the undulating plains. Pinks, creams, yellow white and blue; delicate little things, looking so fragile, but so hardy, it seemed. The sun did not mark them, nor the wind tear ... The mallee was in flower, brazenly red ... There were kangaroos all about, keeping an eye out ears up. The animals looked at them [Fanny and Sandy] and scratched their chests, thinking. Then bounded away with such exuberance ... You could look across, and yeah it was green and soft and undulating; it was what was called hill and dale, with running creeks and tall trees here and there. They were Yate trees, their high crowns glistening in the afternoon sun. And their yellow sap; that yellow sap it tasted like sugar. (179)

Sandy thinks "of all the books he'd read, yet understood that it was people and fire had made this parkland" (179).

In another story told to Harley about Fanny's firsthand knowledge of parks, and the destruction of them by newcomers, Fanny is taking part in an annual Christmas and New Year celebration with Nyoongar and newcomer people at Wirlup Haven. "[T]eamsters and their women," "farm labourers and shepherds," and other "pastoralists in their sulkies and two-in-hands" ride out to the site where the festivities are about to commence (Scott 254). On the way, they come to "a small, grassy plain among trees ... just like an English Parkland, people said" (254). Looking around "at the dry grass, the tight and tangled growth beneath the trees," Fanny knows that the area used to be managed by her people despite the fact that it "ha[s] not been burnt for years" (254).

The main subject of Miriel Lenore's poetry collection, *in the garden*, is a majestic post-1788 park, the Botanic Gardens in South Australia's capital city, Adelaide. The second section of *in the garden* specifically focuses on the subjects of the park's trees. They are, indeed, beautiful beings, to walk, talk, and sit among. They also have not been given the freedoms most humans take for granted: the freedom of movement, the freedom to choose one's visitors, the freedom to converse with members of one's own species. The trees, like many populations of marginalized, imprisoned, and forgotten humans, have analogous histories and experiences, of transportation, colonization, servitude, imprisonment, loneliness, indigenization, naturalization, isolation, hybridization, obloquy, and loss. In the poem "The oak" (Lenore 15) the speaker refers to one of those trees, a Northeast American species of oak (*Quercus macrocarpa*). The speaker recounts that the tree was brought to Australia and planted in the Botanic Gardens at the time of federation, when the governor of South Australia was Hallam, Lord Tennyson, the son of Alfred, Lord Tennyson:

> Branches of the huge Burr Oak
> *(Quercus macrocarpa — East North America)*
> touch the ground on three sides
> the fourth is cut away
> for us to sip tea at white plastic tables
>
> Those plebian birds (or so I think)
> black ducks and seagulls pick up crumbs
> but the tree is noble:
>
> Planted by the State's Governor in 1901
> Hallam, Lord Tennyson
> who carried always (did his mother agree?)
> his father's love for his friend
>
> Reminding me that poetry, love and iced coffee
> are the centre of my city

In understated and prosaic language, which is characteristic of *in the garden* as a whole, Lenore critiques humans' nonchalant uses of and attitudes toward the nonhuman world of flora and the mapping and parceling out of green space between the eighteenth and twenty-first centuries. One of the Burr Oak's long arms has been chopped off to provide a more comfortable seating space for the humans who frequent the Botanic Gardens; it has been "cut away / for us to sip tea at white plastic tables." The description of the severed branch and the tree's remaining long draping branches also evokes post-1788 Australia in the sense that this country became in 1788 one of the most extensive reaches or "branches" of the British Empire and its ties to this empire were severed (to a limited extent) in 1901 under the act of federation. The tree itself is a British symbol. Although the tree that inspires Lenore's poem was transported from the United States, it brings to mind an iconic symbol of British identity, the common species of English Oak (*Quercus robar*). This symbolism is reinforced by the reference in the poem to Alfred, Lord Tennyson, one of England's most beloved poets and read by many English people in a time, the Victorian period, when "more than a quarter of all the territory of the surface of the earth" was directly or indirectly claimed by the British Empire (Greenblatt 2012, 1018).

The final two lines of "The oak" (Lenore 15) seem to sweep aside abruptly the implicit postcolonial ecocritical arguments advanced in the first ten lines as well as to dismiss the main subject of focus of those arguments, the Burr Oak. The speaker finishes that "the centre" of Adelaide for her or him is not the botanical gardens let alone their resident Burr Oak, which has grown big and become cumbersome. Rather, "the centre" is "poetry, love, and iced coffee." The speaker seems to be a visitor who is as indifferent to the tree as is the administrator who instructed a gardener to lopsidedly trim the tree to make room for people and plastic chairs. The Burr Oak and the Botanic Gardens no longer seem to count for much. They are anachronistic, out of place, and in the way of culture and modern life. Yet, the sudden rhetorical dropping of or turning away from the subjects of the Burr Oak and gardens in the final two lines puts into question the disregard or defilement that the given divergence apparently serves.

"The living fossil" (Lenore 14), another poem from *in the garden*, similarly pertinently speaks to the interest of the lives—material, historical, affective, social, and so forth—of trees; its main subject is one of the world's oldest extant tree species, the *Wollemi nobilis*:

> Once animals were captive
> in the centre of the Garden
> now a pine tree is behind bars
>
> Found in the Greater Blue Mountains
> the precious *Wollemi nobilis* stands
> in its cage on the slope above the lake
>
> Known only from fossils till 1994
> rarity and phylogeny combine
> to make this a remarkable plant
>
> Not named for its character, Gondwana's
> forgotten pine honours David Noble
> the Park Ranger who found it
>
> Healthy after its transplanting here
> it will test, with a Mounty Lofty sibling
> The effects of habitat
>
> A child puts his fingers through the bars
> The pine does not bite

As the speaker states, a park ranger first discovered the rare species of *Wollemi nobilis* in 1994 in a region of the Blue Mountains in New South Wales. (Some of this region now is a national park, Wollemi National Park.) The speaker calls the tree "Gondwana's forgotten pine" (14). "Gondwana" is a reference to the tree's ancient lineage, which traces back 200 million years to the time of two supercontinents. One of these, Gondwana, joined the land mass of Australia to other land masses in the southern hemisphere—namely Africa, Antarctica, Madagascar, and South America ("The Wollemi Pine"; "Gondwana"). The *Wollemi nobilis* tree that was brought to Adelaide's Botanic Gardens was initially put "behind bars" to protect it from crowds of visitors. One of the spectators, a child, "puts his fingers through the bars" of the cage that separates pine from public. "The pine does not bite" (14). Over the years, interest waned in the tree, and the bars were removed, as Lenore states in an endnote. The word "forgotten" in "Gondwana's forgotten pine" carries this sense of neglect.

The small but telling detail in "The living fossil" of an ancient tree imprisoned in a cage and the endnote, which tells readers that the bars eventually were removed, emphasize three kinds of ecophobic relationships with and attitudes toward the unknown world of flora and fauna. The first kind associates with, paradoxically, curiosity and delight in that dwindling world and the isolation of it in the effort to protect it (or of what little remains of it) by incarcerating it and putting it on display in private and public parks. The second associates with the neglect of that world when it loses value according to mainstream definitions of use and value. The bars are removed when the tree no longer is a main public attraction. The tree will grow old alone, separated from its own family members and neglected by most of the human populations around it. (Other trees around it, however, may give it companionship and solace.) The third kind of ecophobic relationships and attitudes refers to fear of that unknown world. All three kinds, and many others, have barely begun to be spoken about, learned about, and debated in our public and private institutions.

Although Bobis's cli-fi novel *Locust Girl* is not ostensibly about Australia's pre-1788 vast managed parks, let alone the country's post-1788 colonial and postcolonial parks, these subjects come to mind when reading the novel. Set in an apocalyptic landscape that is identified only as a large area of land controlled by the rulers of the "Five Kingdoms," the novel could be about many other countries and regions of the world affected by climate change inclusive of drought, fire, species loss, and unequal allocation of and use of resources. However, when one reads it in the context of its identity as a work of Australian literary fiction, *Locust Girl* immediately brings to mind suppressed and marginalized arguments about the decimation of Australia's once vast parklands and its post-1788 diminutive public parks. Thus, the novel also resonates with arguments about the destruction of Australia's once extensive grain belts and the attendant loss of ancient milling techniques, estimated to be more than 18,000 years old (Pascoe 47).

Australian grain crops today are concentrated in the southwest and southeast of Australia and located close to or not far off from coastlines. Before 1788, grain belts extended across Australia and covered a much larger area (Pascoe 29). Cultivated by Aboriginal Australians, the grains that made up those belts included Coopers clover (*Trigonella sauvissima*); barley grass or native millet (*Panicum decompositum*), also called cooly or parpar; onion grass (*Cyperus bubosus*); nardoo (*Marsilea drummondii)*; fig; quandong; Australian banana (*Musa acuminata*, subspecies *banksii*); compung (cumbungi); balyan or bulrush; yam daisies (*Microsceris lanceloata*); Vanilla Lily (*Arthropodium milleflorum*), a staple source, like the yam daisies, of starch and protein in Eastern Victoria; Curly Mitchell grass (*Astraleba lappacea*); and native oatgrass (*Themeda avanacea*) (32, 33, 44, 45, 46, 51, 119–120, 146).

Aboriginal Australian aquaculture was as extensive and sophisticated as grain cultivation was before 1788. Abalone—called mutton fish by newcomers—was cultivated all along Australia's western, southern, and eastern coast, from the "south of Perth, across the southern coast including Tasmania and her islands, west to Gippsland in eastern Victoria and north to Wollongong in New South Wales" (Pascoe 67). In southwest Victoria, Aboriginal Australians also cultivated eel, building "vast eel concourses" that took decades and perhaps centuries to refine (55).[3] Many predate the pyramids in Egypt. The "massive fish traps" on the Darling River at Brewarrina in New South Wales, which are among and may be "the oldest man-made structures" on the planet, are as significant as Stonehenge or Easter Island (60). Newcomers did not recognize let alone respect that. They destroyed most of the aquaculture systems "in the first days after their arrival," razing entire villages to the ground by fire along with the aquaculture constructions "in their successful efforts to colonize and settle in Australia" (60).

Up until quite recently, archaeologists who studied the buildings of the oldest people of North America found that at best those people were "complex hunter-gatherers" and at worst "wealthy scavengers ... incapable of the sophisticated cultural development associated with agricultural societies" (Pascoe 61).[4] This erroneous finding was partly due to and compounded by the fact that agricultural work was performed and managed by women, who did not impart their knowledge to outsiders (62). Similarly, in the case of Australia, as late as the 1980s, studies of pre-1788 grain production by anthropologists and archaeologists reflect little or no understanding of the critical role that women played in that production and so a paucity of knowledge of "the vast scale" of the grain harvests (64). Indeed, it is "rare to come across a text after 1880 that describes the existence of intensive Aboriginal food production: the fishing system, or grain and tuber production" (64). Instead, manufacturers of Australiana churn out countless "plaster figurines of Aboriginal men standing on one leg, spear in hand waiting for the windfall kangaroo" (65).

Only a decade ago, in 2010, a member of parliament, speaking out against a State of Victoria Native Title Bill, implied that Aboriginal Australians were largely a nomadic people, therefore they "had no concept of land ownership," and so "Native Title" claims did not apply to Aboriginal Australian land claims (qtd. in Pascoe 77). The member of parliament was repeating perhaps what he had studied at school. In standard school textbooks, Aboriginal Australian people are described as being nomadic. In fact, most were sedentary. In those same books, Aboriginal Australians' houses invariably are called "huts," "hovels," and "hump[ies]" (Pascoe 77, 85). Analogous structures in European countries are called "croft houses" (77).

Newcomers took basalt material from the fish traps built by Aboriginal Australians and used the material to build fences as well as other infrastructure for their own homes and farm buildings. The basalt farm fences, still seen today, "are now subject to heritage protection" (Pascoe 93). Other newcomers' built environments date only to the last century and similarly are protected under heritage laws. Those built environments include Federation-era buildings, 1930s architecture, and 1950s commercial buildings. Many are extraordinarily beautiful structures and resonate with history. Yet, to bestow great cultural and historic value on those buildings and hardly any on cultural sites that hold particularly inestimable value for the descendants of Australia's oldest people is unfair, to say the least. Until today, it is extremely difficult to successfully apply for heritage protection of ancient Aboriginal agricultural structures that predate by thousands of years such designated heritage structures as colonial basalt fences.

Regions of Australia that now are "mythologized as the desolate Outback" once were productive and healthy environment[s] (Pascoe 76). The most inland deserts, and other areas that are infamous according to accounts by European explorers, were "peopled by large numbers of Aboriginal people taking advantage of plains to manage flood dispersal, plant crops, and harvest and store grain" (76). Before 1788, people were affluent, spent most of their time in activities of learning and leisure, not in trying to survive. "Of course there were hungry times [for the oldest Australian people], or [they] would not have managed their resources so carefully," but they were not "hinged" on either "uncertainty" or "toil" (302). Nonetheless, the "tenacity of ... delusion" about the primitive subsistence culture of Aboriginal people continues today to "[impoverish] national debate" (77).

The descriptions in *Locust Girl* of the central territories of the Five Kingdoms, the "biggest country," "last remaining country," and "last green home on earth" (Bobis, *Locust Girl* 101), also bring to mind Australia in the context of its five most densely (human) populated environments—the capital cities of Sydney, Melbourne, Brisbane, Perth, and Adelaide—and its five main centers of power and affluence, which include the first four of the cities listed here in addition to Canberra. The Five Kingdoms' main resources—Waters, Fires, Seeds, Oils, and Colours—evoke, further, the five principal resources in Australia that have been exploited, misunderstood, mismanaged, or eradicated under ecocidal policies. Those resources are water, bushfire, pre-1788 grains, trees (oil-rich eucalypts), and diverse animal and plant species (which, in Bobis's novel, correspond to "Colours"). The abundance of water before 1788 "softened drought, spread resources, and let people walk easily over more of Australia, even in arid regions" (Gammage 106). Top soils all across the continent were so soft, "spongy," and "absorbent" that "horses travelled over their fetlocks in the loose soil" (104). Today, much of the earth is hard, dry, and cracked. More than half of Australia's biggest body of water, the Murray–Darling catchment, has disappeared. Whereas much of Australia today is a dun or brown color all year round, before 1788 it was a riot of color except for during the hottest days of summer. Bushfire was frequent before 1788, but fires were smaller in size and more efficiently managed. Grains, similarly to water and bushfire, were evenly dispersed across Australia before 1788. So, too, trees—inclusive of the ubiquitous oil-laden eucalypts—were fewer in number before 1788 but more evenly distributed (320). Today, Australia leads the world in loss of species diversity (320). After 1788, newcomers, "ran big mobs of sheep on pasture that was never going to last the next dry period; put cattle on fire-prone forest hillsides; and cleared land to plant [introduced] grain crops in thin, nutrient-poor soils that took off and blew away when the rains stopped altogether" (Rigby, *Dancing with Disaster* 120). If people

> did jar the land's regenerative capacity, imbalances were slight and their threat remote. What came after 1788 was much more serious. Damage then was ignorant rather than willful, but revolutionary. (Gammage 313)

Fish-Hair Woman, the novel by Bobis that immediately precedes the publication of *Locust Girl*, refers to human conflict in a relatively narrow sense, the same sense that distinguishes Hazzard's *The Great Fire*, the title of which refers to the Second World War and specifically to the fire-bombing of Tokyo and nuclear obliteration of Nagasaki and Hiroshima. Set in the Philippines against the backdrop of a military dictatorship that evokes the rule of Ferdinand Marcos (president of the Philippines between 1965 and 1986) and brutal crackdown on dissidents, *Fish-Hair Woman* depicts the incalculable human toll of war. Estrella Capili, the "fish-hair woman," one of thousands of innocent people punished under the brutal military regime, is forced to "trawl" a river (Iraya) with her 12-meter-long hair in search of the bodies of civilians who have been murdered. She meets and falls in love with an Australian man, Tony

McIntyre, who subsequently disappears. Thirteen years later, McIntyre's son, Luke, travels to the Philippines from Australia to find out what happened to his father and the mysterious fish-hair woman.

In *Locust Girl*, awarded the Christina Stead Prize for Fiction in 2016, Bobis also writes about military conflict. Differently from *Fish-Hair Woman*, *Locust Girl* addresses the toll that internecine conflict has on the environment as well as the human. A narrative that is seemingly inspired by Bobis's second country, Australia, as *Fish-Hair Woman* is evidently inspired by Bobis's first country, the Philippines, and a novel that carries as many descriptions of dry and burnt earth as *Fish-Hair Woman* does of archipelagic and flooded realms, *Locust Girl* provokes comparison with the abuse, deliberate or guileless, of fire by many people who came to Australia after 1788 and the environmental as well as human losses that Australia experienced in the same period.[5]

Indeed, the most remarkable parallel between *Locust Girl* and arguments about the Australian environment by environmental historians, indigenous studies scholars, and ecocritics is the content that evokes post-1788 bushfire in Australia. Most bushfire before 1788 was unnatural in the sense that bushfires were deliberately set alight by humans (Gammage 318). Fire "was made, not natural" (318). The fires today that escape humans' efforts to control, thwart, or stop them might be called natural in the sense that many are not deliberately caused by humans. At the same time, they might be called unnatural in the sense that they seem to contravene the oldest laws of the planet, call them the oldest human laws or the oldest natural laws.

Certainly, fire defines the Australian continent and its islands before 1788, but people then recognized fire as a friend, not fiend. They collaborated with rather than fought against fire. It was their "closest ally," (Gammage 156). They recognized in it not only a "great challenge" but also a "great opportunity" for partnership (157). After 1788 ("colonial") fire was "lawless and generally ill fitted to existing ecosystems and climatic conditions" (Rigby, *Dancing with Disaster* 119).

Australia has the most pyrophitic environments in the world. Rich in oils, the country's ubiquitous eucalyptus trees—trees that call "exiled Australians" back home more so than any other Australian flora—"greet fire with astonishing ingenuity and diversity, encouraging, tolerating, resisting, deflecting, re-greening, [and] seeding" (Gammage 115, 119). "[T]ough, adaptable, battlers in hard times [and] opportunists in good," the leaves of most eucalypts, which are evergreens and molt all year, "release volatile oils on hot days when fire is most likely" (115, 120). Eucalypts that "dominate dry sclerophyll forests and grassy woodland ... merrily regenerate by putting out masses of new branchlets all up their scorched trunks" (Rigby, *Dancing with Disaster* 121). Others need a major fire to reproduce. One of those species is mountain ash. It grows in wet sclerophyll forests, is one of the stateliest and most regal of eucalypts, is the tallest flowering plant in the world, and is one of the world's tallest tree species, rivaling a more famous tall tree species, the North American redwood (121).

Although mountain ash needs a major fire to regenerate, it only needs that "once every four hundred years or so" (Rigby, *Dancing with Disaster* 121). In such an event, the hard seeds of the trees burst open "in the intense heat," fall from the tops of the trees to the ground, and "germinate in their parents' ashes, moistened by the rains of the cool change and bathed in the sunlight that now falls unimpeded in the absence of the forest canopy" (121). Crown fires in mountain ash forests

> burn more explosively than any other wildfires in the world, building into a roaring tornado of flame that generates its own weather and can be seen from space. Long strips of bark and huge balls of flame and gases break away and are carried by the wind to spot fires kilometers away from the fast-moving front, the radiant heat of which can cause anything flammable within a radius of four hundred meters, including fur and flesh, to combust instantaneously. (121–122)

Australia in the twenty-first century is ravaged by pyric events on a scale not seen before. The worst bushfires on record have occurred since 2000. The "Black Saturday" fire that swept through Victoria in the summer of 2009 was the "most intense" of Australia's "megablazes" to date (122). It released energy equivalent to 1,500 Hiroshima atomic bombs (122). Large domestic water storage tanks simply evaporated (122). The endangered leadbeater's possum, a species that is Victoria's "faunal emblem," "lost 40 percent of its remaining habitat" in the inferno (140). The 2003 firestorm that burnt over 70% of the Australian Capital Territory killed 95% of the wildlife in the parks in the southwest (Gammage 157). The fire "ripped trees 70 cm across into the air and dumped into a back yard a garden shed complete with tools and shelving from so far away that no-one could find where it came from" (157). In 2019 and early 2020, the bushfires that swept through New South Wales, Victoria, and South Australia further beggared belief. They were even more catastrophic than the Black Saturday fires of 2009, wiping out 3 billion animals and 10 million ha of vegetation (Slezak; Wheaton). Researchers believe that "the only comparable wildlife disasters in recent history" are the oil spill in 1989 in Alaska (the Exxon Valdez spill) and the oil spill (and blowout) in 2010 in the Gulf of Mexico (the BP Deepwater Horizon spill) (Slezak). In contrast with the other worst bushfires to date in Australia, the recent 2019–2020 fires are not named after a single day of the week or local region. They lasted so long and were so extensive that they are being called the Black Summer bushfires.

Many bushfires in the nineteenth and twentieth centuries were as horrific from the perspective of those who witnessed and experienced them at close quarters and suffered through them. Preceded by a drought "so severe that thousands of topsoil form western Victoria's Mallee district [blew] into Melbourne" and eclipsed the sun (Rigby, *Dancing with Disaster* 142), the Ash Wednesday fires in 1983 incinerated large areas of land in the states of South Australia and Victoria. A century before that, the Black Thursday fire of 1851 burnt "almost half of Victoria" (Gammage 161).

According to firsthand accounts of settlers and explorers, a main method that Aboriginal people used to manage fire was to selectively burn forests at "low-level burns" (Pascoe 116). Pre-1788 fire was as "planned" as it was "precise" and "could be repeated hence predicted" (Gammage 185). It was "organized locally" but was "universal," and it "united Australia" (185). "After 1788, some newcomers imitated 1788 burning, or thought they did, but most banned fire, which meant abandoning land to erratic fire" (122). Bushfires either "increased in number, severity and extent" or "fire sensitive species were favored" (122). In 1836, a newcomer writes about a part of country in Western Australia where fire management skills were still being practiced relatively unhindered by newcomers:

> the country is kept comparatively free from under wood and other obstructions, having the character of an open forest through most parts of which one can ride freely; otherwise, in all probability, it would soon become impenetrably thick ... This has already been proved in the case of Van Dieman's Land [Tasmania], where, in consequence of the transportation of the Natives to Great or Flinders Island, and the consequent absence of extensive periodical fires, the bush has grown up thick to a most inconvenient degree ... It is true that we might ourselves burn the bush, but we could never do it with the same judgement and good effect as the Natives, who keep the fire within due bounds. (qtd. in Gammage 318)

Other newcomers observed that Aboriginal Australians kept in check with fire various species of cypress pine, a "notorious regenerator" (Gammage 318). When one of those new Australians first arrived in Nymagee, New South Wales, he saw "open box country, covered with a waving mass of herbage" (qtd. in Gammage 319). "I thought it was a pastoral paradise," he writes (qtd. in Gammage 319). "That was before the growth of the pine scrub," he adds (qtd. in Gammage 319). In 1885, by which time the traditional owners of the land were denied management of it, the pine country "had started to spread to an enormous extent" (qtd. in Gammage 319). The newcomer "scrubbed [cleared] the place in 1886, again in 1890, and again in 1894," but by 1900, "some of it [was] ... nearly as bad as ever" (qtd. in Gammage 319).

Newcomer Peter Cunningham describes the countryside of Parramatta and Liverpool in New South Wales in 1827. The land then was "lightly timbered and so clear of undergrowth that you could ride a gig in any direction without hindrance" (Pascoe 117). A short time after, "the countryside was overwhelmed by understorey species" because newcomers prevented "the Aborigines ... from operating their traditional fire regimes" (117).

In causing some tree species to become extinct because of their lack of knowledge of fire, newcomers "liberated" other tree species (Gammage 320). However, newcomers were less learned than older Australian people about which trees species would or would not take over and overdetermine the environment. The species that took over included, in addition to some species of cypress pine, acacias. They are the most common and the most popular species of flora in Australia in addition to eucalypts, and they now are prolifically feral. Their populations once were modest because people kept them in check (Gammage 320).

For thousands of years, Aboriginal Australian people coexisted with fire. They also "worked hard to make [it] malleable, and to confine killer fires to legends and cautionary tales" (Gammage 157). Selectively burning areas of bush, also called "fire-stick farming," and using a "a mosaic of low-level burns" to stop some species from dominating others, the oldest Australian people understood the great alliance between fire and eucalyptus trees (Pascoe 49, 116). Thus, before 1788, "[e]rratic fire," so-called natural fire, was the least "manageable of the variables constraining Australia's plants" and "[c]ontrolled fire," so-called unnatural fire, was the most manageable of those variables (Gammage 121). Before 1788, "fire-diverse communities" also "grew comfortably together" (121). Aboriginal "pyrotechnics kept fires manageable and productive" (Rigby, *Dancing with Disaster* 116). What is "without doubt" is that the first Australians

> ultimately got the hang of living on a ... fire-prone continent and ... most of Australia's megadiverse plants and animals eventually learned to dance along with the sophisticated fire regimes that [the first Australians] established. The outcome of this process of pyro-symbiogenesis was not only a peculiarly pyrophitic biota but a human society that had become extraordinarily adept at [co-existing with fire]. (117)

Aboriginal Australian people's coadaptation with bushfire is an "exemplary" yet greatly underrepresented "tale of pyrosymbiogenesis" (116). Were it to hold great significance for both Australian society and other societies that make up the "perilously warming planet", it would generate felicitous changes in mainstream attitudes toward the environment, inclusive of Australia's pyrophitic environments (116). After 1788, a year that represents the beginning of, and "the height of," "pyrophobia" in Australia, newcomers mostly chose to ignore or were unaware of one of the most "pyrophitic geocultural landscapes on the planet" (116). Today, we are only just beginning to appreciate and understand that and "not least [so] by paying great respect to Aboriginal pyrotechnics" (116).

Les Murray is one of Australia's most distinguished pastoral poets (McCooey 901)—or "bush bard[s]" (Chiasson 136)—as well as one of the country's most technically accomplished poets (Kane 79, Huggan 80). He stands "at the fore" of "Australian literature" in which "the landscape" is "the main protagonist" (Rothwell 33). The poem, "Late Summer Fires" (*Subhuman Redneck Poems* 16), exemplifies that. Read from a postcolonial ecocritical perspective, "Late Summer Fires" evokes in particular, similarly to Bobis's novel, the betrayal of the environment in the context of the clash between pastoralist interests and Aboriginal Australian land rights. Bushfire, an ubiquitous feature of the Australian landscape, is foregrounded in the poem and functions in it as a metaphor for the efforts, unsuccessful but catastrophic to eradicate Aboriginal Australian land rights.

In the final lines of the poem, a pastoralist family leaves an area destroyed by a fire, taking their sheep with them. The horizon is stained yellow from the smoke of the fire, the grass has been burned black, the once naturally red earth now is blackened, and animals have become bloated carcasses of red and black decaying flesh. Their bodies look like the charred stumps of felled trees. Up until the last line of the poem, the poem seems to be an evocative and terrible description of a bush fire, and the poem is that. However, when one reaches the final three words, one sees that the poem can be read as an oblique allusion to Aboriginal Australian land rights and clashes between various interests, pastoralist and non-pastoralist, over those rights. The final climatic words, a direct reference to the Aboriginal Australian flag, yoke together the subjects of bushfire and Aboriginal Australian land rights in the most powerful symbol at the national level of Aboriginal Australian identity, which is inseparable from Aboriginal Australian land rights. The four colors that appear in the poem aid to effect the given yoking: red, yellow, black, and white. The first three describe the Aboriginal Australian flag and Aboriginal Australian identity as well as bush fire; the last color, as it appears in the poem, alludes to white Australia, or pastoral interests that trace back to Anglo-European colonization and settlement of Australia.

Australian history since 1788 is closely intertwined with the history of the exploitation of the Australian environment as well as its oldest people by newcomers. Their colonial-settler pastoralist enterprises transformed the Australian continent into vast stretches of wheat farms and tracts of cattle and sheep stations. The oldest environments were not completely beaten by those enterprises, as the speaker says in "Late Summer Fires" (*Subhuman Redneck Poems* 16), but the lack of understanding about those environments has caused stupendous environmental as well as human misery and loss. This devastation continues today, in the periodic relaxation of building zone regulations, political lobbying of developers to industrially develop or urbanize areas that are prone to bush fires, aggressive acts (both offshore and onshore) of mining companies and nuclear power interests, loss of and disrespect for Aboriginal Australian land rights, and alliance with not opposition to bushfire.[6]

In *Locust Girl*, interminable fire, uncontrollable fire, deliberate abuse of fire, and extended periods of drought are the norm, and water, seeds, oils, and colors (biodiversity) are scarce outside of the borders of the Five Kingdoms. Grandfather Opi, one of the displaced people whom Amedea meets in her desperate search for water and grain, sings stories about the time before "the big dry" when every country had many colors, abundant fresh water from springs, "golden grains" from grasses and other food crops, and a regular supply of meat from animals, who "grazed among the green" (Bobis, *Locust Girl* 102). Opi, Amedea, Beenabe, Espra, Daninen, and thousands of others hail from many small countries in one big estate. Their countries conjure Australia before 1788, when it was a loosely knit amalgamation of countries. Then, there were disputes between people from different regions of country, such as arguments about the boundaries between one country and the next, but typically these were solved through negotiation. Violent clashes were rare. The oldest people of Australian also were more open than not to sharing their country with and showcasing it to newcomers.

Among the many records of newcomers that Gammage cites in his study, a particularly poignant one concerns the testimony of Alexander Mollison. Mollison set up a lambing station in 1837 near Barnawartha, Victoria. An Aboriginal Australian man, called "Jimmy" by white people, introduced Mollison and other newcomers to the area (Gammage 307). He burnt it to prepare it for them, for "[h]e knew what would result: a park abundant with emu, duck and more. He managed his land in every sense, indeed with so much sense that he seemed to have thought that the newcomers would manage and share it equally sensibly" (307). He

> paid fearfully for his mistake. Unknowing how momentous his gift was, unseeing how carefully his land was made, uncaring of his pride, [the white people] displaced him, and within months his people were fighting a losing battle to save his country. (308)

In the final pages of his study, Gammage states:

> There is no return to 1788. Non-Aborigines are too many, too centralized, too stratified, too comfortable, too conservative, too successful, too ignorant. We are still newcomers, still in wilderness ... We use land care merely to mitigate land misuse. We champion sustainability, which evokes merely surviving, whereas in 1788 people

> assumed abundance ... We take more and leave the future less ... When the time comes to choose between parks and people, species and space, food and freedom, 1788's values will be obliterated. (321)

A little later, Gammage writes,

> If *terra nullius* exists anywhere in [Australia], it was made by Europeans ... when [it] came ... an ancient philosophy was destroyed by the completely unexpected, an invasion of new people and ideas. A major achievement ended. Only fragments remain. For the people of 1788, the loss was stupefying. For newcomers, it did not seem great. Until recently few noticed that they had lost anything at all. (323)

Gammage revisits an infamous term that Anglo-European colonizers used to describe Australia in 1788, *terra nullius*, in his argument that if Australia ever was an empty land, then it became that after 1788, in a period of time when newcomers laid waste to the continent and its oldest people. Today, Australia's parks "have gone," and the country's earth "has changed" (Gammage 17, 103). "Topsoil blows away, hills slip, gullies scour, silt chokes, salt spreads, [and] soil compacts" (103). Kangaroos, wallabies, and other grazer species that populated Australia before 1788, unlike the grazer animal species that newcomers brought by the millions to Australia, do "not break up the surface of the soil—or compact it—both of which lead to erosion" (Pascoe 43).

Australia is "a world leader in animal and plant extinction," a consequence in part of the mismanagement of bushfire after 1788 and ignorance of "how ancient and vital 1788s unnatural fires were" (Gammage 320). Gammage uses the term "unnatural" to mean human-engineered. By such use, he calls attention to how the terms "natural" and "unnatural" environments can slip and slide in sense and use. Much of Australia before 1788 "was even a different colour" because of forces that were no less human, or no less unnatural, than the forces that shape Australia today. Differently from the present dominant forces, those older forces reflected humans' willingness to co-exist with other species on their terms as much as their own (human) species' terms (320). Australia "had more green grass in summer" as well as "much less undergrowth" (320). In 1888, a hundred years after newcomers colonized and settled in Australia, it "had more trees," but they were less evenly distributed and posed more fire risk because of the areas where they grew without close human supervision (320). Today, there are "fewer trees on farms, swampland ... but more in forests, national parks and remote places" (320). Further, newcomers mistook the areas where trees were concentrated for fertile land for farming and so deforested those areas while letting other areas, extant parkland, which was cultivated and rich in grasses, become feral (320). Older Australian left to the forests the "inferior soils" and practiced agriculture on the richer soils (Pascoe 116).

The people of 1788 "spent more time each year managing land than Darwin or the [*Sydney*] *Herald* editor in a lifetime"; they "had no hope of encountering such myopia" as that reflected in the words of Darwin when, in 1836, he wrote that Aborigines were "a set of harmless savages wandering about without knowing where they shall sleep at night"; and as that reflected in the words of the editor of the *Sydney Herald*, in 1838, when he declared that Aborigines "bestowed no labour on the land and that—and that only—it is which gives a right of property to it" and how could the "great continent" of Australia ever have been "intended by the Creator to remain an unproductive wilderness?" (qtd. in Gammage 309).

Gammage's *The Biggest Estate on Earth: How Aborigines Made Australia*, "the fullest account to date of Aboriginal place-making, or 'land management'" (Rigby, *Dancing with Disaster* 116), and the winner of the Victorian Prize for Literature in 2012, as with Rigby's *Dancing With Disaster: Environmental Histories, Narratives, and Ethics for Perilous Times* and Pascoe's *Dark Emu: Black Seeds: Agriculture or Accident*, winner of the 2016 New South Wales Premier's Awards Book of the Year and shortlisted for the 2014 Victorian Premier's Literary Award for Indigenous Writing and the 2014 Queensland Literary Awards, speak for current knowledge of Australia's unique pyrophitic ecologies and evolutionary character of "pyrosymbiogenesis" (Rigby 116). That knowledge reflects that to overdetermine the interests of other species or to profess to ethically manage environments in ways that render environments agentless is to embezzle the human as well as the environment and privilege some human populations at the great expense of others. An analogous argument appears in Bobis's novel *Locust Girl*. It portrays a country that is threatened more by bushfires than in the past, is less green than in the past, and is where the rulers have steadily pushed to the side the rights of self-government of the environment, and with that the rights and knowledge banks of its oldest human caretakers.

In an essay entitled "Theorizing in a Space of Ambivalent Openness: Ecocriticism and Ecophobia," Simon C. Estok summarizes the emergence of the discipline of ecocriticism. He notes that in the 1970s, when the discipline was taking shape, the main motivation for its scholars was environmental activism. That waned in the 1980s, at the height of poststructuralism, a movement that weakened scholarly consensus among ecocritics. For some, poststructural theory and practice imprisoned academics in language and denied material realities, and so denied the realities of the environment. For others, poststructuralism was a boon, extraordinarily helpful in illuminating some of the false or suspect ontological claims of mainstream environmentalism, inclusive of anthropocentric and reductive definitions of nature and the environment (Estok 204–205).[7] A quarter of a century on, encouraged more than hindered by poststructural theory, environmental activism is being taken as seriously by ecocriticism's leading scholars as it was by scholars active in the 1970s and early 1980s. As Ursula K. Heise defines the discipline, ecocriticism began as a sub-disciplinary area of English literary theory and criticism, grew into "a field of inquiry and praxis" spanning the humanities and the sciences, and today is held together by "the triple allegiance to the scientific study of nature, the scholarly analysis of cultural representations, and the political struggle for more sustainable ways of inhabiting the natural world" (506).

Estok's implicit call for ecocritics to engage in and support environmental activism and Heise's description of ecocriticism, which states in effect that ecocriticism is not that without political engagement, are a tall order for ecocritics who work and live in regions of the world where to be politically active is to risk imprisonment, rape, torture, and execution. That call and description also ask a great deal from many ecocritics who work and live in so-called democratic countries but identify with politically hounded or marginalized communities. One of those countries is Australia. It has an international reputation for upholding human rights yet routinely betrays those rights in the case of Aboriginal Australian people and other minorities.[8]

In his critical plant studies work, John Ryan visited the Kurongkurl Katitjin Centre for Indigenous Australian Education at Edith Cowan University in Western Australia. In *Green Sense*, he discusses a particular garden at the center. When he visited it, he met with some staff who worked there. One of those staff, Jason Barrow, an education officer at the center, explained that the primary purpose for the garden, which included two balga tree species, balga (*Xanthorrhea presseii*) and mimidi (*Xanthorrhoea brunonis*), and a Western Australian Christmas tree species, also known as mudja (*Nuytsia floribunda*), was to educate the public about pre-1788 human-vegetal relations, Noongar pyro-technology, and the fire season, or *birok*, as it is called in the Noongar language (Ryan, *Green Sense* 310). Today, most Australians have little or no knowledge of *birok* or the fire seasons in other parts of Australia. Indigenous studies scholars, ecocritics, critical plant studies and animal studies scholars, and environmental history scholars are endeavoring to restore, and add to, that knowledge. The next chapter reflects some of that new knowledge as it is generated out of biosemiotics. In addition, Chapter 5 dips into the manifestly humanist area of inquiry of translation studies, which offers insights into translation in the context of the work of translating the languages of other beings beside humans. Those beings are as discursive, or linguistic, as human beings, who are, in turn, as material and embodied as their nonhuman fellow beings.

Notes

1 The firebombing of Tokyo killed about 100,000 civilians and obliterated about half of the city (Carney).

2 While I do not directly discuss Bobis's novel in terms of its status as a work of cli-fi, much of what I do say ties directly to critical investigations of cli-fi literature. Two prominent cli-fi literature scholars, Axel Goodbody and Adeline Johns-Putra, define it as being

> a distinctive body of cultural work which engages with anthropogenic climate change, exploring the phenomenon not just in terms of setting, but with regard to psychological and social issues, combining fictional plots with meteorological facts, speculations on the future and reflection on the human-nature relationship, with an open border to the wider archive of related work on whose models it sometimes draws for the depiction of climatic crisis. (2)

The scholars also note that although cli-fi texts can be distinguished according to their thematic focus on climate change and the "political, social, psychological and ethical issues associated with [climate change]," their "plot formulas" and "stylistic conventions" are too varied for them to be distinguished for forming a distinct literary genre (1–2).

For more on cli-fi, see Johns-Putra's *Climate Change and the Contemporary Novel* and Adam Trexler's *Anthropocene Fictions: The Novel in a Time of Climate Change.*

3 In 2018, the UNESCO World Heritage Site added to its list the Budj Bim Cultural Landscape, a region in Victoria's southwest that includes an "elaborate series of stone-lined channels and pools set up by the Gunditjmara people" for harvesting eels 6,600 years ago (Johnson). In the aftermath of the 2019 bushfires, which included the Budj Bim fires that burned more than 7,000 ha of this part of country, its traditional owners discovered more aquaculture sites in places that were previously concealed by vegetation (Johnson).

4 A study that makes a similar argument in the context of the Americas is Charles C. Mann's *1491: New Revelations of the Americas before Columbus.*

5 Bobis (1959–) was born in the Philippines and came to Australia as a student in the early 1990s. A teacher as well as a writer, Bobis has published poetry and drama in addition to fiction, and writes in the languages of English, Filipino, and Bikol, her native language.

6 The word "subhuman" in the title of the collection in which "Late Summer Fires" appears evokes a lecture delivered by Bernard Smith in 1980. In that lecture, the first of the distinguished Boyer Lectures, Smith used the word "subhuman" in reference to white racist attitudes toward indigenous Australians and to, in particular, an Aboriginal Australian known as Truganini. Murray's "subhuman" distinguishes a white underclass of Australians—namely, poor, rural, and working-class Australians—but the sense in which Smith used it pervades the sense in which Murray uses it. Smith states, "A spectre has haunted Australian culture, the spectre of Truganini...since 1788 Aborigines have [continued to be] treated in their own county as if they were sub-human ...Truganini's story must stand, in these talks, for all those that will never be written" (qtd. in Taylor 26).

7 Two ecocritics who might be used to represent this polarization in ecocriticism in the late decades of the last century are Leonard M. Scigaj and Mark Long. In *Sustainable Poetry: Four American Ecopoets* (1999), inspired by the work of Maurice Merleau-Ponty, Scigaj argues that phenomenological theory is "the most promising philosophical response...to poststructuralism

and philosophical dualism" (65), and he applies it in his reading of four "ecological poets," Gary Snyder, Wendell Berry, A. R. Ammons, and W. S. Merwin. These poets, as Scigaj explains, emphasize that consciousness is always "embodied" (66) and the "referential origin" of "all language" is "extralinguistic" (36, 38). The poststructuralist thinker Mark Long respectfully takes that argument to task in an essay titled "William Carlos Williams, Ecocriticism, and Contemporary American Nature Poetry."

8 For more on activism in environmental contexts, see Estok ("Activist Ecocriticism: An Introduction").

5 Language, Translation, and Communication

As understudied as they are, vegetal and bestial figures in literature tug at the sleeves of scholars who are curious about and otherwise drawn to "earthothers"—namely, plants and nonhuman animals (Gaard, *Critical Ecofeminism* 22). Their languages are overwhelmingly overlooked, misrepresented, or dismissed under mainstream definitions and studies of language, within the arts as well as the sciences. Yet, the evidence is difficult to refute. Referring to a slim sampling of the evidence, drawn mostly from the work of ecocritical biosemiotics scholar Wendy Wheeler, I focus in this chapter on the allusions to other than human language in Peter Goldsworthy's posthumanist novel, *Wish*, about a relationship between a sign language teacher hired by two animal rights activists to tutor a human–gorilla hybrid hominoid ("Wish"), and Robyn Davidson's *Tracks*, an account by the author of her trek in the 1970s with camels—baggage carriers more or less against their will—from Alice Springs in the Northern Territory to the coastal place of Hamelin Pool in Western Australia. In my analysis of *Wish* and *Tracks*, I also refer to work in the discipline of translation studies. A manifestly anthropocentric area of critical inquiry, translation studies nonetheless offers useful insights to scholars interested in the question of translation as that refers to the translation of other than human languages. Ecofeminist Greta Gaard's comments on listening, that most underrated of language skills, also critically underpins this chapter about the discursive realms of the nonhuman world.

Biosemiotics and Ecocriticism

In recent decades, the area of inquiry of biosemiotics has been especially useful for challenging narrow speciesist understandings of language. An outcropping of biology, biosemiotics first emerged in the 1980s, when a group of biologists, looking to the work of scholars in the field of information theory, argued that no information was "semantics-free" (Wheeler, "'Tongues I'll Hang on Every Tree': Biosemiotics and the Book of Nature," 122). They questioned, therefore, conventional biological definitions of "mind" and "knowledge," pointing out their "purely anthropocentric connotations" (122). Further, unable to explain many biological responses under laws of physics, mathematics, and chemistry, they looked back to the work of Charles Sanders Peirce (1839–1914), a figure who proved to be, indeed, "a major scientific and philosophical influence" on the field (122). Using Peirce's work, they hypothesized that "*all* living things" are not merely "information-carrying mechanistic channels" but are beings that communicate with and respond to their environment in highly complex "nonmechanistic" and "nondeterministic" ways, and so engage in processes of creativity, or play, as well as other forms of interpretation (125).

Wendy Wheeler has been particularly powerful in articulating the biosemiotics argument that language extends far beyond human forms of language. She argues that natural language includes human language but is a much vaster area of language, extending far beyond the substratum (of human language) of "words and discourses," so-called articulate language (*The Whole Creature* 17, 19). Articulate language is "just the most recent evolutionary part of a vast global web of semiosis encompassing all living things—from the smallest cell to the most complex multicellular organism" (Wheeler, "Natural Play" 71). "All living forms have communication systems of a kind" (*The Whole Creature* 16); "all life—from the cell all the way up to us—is characterized by communication, or semiosis" ("The Biosemiotic Turn: Abduction, or, the Nature of Creative Reason in Nature and Culture" 270). Thus, any "understanding of human behaviour and reasoning" that does not address the role played by biology, or "the body, emotion and tacit knowledge," is an "incomplete" account (*The Whole Creature* 33).

Disappointingly so, both neoliberal thinking and "the linguistic turn" in cultural studies in the 1970s and 1980s hindered the notice and acceptance of contemporary biosemiotics accounts of language, which challenged the commonplace notion that "articulate language" constitutes all of language (and so stood with, too, older marginalized beliefs about all living beings' capacity for engaging in biological evolutionary processes of "symbiogenetic co-operative communication") (Wheeler, *The Whole Creature* 13, 16, 19). Neoliberalism, in emphasizing "individualism," downplayed the fundamental "sociality" of humans and, by implication, that of all other living beings. The linguistic turn effectively reified the emotionally threadbare panoply of humans' "words and discourses" and sidelined or dismissed altogether evidence for other kinds of language in the natural world.

Most damningly, under the glow of the linguistic turn, "experience of reality" was held to be something "wholly constructed in human language" (Wheeler, "'Tongues I'll Hang on Every Tree'" 126). This "social constructivist" argument, as biosemioticians criticized it, betrayed a profoundly "anthropocentric" bias as well as "idealist" philosophy, for it only focused on human language and only on a small area of human language, articulate language (126).

In other than human species as well as in the human species, systems of communication and exchange include "unconscious" and "gestural" forms of communication. These lie outside of (the sub-realm of human language of) articulate language; nonetheless, they are, as articulate language is, an important basis of "sociality" (*The Whole Creature* 17). They are the "materialist, but non-positivist and non-reductionist bases of affect" (which include, for example, empathy, sympathy, forgiveness, selflessness, protectiveness, and self-identification with "the other") (15). These same systems of communication and exchange manifestly belie the maxim that reason and emotion, the mind and the body, "are best kept apart" (80).

Admittedly, the modern, secular separating of thought and matter is the "result of a long history of philosophical thinking in which rationality—reasonable thinking and behavior—was seen as a way of escaping from brutal conflict" (Wheeler, *The Whole Creature* 80). Such separation enabled humans to reject "primitive superstitions, beliefs, and the unassailable right of powerful groups or individuals to impose their will on others by force" (80). Yet, the bifurcation was instrumental in the dismissal "of the intimate relation between mind and body, reason and passion" and so fostered a disregard for "affective life" (77, 78, 80). Affective life, in fact, is part of "material life ... what happens in people's emotional, psychological, lives is what happens in their material, physiological, lives and futures also" (154).

In *The Whole Creature*, Wheeler put language back into biology by way of biosemiotics—namely, "the study of signs and significance in all living things" (19)—and so back in the natural world (or in circles of the natural world that include but are not limited to human life). She argues that the natural world is a semiotic realm that is as complex and sophisticated as the kinds of semiotic realms that are associated with human language and communication, and other than human beings are no less social, or discursive, than human beings.

In subsequent work, Wheeler goes on to challenge even further the anthropocentric "dominance of materialism and determinism in the natural sciences" in the nineteenth and twentieth centuries ("Tongues I'll Hang on Every Tree" 121). Under the given dominance, as Wheeler argues, scientists deny language to most other beings beside human beings. This repudiation has become a "nearly unassailable truth," defining the "narrowed horizons of contemporary technologized Western cultures" such that any explanations of natural thinking, language, communication, and translation that do not fit reductive, anthropocentric "physico-chemical" models of plant and nonhuman animal behavior are considered to be "scientifically [and] politically incorrect," or spurious accounts (121, 127).

In learning more about and affirming natural language, Wheeler and other biosemioticians (and thinkers situated in such disciplines as critical plant studies and critical animal studies) are finding, for example, that, similarly to human beings, other biological beings model their world, or engage in "natural constructivism" (Wheeler, "Tongues I'll Hang on Every Tree" 127). This is analogous to "social constructivism," or the kind of world building in which humans specifically engage (127). Even cells have "something like awareness," or "phenomenological intentionality," and shape their environs (as much as those shape the cells) (125). "From the single cell all the way to the complex multicellular organism, and ... [to] the super-organisms organic and cultural," every living thing has an "interpretative" and "intentional" relation to "everything potentially meaningful in its environment" (127). "In some very real sense," therefore, all living organisms "know" things and have purposes (127).

Natural constructivism also is analogous to social constructivism in the sense that it involves the wielding of metaphors, or the active recognition of and response to patterns of similarity and difference in the environment. In the natural world, in nonhuman animal spheres and plant spheres as well as human spheres of activity, metaphor, or abduction, is the basis of "creative thinking," "creative reason," and "creative recursivity" (Wheeler, "The Biosemiotic Turn" 270, 273–274). Metaphor is a "a real part of the semiotic fabric of the universe and cognition" (Wheeler, "Tongues I'll Hang on Every Tree" 126). It is neither inferior to nor superseded by the privileged "scientific forms of knowing" of induction and deduction (131). It is not merely a "figure of speech" that humans use in their articulate language (123). It abounds in other languages in the natural world (123). It "runs through all nature," and so through and past that realm of nature that we call "culture" (123).

Translation Studies: Tips for Translating the Nonhuman Other

Translation studies is a manifestly humanist area of critical inquiry; nonetheless, the kinds of work in which its scholars engage beckon scrutiny from ecocritics, biosemioticians, critical animal studies scholars, critical plant studies scholars, and other scholars interested in natural language and communication and questions of translation as it refers to the translation of other than human languages. Such invitation is the result of recent directions in particular in the discipline of translation studies.

Less than half a century ago, when translation studies was still a young and emergent discipline, it merely survived "on the margins of the humanities and social sciences" (Bermann and Porter 2). It was "a minor branch of comparative literary study," hardly a "specific area of linguistics," and situated mostly only "in Europe and the Americas" (2). Today, translation studies is global in impetus and reach, a sprawling and "stimulating field of academic as well as practical interest," and "a vastly complex field with many far-reaching ramifications" (Bassnett qtd. in Bermann and Porter 2).[1]

Most importantly, translation studies today is playing an unprecedented role in the work of "representing self and other in complicated hierarchies of power" (Brodzki qtd. in Bermann and Porter 1).[2] This characterization of the discipline is striking for scholars who are interested in the work of translating the languages of other than human beings and investigating how understandings of these beings have been consistently stymied by short-term anthropocentric interests, a point that will be taken up in more detail later.

The earliest work in translation studies, in the 1960s and 1970s, was led by Roman Jakobson, a linguist and semiotician. A major figure for the discipline, Jakobson emphasized the purely formal, so-called linguistic, bases of translation. These bases involved identifying "two equivalent messages in two different codes" (qtd. in Bermann and Porter 3).[3] Scholars who work with the first code, the "dynamic" code—one of several appellations that translation studies scholars who come after Jakobson use—emphasize the instrumental function of language and stress practical communication. Those who work with the second code focus on the hermeneutic function of language and so pay particular attention to cultural meanings.

As Jakobson and others emphasized, the ideal of "equivalence" that associates with identifying the given two basic codes of translation is just that, an ideal. Equivalence, in fact, is

> impossible to achieve ... [either] in practice (the attempt simply spawned more and different translations) or in theory (languages diverge in sound, script, and semantic structure so that "equivalence" and "transfer" can only be metaphorical as opposed to "scientific"). (Berman and Porter 3)

The ideal of equivalence persists today, even as scholars, similarly to their forbears, recognize the impossibility of its realization. These same scholars also continue to abide by as well as challenge many other of the linguistic bases of translation that Jakobson and others forged 50 years ago. Relatively recent work in translation studies bears the stamp of influence of, in addition to linguistics, literary theory, anthropology, cultural studies, and information technology; it highlights the social and cultural as well as linguistic aspects of translation and emphasizes the need for investigating the ethical dimensions of translation and interrogating the different constructions of those dimensions (3).

Translation studies in recent times also has been indelibly shaped by "poststructuralist views of language," "postcolonial views of literature and culture," theory generated out of "gender and sexuality studies," and sociology theory (Bermann and Porter 3). Translation studies scholars take notice of arguments forged by such figures as Jacques Derrida and Roland Barthes, who refute the idea of an "original" text, hold that within any given putative "original" text there is "ongoing intertextuality," and maintain that readers of a text cannot rely on or turn to "a single 'author' or 'source' of a text" (3). Postcolonial scholars Edward Said, Gayatri Spivak, Homi Bhabha, and Edouard Glissant have steered translation studies in the direction of giving "new, more ethically and politically inflected ways to read language, text, and translation in colonial and postcolonial contexts ... No longer [can] translations be viewed as abstract linguistic entities subject to pure descriptive analysis" (4). To translate any given language, postcolonial scholars point out, the translator must ask such questions as what are the differences between oral and written translations of a language; how is translation shaped by the interests of the political, ethical, or religious groups that use and wield it; and what role does translation specifically play in languages associated with colonial and postcolonial histories (4). Gender studies scholars—Judith Butler, and others—challenge translation studies scholars to think more about "gender hierarchies" and about how and why "heteronormative assumptions affect a wide range of cultural practices, including translation and the role of the translator and reader" (4). Sociologists such as Pierre Bourdieu have influenced translation studies scholars to consider textual agents in addition to those of the translator and author of the text being translated. These other "primary actors" and entities include publishers, editors, illustrators, copyeditors, and readers (4).

Looking beyond translation studies scholars' accounts, definitions, and summaries of the task of translation, ecocritics will soon come across Carmen Flys-Junquera and Carmen Valero Garcés's entry on translation in *Keywords for Environmental Studies* (edited by Joni Adamson, William A. Gleason, and David N. Pellow). Similarly to the accounts of translation that one finds in translation studies, Flys-Junquera and Garcés's account tells us that translation is an activity under which scholars investigate and account for the "linguistic differences in language systems," the uses of language ("pragmatics"), the "rhetorical and stylistic conventions" of language, the "background and knowledge" of the translator, and the theoretical frameworks that translators rely upon and must identify, understand, and more or less balance when they are engaged in translating a language (190). Abiding by one or other of these understandings of translation comes with both losses and gains. For example, if a translator wishes to make it clear that the translation is just that, a translation and not a seamless copy of what is being translated, then she or he may "opt for a non-fluent or estranging translation style designed to make *visible* the presence of the translator," an approach that Lawrence Venuti called "foreignization" (qtd. in Flys-Junquera and Valero-Garcés 190).[4] Another kind of translator will adopt a literal translation approach in preference to an approach that conveys wider cultural contexts. Yet another translator will choose to "domesticate" a translation, or "adapt the original to an idiomatic text" and so "[treat] the 'illusion of transparency' as if no translation process existed" (Venuti, qtd. in Flys-Junquera and Valero-Garcés 190).[5]

In "The Changing Landscape of Translation and Interpreting Studies," in defining translation (of human languages) as any practice through which any cultural group constructs representations of another cultural group and in turn is reshaped by that "other," translation studies scholar Monica Baker hones in on the argument that minority languages—"languages of relatively limited diffusion or languages spoken by politically and economically marginalized populations"—are being threatened in the acts of translating them (into the English language) (17). That is to say, "the hegemony of English and the economic and political power of the English-speaking world now mean that *all* languages other than English have become minority languages" (Cronin qtd. in Baker 17). In "Philosophical/Theoretical Approaches to Translation," translation studies scholar Efrain Kristal summarizes the argument that "the notion of a 'literal' translation is a meaningless concept because there are no criteria to distinguish between a translation that deviates from the original and one that does not"; and "word-by-word translations ... are likely to produce awkward transpositions of the vocabulary of the target language onto the grammar of the source language rather than transparent equivalencies" (29). In other words, "the notion of a 'literal' translation presupposes that a translation could be identical to the original, which is not possible, and this means that all translations are 'free' in one way or another" (29).

The diverse and by no means compatible approaches to translation of human languages, all too briefly sketched out here, reflect that translation is hardly an uncomplicated task. Translating the languages of others ushers in as many shortcomings as it does windfalls, invites one into impenetrable thickets, vaults one over hedges at heights that seem impossible to scale, is closely bound up in discourses of power and issues of multilingualism, cannot avoid issues of "identity, migration, and sexuality," is defined by "collaborative" agencies, and demands compromises at the same time as it dispenses prodigal grants (9–10).

Such understandings of the translation of human languages by translation studies scholars are useful to and exciting for other scholars, too, namely those interested in translating other than human languages. These understandings readily beckon comparison with and indeed are comparable with the questions about nonhuman languages that scholars theorize in the areas of ecocriticism, critical plant studies, critical animal studies, biosemiotics ecocriticism, and posthumanism. Just as the work of translating human languages has been hindered and betrayed in the past by unquestioned prejudices and biases, so the work of translating nonhuman languages has been impeded by unquestioned prejudices and biases. Indeed, in the work of translating nonhuman languages, anthropocentric interests (or short-term anthropocentric ones) typically completely outweigh the interests (whatever they are or may be) of the plants and animals whose languages are being translated into human terms. Such translation work typically gives short shrift to questions about animal and plant capacities that include but extend beyond immediate concerns of survival and reproduction. That same kind of work thus inadequately addresses such issues as the linguistic and other communicative losses of plant and nonhuman animal species when they are hyper-industrially controlled and commodified.[6] If the translation of human languages is by no means a wide and smooth path to the nirvana of linguistic "equivalence," then the route of translating the lexicons of nonhuman beings is as or even more difficult to navigate. Translators of nonhuman languages need to be as careful as or more careful than their peers, those who work with the translation of human languages.

It is doubtful that the human species will be able to accurately and precisely translate the languages of the natural world, or achieve a translation or reading analogous to what in translation studies is known as linguistic equivalence. However, the human species has made the paltriest of efforts to do that in modern times. Our species mostly has backed away from translating the natural world on the basis of what the interests of that world may be. More often than not, we have mistranslated, deliberately or not, the languages of the natural world to suit our interests instead of attempting to faithfully translate those languages. In the process, we have wiped out or whittled away at many of those languages. Were we to attempt more fair kinds of translation, we might see the natural world to be like our own world, made up of discursive as well as material spheres, and full of creatures who are as social, garrulous, and discursive as human critters. Yet, we have been more adept at presuming to speak for nonhuman "earthothers" in ways that are profoundly condescending toward and dismissive of them (Gaard, *Critical Ecofeminism* 22).

For sure, as the present book represents, many people are challenging, and have challenged, acts of translations of the natural world that reflect the human interest of subordinating and controlling the natural world and denying language to it. Literature (as well as other aesthetic and cultural production) registers those challenges. Robyn Davidson's feminist travelogue, *Tracks*, and Peter Goldsworthy's transhumanist posthumanist novel, *Wish*, are two works of Australian literature that reflect both that challenging and silencing. *Tracks* is the author's account of training camels, and at times beating camels into submission, for the purpose of trekking with them from the middle of Australia to its western coast. *Wish* explores human sign language discernibly more so than it does animal rights. Yet, in Goldsworthy's novel about human sign language and a young laboratory female gorilla and in

Davidson's account of her interaction and communication with a small group of camels who are sweetly persuaded, and forcibly cajoled, threatened, and beaten, into servitude—animals who are as shy, outspoken, sweet-natured, rambunctious, docile, obstreperous, liberal, and, aristocratic as humans—the authors implicitly and eloquently mount an argument in defense of animal speech. That argument ties to in turn to the issue of the rights of (nonhuman) animals, and specifically to the issue of what rights are being extended and denied to feral camel populations in Australia and nonhuman hominoids—animals that include apes, bonobos, chimpanzees, gorillas, and orangutans—in Australia and other regions of the world.

Wish

In *Wish*, John James ("J. J.") the human protagonist, falls in love with an eight-year-old female hybrid hominoid, a part-human and part-gorilla, not long after he accepts the position of private sign language tutor to the hybrid hominoid animal, whom he names "Wish." Wish's guardians and keepers are Clive Francis Kennear, a primate scholar and animal rights activist who is working on a book entitled *Primate Suffrage*; and Stella, Clive's partner, also an animal rights advocate, and a veterinarian.[7] The couple take Wish into their home not long after an animal science laboratory technician, a former student of Kennear who has become "disenchanted" with the projects at a primate research laboratory in Melbourne, steals Wish from the lab and brings her to Clive and Stella (Goldsworthy 125). Wish has been biologically modified *in utero*, her mother has been destroyed ("euthanized") following transhumanist experiments on her unborn baby, and the experiments on Wish are such that she no longer fits standard taxonomies of species.

When J. J. first accepts the teaching position, he assumes that he will be giving private sign language lessons to a human hominoid; so, when he does meet Wish in the flesh, so to speak, he is discomfited. However, he does not renege on his agreement with Clive and Stella and, indeed, becomes impressed soon thereafter by Wish's language learning skills:

> Her curiosity seemed inexhaustible, her infatuation with the world and its signs utterly engaging and infectious. We can't think about the world until we have named it, I'd always believed. We can't manipulate it, move it about in our mind until we have clothed it in language. We can't even *see* it, naked. Words provide the costumes, the labels, the categories—words permit us to divide the world, and rule. I was wrong. As the days passed it became clear that the signs I taught to Wish were merely clothing things that she already knew, concepts she had thought about, grasped wordlessly, but could not communicate. (Goldsworthy 188)

In fact, as J. J. eventually learns from Terry, the primatologist who stole Wish from an animal science laboratory, Wish's "intelligence … [and] creativity," inclusive of language skills, which are "light-years beyond" those of so-called pure nonhuman hominoids who have been taught human language (152), and inclusive of the other differences "between Wish and her wild cousins [other primates]" (170), are the result of the experiments performed on her by humans when she is an embryo in her mother's uterus. She has "enhanced intelligence" because of those experiments (287).

To the extent that Goldsworthy's novel endorses common beliefs about human intelligence, which include the belief that hominoids other than humans possess an inferior intelligence in comparison with the sapience of humans—after all, Wish is not a "pure" gorilla but a hybrid human-nonhuman hominoid—Goldsworthy's novel makes a disappointing, predictable, and tendentious transhumanist posthumanist argument. That is to say, the novel rolls out the most commonplace posthumanist dismissal of nonhuman animal capacities for intelligence, a dismissal that depends on anthropocentric theories of self-awareness and language.

At the same time, Goldsworthy's novel generates intriguing questions about other forms of language besides human language. These implicit interrogations challenge the narrow, anthropocentric assumptions about and theoretical frameworks of language, communication, and translation. James Bradley, in the introduction to the 2013 edition of *Wish* (published by The Text Publishing Company), in remarking on the novel's main subject of human sign language, picks up and comments on the novel's implicit critique of mainstream (transhumanist) posthumanist understandings of language as well as mainstream (transhumanist) posthumanist projects of perfecting the human by enslaving the nonhuman, for in Goldsworthy's novel Wish is one of hundreds of nonhuman hominoids experimented on for the purpose of using them to perform menial and other tasks for humans such as domestic work, hired companion work, and baggage carrier work.

In "[demanding that] the reader step out of the realm of verbal language and engage with [sign language] as a physical, gestural system," Bradley writes, "[*Wish*] underlines mainstream society's casual marginalizing of the deaf and their culture—and how our ignorance of deaf culture points to a failure to comprehend the possibility of other, quite different ways of being that are all around us" (ix–x). He then says, "For even as we strive to teach dolphins and birds to speak and apes to sign, our solipsism blinds us to the possibility that these creatures may exist in rich complex worlds of meaning quite unlike our own" (xii).

If *Wish* focuses evidently on human language, and mostly on human sign language, then, as Bradley observes, through the novel's two main hominoid characters Goldsworthy forays into realms of natural language extending beyond human language. The novel indirectly speaks to efforts to cultivate more respect for and interest in aspects of human language that lie outside of (in biosemiotics terms) articulate langue. As Wheeler tells us in her investigations of the bodily (or biological) bases of human communication and language, biosemiotics is a good start to those efforts. In Goldsworthy's novel, the character of J. J., who describes "the (human) body" as being something that is "its own polygraph: a visual display—a leakage—of signs and shapes" (40), speaks to efforts to understand the languages of the world beside those of the human and the human body.

J. J.'s musings on the differences between languages that rely on sight and those that rely on sound provoke questions not only about the specific frequencies of sound and light spectra that are detectable by most humans but also about the uniqueness of these languages, or what they do differently. Fluent in Auslan sign language, J. J. reflects on what silence means to those who communicate mostly without using sound: "The hearing have a hush-sign for silence," he says, "a single finger pressed to pursed lips," but "[this] shape means nothing to the Deaf [and] has no entry in the dictionaries of Sign. What is Silence" (Goldsworthy 26). J. J. also reflects on what sign language does that verbal language does not do when he says that sign language is as expressive as spoken language and oftentimes more so. There are "countless shapes for 'sorry,'" he says, "far more shapes than there are words of apology in English" (86).

The characters of Jill, J. J.'s ex-wife, and Mrs. James, J. J.'s mother, also provoke questions about other than human languages. These interrogations tie to the issues of the loss of plant and animal languages and the many plant and animal languages that continue to be threatened with extinction as human language becomes the de facto universal language. Jill is pursuing graduate studies in Aboriginal Australian languages at the Massachusetts Institute of Technology. Her research focuses on the efforts to preserve and restore Aboriginal Australian languages, many of which were banned in the past from being spoken because of racist policies. This content in the novel elicits questions about the countless plant and nonhuman animal languages that are denied, misunderstood, or ignored because they are regarded to be primitive or to interfere or threaten dominant, so called progressive social and economic trends. Mrs. James is a volunteer staff person at the local "Deaf Library" and has been deaf since birth (Goldsworthy 26). For her, ears do not serve any purpose (except perhaps to hang one's glasses or a hygiene mask). They are merely "[c]ongenital deformities" or "[o]rnamental flaps" (16). How often have humans disregarded the languages of other species because those languages identify with morphologies utterly unlike those associated with human communication?

The eponymous heroine of *Wish* joins the list of other more or less famous nonhuman hominoid characters in literature and film: King Kong in the 1933 film *King Kong*, directed by Merian C. Cooper and Ernest B. Schoedsack, and King Kong's many avatars in the cinematic spinoffs of that film; Red Peter, the ape in Franz Kafka's short story "A Report to an Academy" (a character who also makes a cameo appearance in J. M. Coetzee's novel *Elizabeth Costello*); Orange Juice, the orangutan in Yann Martel's novel *Life of Pi*; Amy, the gorilla, in Michael Crichton's novel *Congo*; Caesar, the chimpanzee in the film *Rise of the Planet of the Apes*, directed by Rupert Wyatt; and the bonobos in Audrey Schulman's *Theory of Bastards*.[8] In different ways, these texts trouble the separation along speciesist lines of human and nonhuman hominoids. Commenting on another of those texts, David Garnett's novel *A Man in the Zoo*, Timothy Clark observes that such animal characters "are not just objects of thought, they have always been used to map out constitutive features of human culture" (184). Such characters incite questions about who and what constitutes a subject with rights and about the many legal battles to extend "non-human person rights" to other hominoids beside human hominoids.[9]

In J. M. Coetzee's novel *Elizabeth Costello*, the eponymous hero, a distinguished scholar, delivers a lecture to a small group of academics and to members of the public while on a lecture tour in the United States. In her talk, as part of her questioning of the factory farming of animals and her comparison between that farming and the genocide of Jewish people in Germany under the Third Reich, Costello comments on a captive ape who performs "apeness," or an "ape identity," for his human captors. This ape identity, as Costello makes clear, is not the ape's own identity. It is a speciesist construction forced (by coercion, manipulation, fraud, and torture) upon the ape by the animal's human captors. Like enslaved humans who perform identities in order to survive, so too, other enslaved animals perform identities foisted upon them. Performing animals are used for entertainment in such places as SeaWorld, or in zoos, or in street performance work; they include, for example, dolphins and other cetaceans, dancing bears, and parrots trained to speak a human language; they also include the animals who are incarcerated in animal science laboratories for the purpose of being trained to perform more or less menial tasks for humans, that is to say, to become servants. Coetzee's novel is, as Goldsworthy's novel is, about these animals; in it, the main character, Costello, refers to a study entitled *The Mentality of Apes*. Coetzee here alludes to an actual study, so titled, by the German psychologist Wolfgang Köhler. It was an important study of chimpanzees that was published in Germany in the early twentieth century. In Coetzee's novel, Costello suggests that Köhler might have been familiar to the German-Jewish writer Franz Kafka and the inspiration for a short writing by Kafka entitled "Report to an Academy." As Costello argues, the experiments that Köhler and other humans performed on the ape ("Sultan") in order to determine what feats the animal was capable of performing proved merely to show the least of the animal's cognitive and other capacities. The experiments betrayed not the lack of sophistication or limitation of the (other-than-human) animal but rather the shortcomings, including lack of imagination, of the human (animal). Sultan's human captors cajole, bully, and torture him to perform acts that are not of his own choosing and merely mimic human capacities; his jailers then conclude that those acts are the limits of Sultan's own species' capacities:

> At every turn Sultan is driven [by his human captors] to think the less interesting thought ... he is relentlessly propelled towards lower, practical, instrumental reason ... and thus towards acceptance of himself as primarily an organism with an appetite that needs to be satisfied. Although his entire history, from the time his mother was shot and he was captured, through his voyage in a cage to imprisonment on this island prison camp [Tenerife] and the sadistic games that are played around food here, leads him to ask questions about the justice of the universe and the place of this penal colony in it, a carefully plotted psychological regimen conducts him *away* from ethics and metaphysics towards the humbler reaches of practical reason. (73–74)

Costello then turns to Kafka's story about an ape named Red Peter who has become proficient in the speech, habits, and gestures of humans also in order to survive. She describes Red Peter as follows:

> Measure the distance back from Kafka's ape, with his bow tie and dinner jacket and wads of lecture notes, to that sad train of captives trailing around the compound in Tenerife. How far Red Peter has travelled! Yet we are entitled to ask: In return for the prodigious overdevelopment of the intellect he has achieved, in return for his command of lecture-hall etiquette and academic rhetoric, what has he had to give up? (75)

As Costello's words imply, Red Peter has had to give up a great deal. Similar to the historical Sultan kept in captivity for years, Red Peter performs "the human" in order to survive. He is the "other performer."[10]

Wish carries allusions to another simian text, George Bernard Shaw's play *Pygmalion*, and the musical adaptation *My Fair Lady* about an English philologist, phonetician, and grammarian, Henry Higgins, who makes a bet with another linguist, Colonel Pickering, that he can transform into impeccable upper-class English the Cockney accents of a woman who makes a living selling flowers on the streets of London. Pickering is both amused and incredulous. He does not believe that the lower classes are capable of being taught or can acquire such language skills and competencies, and Eliza Doolittle, the flower seller, is from those classes. In *Wish*, before J. J. names (or renames) Wish, Clive and Stella give her the name of "Eliza."[11] Goldsworthy here makes an implicit comparison here between a class prejudice that ties to language—namely, the prejudice of correlating intelligence with privileged forms of a spoken language—and a speciesist prejudice that ties to language—namely, the belief that nonhuman animals possess rudimentary intelligence because they do not wield human language. Goldsworthy highlights the spuriousness of those beliefs, or he seems to do that, for Wish's capacity for learning another species' language—namely, human language—evidently is because she is part human. Nonetheless, Goldsworthy brings up the question of the capacity for language of other species. The question is exemplified in the epigraph that introduces the second part of *Wish*, "Book Two," which opens when J. J. meets Eliza (later renamed "Wish") for the first time.

> It is a great baboon, but so much like man in most things, that though they say there is a species of them, yet I cannot believe but that it is a monster got of a man and a she-baboon. I do believe that it already understands much English, and I am of the mind that it might be taught to speak or make signs. (Pepys qtd. in Goldsworthy 118)

Unlike the hominoid described in Samuel Pepys's (*The*) *Diary* (of *Samuel Pepys*), Wish *is* "got of a man and a she-baboon" (Pepys qtd. in Goldsworthy 118). She has been biologically modified by humans in an animal science primate research laboratory when in her mother's womb. However, in giving to us such a character, Goldsworthy asks us to consider "pure" (for want of a better word) nonhuman hominoids inclusive of Wish's murdered mother and the "baboon" whom Pepys describes with a mixture of eco-philic empathy and curiosity and eco-phobic disgust. Nonhuman hominoids are, from moral and ethical perspectives, indeed, "so much like man [humans] in most things" (118).

Tracks

In Australia as elsewhere in the world, camels have yet to be given the kinds of rights that now are being extended to nonhuman hominoids. The bestowal is on the basis of how similar nonhuman hominoids are to human hominoid animals. For animal advocacy thinkers such as Wolfe, the conferment betrays a profoundly speciesist bias. For other animal advocacy thinkers, whom Wolfe distinguishes as "humanist posthumanist" thinkers (*What Is Posthumanism?* 125), the bestowal constitutes the thin edge of the wedge that is prizing open the door to acknowledging the rights of other animals beside nonhuman hominoids.[12] *Tracks* functions as one of those salutary chocks. An account of the author's journey across the center of Australia with camels and her beloved canine companion, Diggity, *Tracks* portrays camels in ways that one does not usually see in Australian dromedary literature, either fictional or non-fictional. The animals are described in more detail and are as individual as any human being. They are hoity-toity, strong willed, unbending even when struck viciously by their (human) masters, submissive, delicate, dainty, disdainful, clownish, funny, serious, comic, shy, lugubrious, and so forth. The memorable four among those whom Davidson writes about are Zeleika ("Zelly"), the band's matriarch, aged between four and five years old, a "street-smart, crafty, unfazable, self-possessed leader"; Goliath, Zeleika's newborn son; Dookie, almost four years old, "nominally king ... but ... the first to hide behind [Zeleika's] skirts" when there is trouble; and Bub, three years old, "in love with Dookie," and a natural clown (84, 123).

When Davidson first arrives (by plane from Queensland) in Alice Springs, a town in the Northern Territory, at 5:00 a.m., "with a dog, six dollars and a suitcase full of inappropriate clothes," she experiences almost immediately discrimination against her because of her gender (Davidson 19). (Just as quickly, she registers the racism of the majority of the white townspeople toward Aboriginal Australians.) Reflecting on her vulnerability, she compares herself to the common unwanted animal species of rabbits. Like rabbits, she desperately looks for a "safe place to stay" away from humans (23). "Rabbits, too ... have their survival mechanisms," she says to herself (23). Later, when she is traveling near Uluru and the sister Olga rocks, she meets an Aboriginal Australian man, "Mr Eddie" (162). He offers to be Davidson's guide in the following days, when she treks to Pipalyatjara (162). She imagines that she appears to him as a kind of rabbit because her first name, "Robyn," sounds like the word for rabbit in the Pitjantjara language (162). Davidson's self-identification with a vermin species carries with it a tacit critique of her people, Anglo-Europeans, who overran Australia along with rabbits after 1788. Similar to rabbits, camels were introduced to Australia and did so well that soon thereafter they became an unwanted species. Between 1840 and 1907, successive governments (British colonial governments and later post-federation governments) brought into Australia "up to 20,000 one-humped dromedary (*Camelus dromedaries*) camels."[13] The majority, from India—fewer camels came from Afghanistan, Egypt, and Turkey—were used as in transport, in exploration, and in the goldfields. The male camels carried up to 600 kg of baggage (Government of Western Australia). By 1930, motor and rail transport made the use of camels for transport largely an obsolete practice (Government of Western Australia). Some of the camel populations were "destroyed" (Government of Western Australia). Most were "simply released into the wild," where, even in the driest areas, "they thrived and bred prolifically," and so much so that in 2009 the government responded by introducing organized culling operations (Government of Western Australia). As many as 800,000 feral camels were killed under these operations in 2009 (Government of Western Australia). Between 2009 and 2012, the Australian government authorized the killing of 160,000 more; 135,000 were killed by men armed with long-range rifles in aircrafts; 25,000 were handed over to commercial buyers, who sold their carcasses in the form of meat products (Milman). Today, Australia's feral camel population numbers between 1,000,000 and 1.2 million (Invasive Animals Ltd.). Forty-five percent of these animals live in Western Australia, home to the largest herd of feral camels in the world (Government of Western Australia).

Davidson's dromedary narrative obliquely critiques reductive speciesist assumptions about camels even as the author writes about depending on and using camels for the main purpose of lugging her and her gear across central Australia. In her accounts of her relationships with camels, as temporal and truncated as those ties are, lasting for the period of the trek, Davidson makes a poignant argument for cultivating human–camel relationships that have little to do with most human–camel relationships in Australia. Those refer to the culling of thousands of feral camels by licensed shooters in helicopters and workers in abattoirs.

The detailed descriptions of several individual camels in Davidson's narrative throw into relief the question of dromedary rights and related questions of indigeneity, ferality, right to existence, ecocide, and humans' use of animals solely to serve humans' interests. Ostensibly a travel narrative, as well as a feminist text and a witty and incisive critique of the federal Australian government that at the time was under the leadership of Malcolm Fraser (1975–1983), the Liberal Party M. P. (Member of Parliament), *Tracks* is a moving tribute in particular to a small troupe of camels whom Davidson trained for two years and then relied on as carriers in order to trek more than 2,000 kilometers across the central deserts of Australia. In particular, *Tracks* broaches the subject of language across species in the context of Davidson's relationship with the camels and implicitly rebukes common, speciesist, patriarchal, gross underestimations of the "experiential," "tacit," and "skillful phenomenological knowledge" of all living things (*The Whole Creature* 47). One of the many nights in the desert that Davidson spends chasing after "Zelly," Dookie, and Bub when they renege and bolt for freedom, exemplifies the given aspects of *Tracks*. When at last Davidson finds all of the camels and brings them back into the camp, she is torn between wanting to berate them angrily and joyfully hug them. The camels also exhibit conflicting feelings toward Davidson. One the one hand, they are happy to see her, for as well as being their captor she is their friend, companion, and protector. On the other hand, they retain considerable desire to be free of Davidson's company and her ropes, tackles, saddles, and bags. Davidson records: "They hung around me like flies, shuffling their feet, looking embarrassedly at the ground, or coyly through their … lashes, acting apologetic and loving and remorseful" (91–92).

In *Tracks*, Davidson states that camels are "the most intelligent creatures [she knows] except for dogs" (29). She might be faulted for her statement insofar as she measures camel (and canine) intelligence against human intelligence (noting that camels have the intelligence of an eight-year-old human). To argue for the rights of animals based on the similarities they share with humans "only ends up reinforcing the very humanism" that places nonhuman animals in a position subordinate to human animals (Wolfe, *Animal Rites* 192). In other words, this argument is that certain species of animals "possess the capacities that we possess, but in *diminished* [or immature or childish] form" (192). Thus, these species (along with all other nonhuman animal species) "end up [being] ethically [recognized by us] not because of their wonder and uniqueness, not because of their difference, but because they are *inferior* versions of ourselves" [emphases added] (192). This reasoning, logic, and so forth, what Wolfe distinguishes as humanist posthumanist thinking (*What Is Posthumanism?* 125), "was the problem from the outset" and "simply gets reinforced and reproduced on another level" (of animal advocacy!) (Wolfe, *Animal Rites* 192). Yet, in defense of this (mainstream animal advocacy) reasoning, as Wolfe himself is the first to acknowledge, it has been by far the most successful, in an era when "the stakes here—as everyone from Derrida at one end to Singer at the other has noted—are frighteningly high for ... *billions* of nonhuman animals" (192).

Hundreds of thousands of nonhuman animals have died in Australia for reasons attributable to avoidable and unnecessary ignorance, indifference, and antipathy. The attrition haunts the country's literature from the time of the earliest foundation texts by newcomers; nowhere is it more apparent than in Xavier Herbert's *Capricornia*, one of Australia's most celebrated foundation texts, and an anti-foundation text as well. A "thinly disguised version of the post-Federation region of what is now the Northern Territory" (Huggan 93), the novel describes a world that still teemed with other than human life a hundred years ago, a world that was not yet decimated by newcomers, a world that the contemporary writer Lucy Treloar describes (in her novel about country along the southeast coast of South Australia in 1850s) as being "as cacophonous as a group of musicians tuning their instruments" and as "conversational [and] social" (110). Ostensibly, *Capricornia* traces the fortunes and misfortunes of Norman Shillingsworth, a man who has a white father and a black mother. The themes of half-caste identity and racism are shadowed by a second theme, ecocide. Herbert describes the meeting of two Australian identities—one older, pre-1788, and dominated by other-than-human life; one younger, post-1788, and dominated by human life. *Capricornia* opens thus:

> Although that northern part of the Continent of Australia which is called Capricornia was pioneered long after the southern parts,

> its unofficial early history was even more bloody than that of the others ... [one of three reasons for this] is that the pioneers had difficulty in establishing permanent settlements, having several times to abandon ground they had won with slaughter and go slaughtering again to secure more. This abandoning of ground was due not to the hostility of the natives, hostile enough though they were, but to the violence of the climate, which was not to be withstood even by men so well equipped with lethal weapons and belief in the decency of their purpose as Anglo-Saxon builders of Empire. (1)

The language of irony and satire that Herbert uses brings to mind a mode of thinking that animal rights philosopher Cora Diamond calls "deflection" (57). (Diamond borrows this term from the work of the philosopher and literature scholar Stanley Cavell.) Diamond defines "deflection" as the means by which "we [distance] ... ourselves from our sense of our own bodily life and our capacity to respond to and to imagine the bodily life of others" (53). Deflection "describes what happens when we are moved from appreciation of a difficulty of reality to a philosophical or moral problem apparently in the vicinity" (57). In *Capricornia*, Herbert self-consciously uses the language of deflection of irony and satire to critique the horrific ecocidal as well as genocidal projects of Anglo-European settlers and colonizers.

Had Herbert chosen any other kind of prose style, had he traded in a less ebullient language for a harder, plainer, and soberer language, he would not have been able to succeed in fully representing the experiences of human and other beings under the projects of genocide and ecocide. The reason is that any form of humans' written language, what Wheeler characterizes as belonging to "articulate language," or "words and discourses," is limited (Wheeler, *The Whole Creature* 17). A fraction of natural language, human language, both written words and oral expression, can only approximate those experiences. At the same time, *Capricornia* reflects recognition of the many languages, subjectivities, sensitivities, communicative capacities, affects, and moral economies that are located in the Australian environment. Such recognition and respect are seen in countless instances in the text. Here are a mere two of those bounteous instances.

> A kangaroo leapt off the road and thud-thud-thudded into silence. A family of kangaroos, same number as the [human O'Cannon family] and about the same size, bounded ahead through a cutting. A buffalo dozing in Chinaman's Creek woke with a start and bolted. A shower of white cockatoos fell out of a bloodwood tree, yelling, "A man—a man—a Disturbing Element!" A large admiral lizard leapt up on a rail, stood on hind legs with fore legs raised like hands and watched for a moment the trundling Thing, then loped down

> the cess-path with arms swinging and iridescent frill flying out like a cape. (202)
>
> ...
>
> On a flooded plain through which the road ran high on an embankment a group of long-legged brolgas stood. They stared at Tim, who, as he always did, took off his hat and bowed and cried to them, "Goo' mornin' ladies—lovely day!" And they, as if in courteous reply, extended pearl-gray wings and curtsied, stared after that strange creature that neither walked nor crawled nor flew but glided so fantastically with creaking limbs. (202)

Herbert represents, as Davidson does, animal perspectives. Those perspectives are both real and constructed by humans. The authors do not try to escape the pathetic fallacy; they anthropomorphize the animals and plants that they see. However, speaking for, representing, and even vaingloriously attempting to translate the languages of those beings are not the same as establishing that they have no languages and lives of their own. On the contrary, resorting to or falling into the pathetic fallacy carries with it a tacit recognition of common bonds of language and communication between humans and other beings.

Listening

In *Critical Ecofeminism*, a thorough and detailed summary of the history of and directions in ecofeminism, author Greta Gaard traces its four main stages. First-wave ecofeminism names "the gender/race/species/ecology/nation connections operating in hierarchical dualist thought and the logic of domination" (xiv). Second-wave ecofeminism both influences and is shaped by the work of environmental justice activists and scholars and arguments coalescing around the issues and terms of speciesism, the politics of reproduction, globalization, biodiversity, and vegan critiques of "traditional euro-western environmentalisms" (xv). The third wave reflects critical challenges to first and second wave's essentialist and Eurocentric biases (xv). The fourth wave, represented by Gaard's study, brings to the field further caveats and qualifications. One of these critically ties to what Gaard calls "the practice of attentive listening" and her critique of the underestimation of the capacity of listening in contrast with the emphasis placed on speech (and writing) (xvi).[14]

Speech is a mode, agency, function, and agential power that represents the right of the speaker. Listening represents the giving up of one's right of speech to make room for another to speak. Gaard makes this point in the context of studies by English language and communication scholars. Under the heteronormative frameworks of power that hold up society today, speaking means "power, knowledge, and dominance," while listening identifies with passivity, weakness, and "subordination" (xvii).

Feminist and ecofeminist theories challenge these frameworks; they emphasize that listening

> is a hallmark of good scholarship—listening to one's research subjects, to the oppressed, to one's activist and scholarly community—and creating structures for collaboration, whereby the research subjects can themselves set the agenda, express needs, and benefit from the scholarly endeavor. (xvii)

In support of her arguments that cross over into the areas of language, translation, and communication studies, Gaard cites the work of Val Plumwood and Deborah Bird Rose inclusive of an essay by Rose, entitled "Val Plumwood's Philosophical Animism: Attentive Inter-Actions in the Sentient World." In this essay, Rose writes:

> The backgrounding of listening (receiving information) is ... part of the structure of hyperseparated dualisms ... to speak is the human prerogative ... it is the active mode of being: listening (or being spoken to) is the passive or recipient position. The power relation is clearly hierarchical: those who speak are more powerful than those who are spoken to. I am proposing that listening, and more broadly, paying attention, should also be considered an active verb; indeed, in multispecies creature communities, it must be so considered. To pay attention is to exercise intelligence, to know so as to be able to inter-act. (qtd. in Gaard xvii–xviii)[15]

Material ecocriticism scholar Serpil Oppermann makes a similar point about the deficits and boons associated with listening skills in ecocritical contexts. "Because nature is thought to be 'silent,'" Oppermann states, "it is spoken for by human 'interlocutor[s]'" (108).[16] Material ecocriticism scholars as well as ecofeminism scholars represent some of the work of "telling politicians and business leaders how [nature] is breaking and tearing under the burden" of the denial of speech to the nonhuman other (108).

Human exceptionalism has stymied efforts to understand other than human "signifying systems" (unless those efforts are guided by venal or short term motives) (Oppermann 109). Humans' articulate language continues to be the yardstick for measuring the "communicative capacities of nonhuman others," playing a largely innocent but nonetheless significant role in perpetuating humans' "narcissistic way of thinking about the world" (Gagliano qtd. in Oppermann 109). In order to contest this understanding of communication, critical plant studies scholars, biosemiotics ecocriticism scholars, material ecocriticism scholars, and ecofeminism scholars emphasize that "all life is semiotic" and all biological processes involve "countless organisms that are constantly interpreting and remaking the world they inhabit" (Maran qtd. in Oppermann 109). As these scholars argue, the "assertion that only humans can make sense of the world through language and nonhuman species are devoid of this capacity is simply wrong" (Oppermann 109). As they also champion, more humans should "learn the languages of plants [and many other nonhuman beings] as a second tongue" (Ryan, *Green Sense: The Aesthetics of Plants, Place, and Language* 7).

Translation studies, while it is manifestly concerned with human languages, offers useful insights to scholars interested in issues of language, translation, and communication across species and within other species beside the human species. One of these insights ties to the notion of the impossibility of *equivalence*. Another has to do with the strengths of different and by no means compatible translation practices and so the hard choices that the translator inevitably must make in her or his acts of translation. The bold claim by translation scholars that translation (of human languages) "underwrites all cultural transactions, from the most benign to the venal" (Brodzki, qtd. in Bermann and Porter 1) also draws ecocritical notice.[17] Such notice, which overlaps with work in the areas of critical animal and critical plant studies, and posthumanism studies (in particular posthumanist theory that identifies with what Wolfe calls "posthumanist posthumanism" [125]), includes efforts to re-embrace natural language and prize modern science away from its stubborn, barnacle-like attachment to the rejection of natural signs, a "semiotic disavowal" that traces to the Protestant Reformation and "the seventeenth-century scientific revolution that grew from it" (Wheeler, "Natural Play, Natural Metaphor, and Natural Stories: Biosemiotic Realism" 70). The given efforts bring attention to humans' silencing of many nonhuman beings as well as many groups of human beings and so call for more listening (Gaard xvi–xxii, 18, 41, 110, 119). It has been but need not be in short supply. Plants and nonhuman animals are discursive beings. They possess language, and the ability to communicate and translate others' languages; they have and manifest will, choice, altruistic behavior, "creative reasoning" (Wheeler, "The Biosemiotic Turn" 270–282), and "play" (Wheeler, "Natural Play" 75–78). We have barely begun to resume the monumental task of translating the languages of the nonhuman other in ways that avoid primitive comparisons between those languages and human languages. Understandings of nonhuman animal and plant language continue to be saddled with reductive, "orthodox materialist" claims (Wheeler, "Natural Play" 68).

Notes

1 See Bassnett 1.
2 See Brodzki 2.
3 See Jakobson 127–128.
4 See Venuti, *The Scandals of Translation* 11.

5 See Venuti, *The Translator's Invisibility* 11.

6 For more on the subject of loss of language and communication among trees in commercial forests and among trees planted on the sides of roads in cities and other urban environments, see Peter Wohlleben's chapter "Street Kids" in his book *The Hidden Life of Trees: What They Feel, How They Communicate* (169–180).

7 The initials of Clive's name, C. F. K., carry an allusion to the initials spelled in reverse of the fast-food chain Kentucky Fried Chicken. It and similar fast-food companies that rely on industrial farmed animals are the nemesis of Clive, who is heavily involved in the "animal liberation" movement inclusive of efforts to free animals from industrial farming facilities (Goldsworthy 43). J. J.'s nickname for Clive is "St Francis of the Animals" (45, 49), an allusion in turn to the perdurable association of St. Francis, founder of the thirteenth-century Franciscan monastic order, with "partisans of leftist causes" and animal rights and environmental rights activists in particular (Acocella 72).

8 For a discussion of Crichton's novel, see Wolfe's chapter "Faux Posthumanism: The Discourse of Species and the Neocolonial Project in Michael Crichton's Congo," in *Animal Rites: American Culture, the Discourse of Species and Posthumanism* (169–189).

9 Some of these rights are being acknowledged and legislated in countries following a legal decision centering on an Indonesian orangutan (born on the island of Sumatra and imprisoned first in a zoo in Germany and then in a zoo in Argentina, where the animal was at the time of the decision) (Samuels). For an extended discussion of this subject, see Neel Ahuja's essay, "Rhetorics of Endangerment: Cultural Difference and Development in International Ape Conservation Discourse." Ahuja critiques The Great Ape Survival Project (GRASP), a United Nations Environmental Program (UNEP) partnership that was launched in 2001 by Klaus Toepfer, former UNEP director (126). In its effort to bring together the need for both biodiversity and cultural diversity, it both bends and verges on the discourse of "simian orientalism," a "central imperial discourse for eugenic projects to tame and uplift both humans and domesticated animals" in the twentieth century and a discourse that long racialized indigenous Africans (125). Two further points that Ahuja makes in arguing that biodiversity is fundamentally related to cultural diversity are "*all* great apes—human and nonhuman—have a linked interest in cultural diversity for the preservation of their species" and "both ape and indigene are endangered by the homogenizing and unsustainable force of economic production" (125).

For more discussion of the issue of the other performer where "the other" is a nonhuman being, see Iris Ralph's "Performing others, other Performers, Mark Twain, and Elizabeth Costello."

10 For a different kind of performance, a remarkable performance of the lecture that Costello delivers, see Polish director Krzysztof Warlikowskim's dramatic adaptation of the lecture in the brilliant production, *(A)pollonia*. The play also incorporates scenes from Euripides's *Alcestis*, Aeschylus's *Oresteia*, Hanna Krall's *Apolonia*, Jonathan Littell's *Les Bienveillantes*, Marek Edelman's *Love in the Ghetto*, and Rabindranath Tagore's *The Post Office*.

11 In turn, Wish names J. J., an amply proportioned human, "Sweet-Tooth," because of his penchant for sweets.

12 For more on Wolfe's distinctions between different kinds of posthumanist thinking, see the first chapter of the present study.

13 Most Australian camels belong to the *Camelus dromedaries* species. A small number belong to the *Camelus bactrianus* species (Government of Western Australia).

14 Summarizing and supporting arguments that Judith Halberstam makes in a study entitled *Female Masculinity*, Gaard points out that ecocritics and other scholars have tended to construct or understand masculine gender identity as being something that is "*anti*ecological" (*Critical Ecofeminism* 167). In refuting this construction, Gaard includes an extensive discussion of masculine forms of environmental thinking and praxis, so-called "ecomasculinity."

Referring to Karen Warren's essay entitled "The Power and The Promise of Ecological Feminism," Gaard argues that normative, Western-European heterosexual, masculinities emphasize abstraction and individualism. She contrasts this with marginalized, feminist, queer, and ecocritical masculinities, which in effect "recognize that all human identities and moral conduct are best understood 'in terms of networks or webs of historical and concrete relationships'" (Warren qtd. in Gaard 168). The mainstream, "Euro-Western cultural constructions" of masculinity are predicated on themes of maturity-as-separation, with male self-identity and self-esteem based on dominance, conquest, workplace achievement, economic accumulation, elite consumption patterns and behaviors, physical strength, sexual prowess, animal meat hunting and/or eating, and competitiveness. (163).

In contrast, ecomasculinity replaces an "ethic of daring" (based on dominant male values such as rationality, reductionism, power and control, confidence, conceit, selfishness, competitiveness, virility) with an "ethic of caring" for self, society, and environment (with associated values of love, friendship, trust, compassion, consideration, reciprocity, and cooperation with human and more-than-human life) (Pulé qtd. in Gaard 168).

15 See Deborah Bird Rose's "Val Plumwood's Philosophical Animism: Attentive Inter-Actions in the Sentient World" 102.

16 See, also, Christopher Manes' "Nature and Silence," an essay first published in 1992 in the journal *Environmental Ethics*.

17 See Brodzki 2.

6 Conclusion

Ecophobia

What has changed in the discipline of ecocriticism since Simon C. Estok's article "Theorizing in a Space of Ambivalent Openness: Ecocriticism and Ecophobia" first appeared in print in 2009, in the journal *ISLE: Interdisciplinary Studies in Literature and Environment*, the outlet journal for the Association for the Study of Literature and Environment (ASLE)? What has shifted in institutionalized practices of ecophobia, a catch-all term for aversion to and avoidance of the nonhuman ecogenic other. In the past ten years, Estok's use of the term has gained currency. Most recently, Routledge published a full-length study of ecophobia by Estok, *The Ecophobia Hypothesis*. He and other scholars whose work identifies with postcolonial ecocriticism, Marxist ecocriticism, ecofeminism, and queer ecology address ecophobia by theorizing about the ideological links between it and intraspecies kinds of odium and dread. Yet, discussion of ecophobia is not a household term in ecocriticism judging from the omission of it in such distinguished anthologies of ecocriticism as Hubert Zapf's *Handbook of Ecocriticism and Cultural Ecology*, Serpil Oppermann and Serenella Iovino's *Environmental Humanities: Voices from the Anthropocene*, and Joni Adamson's *Keywords for Environmental Studies*. Is the omission due in part to the "shrill reaction" (Brayton 205) to the article in which theorizing about ecophobia made a debut with a bang? Do scholars want to stay out of the fray of the debate between theory and practice and so eschew one of the key terms of that debate, for Estok used the term to call for more "critical theory" in a discipline, ecocriticism, that had taken shape by in effect distancing itself from "continental philosophy and its twentieth-century academic legacy" (205). Is the marginal status of ecophobia because it is too confrontational, brazen, accusatory, and shaming a term?

With the exception perhaps of "ecophobia's" Latinate syllables, there is little about the "ungainly neologism" (Brayton 205) that is remotely discreet, euphemistic, conciliatory, charitable, or decorous. Unabashedly and unceremoniously, with little trace of refinement, piety, or goodwill, the term "ecophobia" calls out what society largely conceals, underplays, and underestimates. Using more sedate language to persuade society to embrace ecocentrism and reduce anthropocentrism might be more effective than an all-out verbal assault on society's ecophobic and anthropocentric values, practices, and institutions. Yet, precisely because the term is brutally honest and confrontational, shaming, judgmental, and accusing, using it judiciously stands to productively contribute to efforts to nudge and haul society out of the rut of habitual abuses of the nonhuman ecogenic other. Critically engaging with the term might not bring about the end of what it names. However, such engagement would, and already is, bringing more attention to scores of ecophobic practices. Perfectly legal today, they may be criminalized in the future because of that attention, consigned to the dung heap in the form of thick legal tomes, shunned in practice, and shelved for the record.

For literary studies scholars, teaching and studying texts by examining either their ecophobic content or their rebuke of it is an obvious strategy for making "ecophobia" and its like (for example, "speciesism" and "ecocide") commonplace words in schools, offices, airports, gas stations, corner stores, food courts, and shopping malls. Ecophobia today is vast, and it is more insidious and pervasive than it was a century ago. It is as monstrous an institution as the enslavement, trafficking, and commodification of human flesh.

In 2009, in "Theorizing in a Space of Ambivalent Openness: Ecocriticism and Ecophobia," Estok called for more theoretical engagement in the discipline of ecocriticism, and so he re-galvanized debate among ecocritics about the conflicting pulls of activism and scholasticism. In part the result of that call, a special issue of *ISLE* that addressed ecocriticism and theory was published in the spring of 2011. More articles, and monographs, followed soon thereafter.[1]

Estok's article also highlighted questions about the need for a more forceful ecocritical language and vocabulary in the ongoing environmental work of challenging seemingly universal but actually anthropocentric hierarchies in modern times. The kind of rhetoric that Estok's article called for included foremost the term "ecophobia." Many ecocritics embraced it, as a search of the word on the internet reflects. Others ignored or rebuked it, judging from the omission of it in the indices of anthologies of ecocriticism published in the past ten years.

The use of the term "ecophobia" outside of ecocriticism is almost nonexistent but more understandably so. Yet, it names a patently obvious set of prejudices. "Ecophobia" should be as common a term as "racism," "classism," "sexism," and "homophobia." As ecocritics point out in their work of confluent theory, engaging with the first term aids in the fight against the interspecies prejudices that the second set of terms names. Ecofeminists theorize the links between fear and loathing of animals and the environment and sexist attitudes toward and treatment of women (Gaard); postcolonial ecocritics scrutinize the shared ideological grounds of colonization and exploitation of the nonhuman and human other (Huggan and Tiffin, Roos and Hunt; DeLoughrey and Handley); and queer ecology scholars interrogate the ties between hatred of the natural world and homophobia and hatred of the natural world and scientifically spurious and ungrounded dismissals of findings of sexual diversity across species (Mortimer-Sandilands and Erickson). Marxist ecocritics investigate the ties between ecophobia and corporate capitalism (Bellamy; Klein), critical links that Estok also examines, among many others, in *The Ecophobia Hypothesis*. These kinds of confluent theorizing, which also are known as "intersectional" theory (Gaard, "Ecofeminism" 68), emphasize that attitudes and stances of fear and hatred toward the nonhuman other are "rooted in and dependent on anthropocentric arrogance and speciesism" (Estok, "Theorizing in a Space of Ambivalent Openness" 216). Such attitudes and positions are both hardwired (genetic) and constructed. Learning more about them helps scholars to understand how interspecies antipathies—racism, classism, sexism, homophobia, and so forth—function. Theorizing ecophobia advances discussion of environment "alongside discussions of race and gender and sexuality" (217).

Interrogating ecophobia and the links between it and other prejudices is uphill going in a society preoccupied with human internecine conflict and unwilling to consider that that conflict is as rooted in as it is magnified and intensified by ecophobia. To tackle the critical connections between ecophobia and human conflict is to question some of our most basic concepts of personhood. Theorizing ecophobia also includes exploring the causes as much as the effects of ecophobia. Estok does just that in *The Ecophobia Hypothesis*, amassing and sorting through evidence for the genetic as well as socially and politically constructed bases of ecophobia. If ecophobia has "functioned, in part, to preserve our species (for instance, the fight or flight response)," then "growth economies and ideological interests" have grossly capitalized on it (Estok, *Ecophobia* 1). Theorizing ecophobia means comprehensively as well as rigorously questioning those economies and interests. They include the fossil fuel and nuclear power industries and industrial food production inclusive of industrial pastoral.

While terms such as Morton's "dark ecology" (*The Ecological Thought* 16) and Stacy Alaimo's "trans-corporeality" (*Bodily Natures* 3) also intersect with important discussions about speciesism, the term "ecophobia" *outs* morally complex and questionable acts of speciesism through more focused and stronger ethical lenses.[2] Do scholars averse to using it think that it belies and reduces complex relationships? Perhaps. Does the term "ecophobia," like "racism," "classism," "sexism," and "homophobia," rhetorically belie gnarly, knotted, entangled, and complex relationships? No. Like those terms, "ecophobia" directly challenges society's most morally questionable, and arguably most reprehensible, relationships between humans and other species.

Euphemisms such as "global warming" and "climate change" are effete stand-ins for the more robust nomenclature of "ecophobia." "Ecophobia" is to "global warming" and "climate change" what a bare bulb is to light softened by a lampshade. As Estok argues in "Virtually There: 'Aesthetic Pleasure of the First Order,'" "[t]he problem … is more serious than climate change" (5). If "ecophobia" were to become a commonplace word in our educational, legal, and civic institutions, and on our weather channels, it would generate more debate about environmental policies and practices. Moreover, engaging with the term and like language helps in combating interspecies forms of hatred and fear. That is a point that already has been made here but bears repeating.

Thirty years ago, the biologist Edward O. Wilson brought attention to ecophobia's proximate antonym, "biophilia," defining it as referring to "the innate tendency to focus on life and lifelike processes" (*Biophilia: The Human Bond with Other Species* 1); "the urge to affiliate with other forms of life" (85); and "the connections that human beings subconsciously seek with the rest of life" (*The Diversity of Life* 350). If, by emphasizing biophilia, a set of behaviors that is a subset of ecophilia, Wilson and others sought to garner support for arguments and acts in defense of the nonhuman ecogenic other, then their efforts did not succeed spectacularly. If anything, emphasizing acts of biophilia in the popular imagination seems to have had the effect of excusing, eliding, erasing, ignoring, and underestimating institutionalized ecophobic practices. Here is Estok's argument:

> the biophilia hypothesis alone cannot account for the realities of the world, for the kinds of things that are going on in the world, the factory farms, the rainforest destruction, the biodiversity holocaust, and it cannot make the connections with theories about exploitation, about people who gain while others (human and nonhuman) foot the bill, or about intersections among ecophobia, homophobia, speciesism, and sexism. (*Ecophobia* 9)

Picking apart arguments in a later work by Wilson, *The Biophilia Hypothesis* (coedited with Stephen Kellert), Estok argues that "the problem with the uses to which biophilic theories have been put is that they have failed to recognize that biophilia is a point on a spectrum" (*Ecophobia* 9). They neither "explain why environmental crises are worsening" nor "adequately encompass the complex range of ethical positions that humanity generally displays toward the natural environment" (10). Moreover, the rhetoric of biophilia most often appears in places where biophilia is least evident: on the labels, websites, and advertising slogans of the fossil fuel, nuclear power, and meat industries. They regularly venally deploy the language of biophilia to sell ecophobic policies and practices to the public.

The ecophobia hypothesis unapologetically and unabashedly confronts kinds of suffering and death directly caused by aversion to, hostility and indifference toward, and avoidance of nature. It is analogous to "the Love that dare not speak its name" in Alfred Lord Douglas's poem about homosexuality in England in the late nineteenth century (28). "Ecophobia" names a hate that other vocabulary weakly names or utters in *sotto voce*; calls out more loudly for major concessions in humans' use of and dependence on ecogenic nonhuman beings; cajoles environmental thinkers to further question the limits of ecocriticism's "essentially pastoral, conservationist, and preservationist sensibility" (Rozelle 376); and asks ecocritics to consider being more of a sharp thorn than a nettlesome one in the side of anti-environmentalists.

Promoting more awareness of ecophobia has been going on since ecocriticism first emerged as a discipline in its own right, but the term itself, ecophobia, has become a recognizable term only in the last ten years or so. The language of ecophobia theorizing promotes the given scrutiny in bolder and more urgent terms than other language does. Probably, there is not a single work of literature that does not betray or grapple with ecophobia in some shape or form. Giving more currency to the language of ecophobia in literary theory and literature studies, whether for the purpose of denying or affirming ecophobia, opens the doors to asking more serious moral questions about our use of the planet inclusive of fellow animal and vegetal species.

Ecocriticism and Object-Oriented-Ontology

Timothy Morton critically deconstructs, according to Derrida's famous theory of deconstruction, the many dyads that fuel ecophobia. He also uses Object-Oriented-Ontology (OOO) theory to tackle ecophobia. OOO, as the name highlights, focuses on why objects are identified as such, or why they are understood to be essentially and ontologically objects as opposed to subjects. In an essay entitled "Here Comes Everything: The Promise of Object-Oriented-Ontology," Morton ecocritically deploys OOO-theory in his critique of the subject/object dyad and in doing that turns inside out, upside down, and back to front, anthropocentric distinctions between objects and subjects, things and beings, exteriority and interiority. These distinctions lurk within as well as parade outside of the disciplinary halls of ecocriticism. OOO-ecocriticism, as Morton demonstrates, helps to keep hubris under the high heels of ecocriticism as well as humility on its toes. Just as posthumanism theory *avant d'lettre* declares that "radically different material conditions of existence prove incompatible subjectivities" (Badmington 5), OOO-ecocriticism effectively tackles questions having to do with how and why society holds that the natural environment inclusive of plants and nonhuman animals constitutes a limited, vacuous, thoughtless, affectless, inchoate, subject-less, object-full realm. Morton addresses those questions by attacking two main directions within ecocriticism itself. As he argues, both betray fealty to the subject/object dyadic lord.

The first, older direction of ecocriticism, "normative ecophilosophy," holds to an outdated belief in stable and clear-cut distinctions between the human and the environment. Under this belief, scholars reify nature ("Nature") (Morton, "Here Comes Everything" 164). The second, younger direction reflects a form of "speculative realism" that is no less specious (163). Ecocritics who follow this direction "ingeniously" but misguidedly "[assert] a reality independent of minds" ("Non-Nature") in the effort to challenge claims by ecocritics who follow the first direction ("Nature") (164). Morton's brand of OOO-ecocriticism follows neither path; it does not contend that "There is no Nature" but also does not aver that "There is a Non-Nature" (166). "What we should think," Morton states, "asserts neither Nature nor Non-Nature, single, solid, and 'over yonder'" (166). What we should think is far from the nihilism of Non-Nature and no less distant from the idealism of Nature.

The "regular" direction ("normative ecophilosophy") "conjures up the good old days when things meant what they said and said what they meant" (Morton, "Here Comes Everything" 163). Here, the first "forays into literary ecocriticism were Trojan horses for a replay of 1970s and 1980s theory wars" (163). The "cool ... effervescent philosophical movement" ("speculative realism") is no less persuasive:

> The cool flavor fizzes with the future—the bliss of new thinking, more at home with the shock of ecological reality. The regular flavor is somewhat theistic, while the cool flavor is somewhat nihilistic. The regular flavor establishes Nature as an object of reverent admiration; the cool flavor asserts the deep mystery of a Non-Nature. (163)

In other words, normative ecophilosophy refers to an obsolete anti-poststructuralist idea of nature (163), holds that nature is something that is detachable from or lies outside of the human (164), and is a theistic form of ecocriticism that "asserts that 'There is a Nature'" (176); and speculative realist ecocriticism is a form of non-believing ecocriticism, is cavalier in its poststructuralist adherence to Non-Nature, and touts spurious post-Kantian theories of correlationism—"the belief that things can only exist in relation to (human) minds or language" (164). OOO-ecocriticism, as Morton goes on to argue, "decisively departs from" both the normative ecophilosophical position of "Nature" and the seemingly radical speculative realist one of "Non-Nature"; it does that by "enabling a ruthless rejection" of either the belief that nature lies outside the human or the belief that nature does not objectively exist (164).

OOO-ecocriticism also challenges the material turn in ecocriticism; it argues in effect that this turn potentially accelerates rather than slows debasements of nature. That is to say, material ecocriticism opens the doors to anti-environmental arguments that nature is just one kind of matter among others and not more valuable than the kinds of matter produced by or mostly through human agencies and interventions—for example, plastic, petroleum, and nuclear energy. OOO-ecocriticism disputes the notion of "essentialist Matter" that propels material ecocriticism (Morton, "Here Comes Everything" 164). Although the OOO-ecocritic asserts that "real things exist" and that those things "are objects" as opposed to "amorphous 'Matter'" and are of "all shapes and sizes, from football teams to Fermi-Dirac condensates or, if you prefer something more ecological, from nuclear waste to birds' nests," the OOO-ecocritic preserves moral distinctions among different kinds of matter (165). OOO-ecocritics thus "capitalize both Nature and Matter," or "de-nature them," in their argument that Nature and Matter are not the same as nature and objects; and they steer "a middle path" between "the philosophical impasse of essentialism" that lurks in material ecocriticism and betrays older forms of normative ecocriticism and the "nihilism" of speculative realist ecocriticism (164).

OOO-ecocriticism thus also reflects Jacques Derrida's notion that "there is no outside-text," a claim that ecocritics have often mistaken for "nominalism: we can only know things by their names" (Morton, "Here Comes Everything" 179). "Far more drastically," Morton states, Derrida's axiom means that "any attempt to establish rigid boundaries between reality and information results in unsustainable paradoxes" and "language is radically nonhuman—even when humans use it" (178). OOO-ecocriticism thus encourages ecocritics to be even more tentative than are speculative realists in the effort to understand nature (and its languages).

Finally, as Morton explains and wields OOO-ecocriticism, it holds in effect that all things have "an irreducible dark side" to them, a notion that owes to the phenomenological thinking of Edmund Husserl and Martin Heidegger and to Graham Harman's notion of the "withdrawn-ness of objects" (Morton, "Here Comes Everything" 165, 183). In OOO-theory, "withdrawn-ness" refers to the idea that all relationships are not between subjects and objects but between objects and all objects have the feature of "withdrawnness" (183–184). The object thus "can never be fully seen ... we can never see the whole of it, and nothing else can either (165)." The object is "irreducible" in the sense that its "inside is radically unavailable" (166, 177).

As with all ecocritical positions, OOO-ecocriticism is not without leaks in its water tanks. In its expressions of loyalty to the object, the real, and things, OOO-ecocriticism might be compared to a handsome dowager reinventing herself by more and more ingenious and fantastic means. Nonetheless, OOO-ecocriticism does push ecocriticism in exciting directions. It is somewhat analogous to "the new objectivity" movement and revolt against abstraction in the early decades of the last century. In Germany, the movement was dubbed the *Neue Sachlichkeit*. Borrowing the German words for "thing" ("sache") and "matter-of-fact" ("sachlich"), new objectivity artists "understood the artwork, not as an expression, not as the ... vessel of ... [a] psychic state, but as a self-standing non-contingent object, equal in dignity to other phenomena in the world" (Albright 54). These artists turned against Romanticism, Expressionism, and other aesthetic and philosophical positions that reflect interest in the psyche, the subjective condition, interiority, emotion, affect, and so forth. Examples of the art of the new objectivity movement are Ezra Pound's *The Cantos*; the ballet *Pulcinella*, composed in 1919 by Igor Stravinsky for Sergei Diaghilev's ballet company *Ballets Russes*; Jean Cocteau's *Cock and Harlequin*, written in 1918, "a call to a new aesthetic of the spare, the simple, the linear, the sturdy, and even the ordinary"; Bertolt Brecht's "epic theater" and "smoker's theater," or performance and performance spaces that dispel any suspension of disbelief of where one is or in what one is participating; Arnold Schoenberg's early 12-tone compositions; and T. E. Hulme's 1911 essay "Romanticism and Classicism," which decried the sloppiness and indulgences of Romanticism and "advocated instead a Classical art, hard and dry" (54). Similarly, Bertrand Russell "tried hard to liberate the objective world from entanglement with the human psyche ... [and safeguard] the continuity and reliability of physical objects in time and space" (54). The intent was to make "[T]he object ... truly respectable in itself" (54).

Modernism scholar Daniel Albright's summary of the new objectivity movement includes a description of the *Neue Sachlichkeit* compositions that Schoenberg devised for his one-act monodrama *Erwartung*. Albright's account of those compositions especially conjure Morton's OOO-ecocritical descriptions of the *strange strangeness* of things ("Here Comes Everything" 165). The "very urbanity and simplicity" of the compositions "[make] the lack of a tonal center all the more disorienting ... like an exercise in the Freudian uncanny" and "the displacement of the *almost*-familiar feel stranger than the bland incomprehensibilities" (Albright 55). OOO, like the new objectivity movement a hundred years ago, defends much that associates with and is defined as being exteriority (as opposed to interiority), objectivity (as opposed to subjectivity), and function (as opposed to meaning). OOO-ecocriticism focuses especially on beings and things that humans have often denied consciousness, will, freedom, and subjectivity (interiority) to simply because they are not human. OOO-ecocriticism also highlights calls for respecting the unfathomable and unforthcoming aspects of nature and so respecting the unwillingness as well as the willingness of nature to divulge itself to and be used by others.

Like the new objectivity movement, a slightly later movement, that associated with the Frankfurt School, also challenges in effect the debasement of putative objects. Such confrontation appears in an essay by Theodor Adorno entitled "Subject and Object." In this posthumous work (first published in 1969), Adorno attacked the hypostasized separation between the subject and object that stamped metaphysical inquiries and epistemological claims. He addresses, indeed is preoccupied with, human inequities, yet his argument incites with minimal provocation an ecocritical reading, or a reading that highlights the anthropocentrism of common separations of and differentiations between so-called subjects and objects. According to these common divisions, human beings are granted the trait of subjectivity—consciousness, access to metaphysical realms, interiority, and so forth—and nonhuman beings are deemed to be marked by objectivity in the sense of possessing limited knowledge and limited forms of life.

In epistemology, as Adorno explains in the opening paragraphs of "Subject and Object," the term "subject" typically refers to "the particular individual" as well as "consciousness in general," and the term "object" refers to what is separated from the subject (497–498). As he also explains, the concepts of subject and object "have priority before all definition," since to define something means that "something objective, no matter what it may be in itself, is subjectively captured by means of a fixed concept" (498). However, this process, or project, of separation of subject and object is "hypostasized"; it is "transformed into an invariant" when it ought to be approached as being at once "real and illusory" (497–498). The "false" separation is "no sooner established directly, without mediation" then it becomes "ideology" (498). "[P]arted from the object," the subject "reduces [the object] to its own measure" (498). The subject "swallows the object, forgetting how much it is an object itself" (498).

Adorno argues against this hegemonic epistemology by pointing out that the "primacy of the object" must remain paramount even though the object cannot be conceived without the subject, and the object is not "so thoroughly dependent on the subject as the subject is on objectivity" ("Subject and Object" 502). He thus emphasizes that the object is always the "corrective of the subjective reduction," and the subject, while it is the "epitome of mediation," is the "How—never the What" of the relationship or mediation (502). In challenging conventional notions of the superior subject and inferior object, Adorno further argues that the relationship of subject and object if this were "in its proper place, even epistemologically," would be one that would reflect "peace among men as well as between men and their Other," or "the state of distinctness without domination" (500).

For ecocritics, Adorno's "Other" refers not only to the "other" of marginalized human individuals and populations but also to the "other" of marginalized nonhuman beings and populations. They are mistaken for something that is extraneous, "residual," and for being of secondary value instead of for something that is central, main, and of primary value ("Subject and Object" 505).

Riders in the Chariot

In the context of Australian literature, the object/subject dyadic discourse and the renunciation of its most common inflections is apparent in the work of a close contemporary of Adorno, Patrick White. A theistic thinker, White does not reinvest or redeem the objective world according to the anti-subjective and anti-metaphysical thinking of either Theodor Adorno or Timothy Morton and fellow OOO-ecocritics. Rather, in his novels, White makes everything a subject inclusive of any given putative object, and so envisions a world that identifies with what Adorno calls "the state of distinctness without domination" ("Subject and Object" 500).

As numerous critics have written about, White was deeply interested in intensively subjective realms and what might lie beyond the physical world (White, "Australians in a Nuclear War" 116). Religion was part of that interest and critically funds all of his books and their main theme of the "the relationship between the blundering human being and God" (qtd. in McGregor et al. 218). Peter Beatson explores this aspect of White's work in a study entitled *The Eye in the Mandala. Patrick White: A Vision of Man and God.* In *Patrick White's Fiction: The Paradox of Fortunate Failure*, Carolyn Bliss also examines this subject. Michael Giffin, in a study entitled *Arthur's Dream: The Religious Imagination in the Fiction of Patrick White*, writes about White's orthodox Judeo-Christian world view. In "The ethics of abjection: Patrick White's *Riders in the Chariot*," Andrew McCann discusses White's habit of appropriating Judeo-Christian symbols to flesh out a given character. In "Towards an Ecology of Australia: Land of the Spirit," Veronica Brady analyzes White's characteristic symbolist's as opposed to realist's use of language in her argument about White's faith in spiritual realities. Helen Verity Hewitt's study *Patrick White, Painter Manque: Paintings, Painters and their Influence on his Writing* draws critical attention to the strain of Romanticism that runs through White's work and particularly so in the middle to late novels (which include *Riders in the Chariot*). James Bulman-May, in a study entitled *Patrick White and Alchemy,* and Brian Kiernan, in an essay entitled "Coloring in White," scrutinize in particular the "alchemical manifestations, Jungian philosophy and mandalic images" in White's work (Kiernan, "Coloring in White" 196). White's fictions characteristically are about worlds that are more than "physical fact" (Brady, "Towards and Ecology of Australia" 148).

Yet, the metaphysical worlds of White's fictions are not manifestly saddled with or betrayed by anthropocentric trappings. White does not as a matter of course elevate the interests of human so-called subjects above the interests of nonhuman so-called objects. He confronts the trenchant anthropocentrism legitimized in the modern period by the Enlightenment and post-Enlightenment metaphysical philosophical inquiries. These inquiries, which split or differentiate between the subject and the object, characterize both Cartesian rationalist metaphysical pursuits and anti-Cartesian, Romantic metaphysical pursuits. In their most common forms or acts of expression, both inquiries betray a profound condescension toward and dismissal of the environment.

The dominant discourse of Romanticism is that the nonhuman world is not an autonomous being or subject but a product *of*, a corollary *to*, the thinking (human) subject, or *consciousness*. So-called objective reality is understood to be under the aegis of the subjective reality of the human. Such thinking colors Hegelian consumptive claims of a system's "totality," which will "suffer nothing to remain outside of" and emphasizes "the primacy of the whole" (Adorno, "The Melancholy Science" 81, 83).[3] This same thinking associates with the Hegelian characterization of objective reality as being "foul existence" (Buck-Morss 72). The dominant strain of Cartesian rationalism, no less so than the dominant products of Romantic anti-rationalist discourse, has been one that in effect disdains and rejections nonhuman beings. They are considered to be limited, incomplete, subject-*less*, *without self*. The "Cartesian illusion" of denial of existence of the object (-subject) outside of the subject (-object), that is, outside of the "thinking [human] subject," underlies even Edmund Husserl's phenomenology, one of the most formidable challenges to Hegelian thought (Adorno, "Introduction" 114). Husserl's phenomenology reflects the attempt to reach knowledge of the object. Nonetheless, in this attempt, many thinkers do not let go of the Hegelian premise, which is that the object is superseded or transcended by the subject.

White's love of objects inclusive of the putative objects of plants, nonhuman animals, and the environment appears in his earliest work and continues up through his last works. In *The Aunt's Story*, published in 1948, the central character, Theodora Goodman, speaks for the value of the object-subject world, not only human-made (anthropogenic) things such as "sensible shoes" (56), "chairs and tables"—the "sanity" of them (162)—but also nonhuman-made (ecogenic) things such as the "big pink and yellow cows cooling their heels in creek mud" (16), a red-eyed hawk, and a dog who senses that Theodora will not treat him as a subordinate at her father's property Meroe. In *The Tree of Man*, published in 1955, the main character of Stan Parker represents the possibility of humans "integrating into the natural world" (Mark Williams 53). Laura Trevelyan, one of the two main characters in *Voss* (published in 1957), complements, and contravenes, the metaphysical and transcendentalist ambitions of another main character, the novel's namesake and Laura's betrothed, Voss. The German explorer willfully sacrifices the object-subject world of the Australian environment in his metaphysical and transcendentalist search for "Gothic splendours" (*Voss* 264, 267). He disparages as being weak and self-deluding any veneration of the so-called objective condition. His is the obsessive search by the human for a "pure, undivided light which is outside nature, not something recreated along with grass and trees and animals but a transcendent principle which is superior to and opposed to creaturely things" (Mark Williams 67).[4] Trevelyan, who associates with the color green (White, *Voss* 54, 158, 198, 259), a color that has a very long and rich history as a referent for "nature" and nonhuman ecogenic identity, prevails upon her fiancé to take a more humble human stance toward the object-subject world. This includes "the immediate world" "clothed in green" of the ecogenic realm that Voss simultaneous explores and denies (198).

Mary Hare, one of the four principal characters in *Riders in the Chariot* (published in 1961), is one of the most pronounced of White's ecological avatars. She is a *green* interloper in the "glass house" of Xanadu, an imposing estate erected by Mary's father, Norbert Hare, on the outskirts of Sydney (White, *Riders in the Chariot* 35). Norbert's metaphysical thinking and transcendentalist ambitions, which are similar to those of Voss, are deeply anthropocentric and blind him to the beings in the ecogenic environment around him. He exploits it or disregards it in his design of Xanadu. Mary Hare loves the estate she inherits from her father—its "great, tatty, brilliant rooms" (96); "voices of marble and gold" (42); "gilded mirrors," "marble staircase," and "malachite urns" (21); "golden walls of stone" (17); frills of "iron lace" (16); and "dome of faintly amethyst glass" (16). However, she does little to upkeep the place during her incumbency. Eventually she abandons her father's "grandest gesture" and "building of his folly" (15).

Norbert Hare's estate, "His Pleasure Dome, he called it" (White, *Riders in the Chariot* 15), carries allusions to the "stately pleasure dome" of the English Romantic poet Samuel Taylor Coleridge's poem "Kubla Khan" and to the figure of Coleridge himself, a powerful spokesperson for the British Romantics and the most metaphysical of this generation of poets. As ecocriticism scholar Laurence Coupe points out, the British Romantics strenuously challenged callous Enlightenment approaches to the natural world, attacking the "dead universe" of Newtonian physics, which effectively treated the nonhuman world as a subject-less object and a non-being (13). But the anti-Enlightenment Romantic imagination also often endorses and promulgates condescending attitudes toward and relationships with the natural world (Caddel 139–150).[5] Norbert Hare represents that kind of Romantic imagination, in particular as it associates with Coleridge. Hare's regard for the natural world as being either an interference or imperfect condition brings to mind Coleridge's own views. He was at the very least ambivalent toward, if not decisively dismissive of, natural phenomena. He frequently endorsed the Hegelian notion that nature, so-called objective reality, was illusory and merely supplementary (Gravil; Roe). In contrast with the "entrenched literal-mindedness" of his colleague William Wordsworth, Coleridge's thinking was that of a transcendentalist and symbolist and reflected his dismissal of the primacy of the objective world (Newlyn 127). Such thinking is manifest in a seminal writing, "The Subjective & Objective." In this essay, Coleridge distinguishes between the so-called objective condition, or "the sum of all that is merely objective," and the so-called objective condition, or "the sum of all that is subjective" (21). He names the objective condition "Nature" and the subjective condition the "Self or Intelligence" (21). "Nature" he states, is "without consciousness"; the "Self or Intelligence," he states, "is conscious" (21). "Nature" is "exclusively represented"; the "Self or Intelligence" is "exclusively representative" (21). Coleridge goes on to assert that neither the subjective condition defines the objective condition nor the objective condition trumps the subjective condition, but then he resolves this "apparent contradiction" by asserting that the objective condition is "unconsciously involved in the latter" and is "not only coherent but identical, and one and the same thing with our own immediate self consciousness" (22) [emphasis added]. Further, this credo must be "the office and object" of the "Transcendental philosopher" (22).

Coleridge's essay turned the nineteenth-century wheels of an already well-established anthropocentrism. In the nineteenth century, "Self or Intelligence" identifies the human and "Nature" any state or being *without* the human and, therefore, without consciousness. Yet, if Coleridge accepts and promulgates the split between the putative insubstantial, nonhuman, subject-less object of "Nature" and the primordial anthropomorphic "Self" or "Intelligence," then he is never fully reconciled to this bifurcation. The poem "Kubla Khan" betrays his anxiety about his and the metaphysical philosopher's subordination of the objective condition to the subjective condition. Kubla Khan's palace Xanadu, "a miracle of rare device, /A sunny pleasure dome with caves of ice!" (Coleridge, "Kubla Khan" 347), is perilously unstable, divisive, and disembodied. It describes an intensely subjective condition or state that is unanchored by objective reality. The sense of radical instability is augmented by the shape of the poem itself—the unevenness of its lines, its overall disjointedness—and also is hinted at in the subtitle, "Or, A Vision in a Dream. A Fragment" of the poem. The main parts of Xanadu, if indeed they exist, never materialize in the poem. All movements or indications toward it produce or result in a violent, even apocalyptic, upheaval. Only Xanadu's external, non-essential, secondary, physical features—its "walls and towers ... girdled round," its "gardens bright with sinuous rills, /Where blossomed many an incense-bearing tree," its "green hill athwart a cedarn cover"—exist. "Kubla Khan" is a paean to but also and critique of the separation—the "deep romantic chasm"—of the human and the environment, and the subordination of the object world—the environment—to a putative central subjectivity.

Riders in the Chariot's recurrent images of shattering glass and splintering stone allude to Coleridge's "Kubla Khan's" Xanadu and the Romantic metaphysical imagination that erects false, anthropocentric conceits in blatant disregard of the environment. Norbert Hare's Xanadu, situated on a parcel of property on the edges of the suburbs of Sarsaparilla and Barranugli, represents the ambitious desire to both transcend and wall oneself off from the ecogenic realm. Xanadu is an anthropogenic thing, highly reified, imposing, audacious, adamantine. Built mostly out of relatively stable, inorganic ecogenic materials, the semi-precious stone and glass estate symbolizes Hare's desire for a permanent, preternatural, irrefragable, or eternal condition. Thus, Xanadu is a tragic, doomed, ill-fated entity. When Mary is still a young girl, Norbert, in a fit of rage over a supper of slaughtered "cold fowl" spoiled by a swarm of "flying-ants," fires a pistol at Xanadu's prize possession, a crystal chandelier "imported from some dismembered European house" that hangs in the drawing room of the mansion (*Riders in the Chariot* 36, 37). The shattering of the "crystal fruit" presages the demise of the estate as a whole and represents the revolt against the hubris of anthropocentrism (37). (The figure of the crystal chandelier also carries allusions to London's nineteenth-century Crystal Palace, which for many visitors represented human domination over nature through the modern instruments of science and technology.)

In contrast with Norbert Hare and his conceit, Xanadu, Mary Hare, a "nature mystic" (Chapman 112; Morley 158), represents the antithesis of the belief, reflected in Coleridge's essay, that consciousness, intelligence, the self, or "the sum of all that is subjective," is split from matter, or "the sum of all that is merely objective" (Coleridge, "Subject & Object" 21). Mary Hare speaks for the faith that the human is interdependent with, not superior to, the nonhuman. She is not particularly distinguishable from her native surrounds. She is "[s]peckled and dappled, like any wild thing native to the place" (*Riders in the Chariot* 16). She "[loses] her identity in 'trees, bushes, inanimate objects'" (91). She "enter[s] into the minds of animals" (91). She "never approach[es] her legal property by following the official road to the gates" (13). Instead, she takes a "tunnel" through the native vegetation (which she has allowed to overtake her father's landscape park [16]). She tells her housekeeper, Mrs. Jolley, that people "cannot live together unless they respect each other's habits" and she has done that "by painful degrees" in her "relationships with birds and animals" (59). She tells Mordecai Himmelfarb, a recent newcomer to Sarsaparilla, that "the earth is wonderful. It is all we have" (172). When Himmelfarb questions Hare's ecocentricity, asking "And at the end? When the earth can no longer raise you up?," she answers him: "I shall sink into it [the earth] ... and the grass will grow out of me" (172). She attends the bush instead of church on a Sunday (69). It is natural for her to "adopt a kneeling position in the act of worship" of the earth, in particular when she is knee-deep in the "good, soft loam, and velvet patches of leaf mold [...] from which [...] rise the scent of fungus and future growth" (13). Her richest "companions" are "sticks, pebbles, skeleton leaves, birds, insects" and the "hollows of trees" (24).

As an ecogenic figure, a "country beauty" that is "botched and brown and quickly gone" (White, *Riders in the Chariot* 61), Mary Hare speaks for the ecological values of decomposition and excrement in contrast with the non-ecological values of permanence and purity, represented by the reputedly perdurable Xanadu.[6] She does not interfere with Xanadu's disintegration, caulk its cracked walls—"lizards [run] in and out of [them]" (40)—or replace the "drunken brown festoons" of imported silk wallpapers with new wall coverings (86). Leaves and other flora become residents of the palace. They "plap" and "hesitate," "advance" and "retreat" in "whispers and explosions of green" (326). "[O]ld birds' nests" lie "on the Aubusson, or what had become, rather, a carpet of twigs, dust, mildew and the chrysalides of insects" (46). "On one side of the dining room" an elm "enter[s] in" (46). Its "early leaves [pierce] the more passive colors of human refinement like a knife" (46). In the gaps in the walls and roof, "little rags of blue sky [flicker] and [flap] drunkenly" (46). In other places "rain [has] gushed" and in others again it has "trickled down the walls, and over marble, now the color of rotten teeth" (46). Indeed, as the narrative tells us, Xanadu itself "enter[s] into a conspiracy" (325) with the flora and fauna, and Mary's tacit approval long before the heir incumbent defects from her father's house.

The understory figures of Mary Hare and her fellow organic flora and fauna bespeak relatively gentle, repeatable acts of license and transgression—the insurgency of the carnival as opposed to apocalyptic acts. In contrast, the figures of Norbert Hare, Xanadu, and "light" and "time" in the novel represent irreversible, permanent, absolute, universal, fixed states and conditions. Paradoxically, the latter figures are radically unstable. Light is "crumbling gold," "slips of elusive feldspar," "deposits of porphyry and agate" (449). It "[finishes] the job" of the disintegration of Xanadu where "time" has not already "slashed" the halls and rooms (46). The mansion's "golden walls of stone" (17) are "split by sun and fire" (40); "[c]abinets and little frivolous tables seem to splinter at a blow"; and "Even solid pieces in marquetry and the buhl octopus" are "stunned" (46) by the figures of light and time.

If Mary Hare represents a "green" flaw, a mortal "brown" spot in the Romantic metaphysical conceit of the "crystal glass" of Norbert's Xanadu and if she is atypical of the human community in her self-identification with the ecogenic realm, then she is not conscious of or does little to actively promote her ecocentricity. Before she disappears from or abandons

Xanadu, she makes no provisions for the land and the flora and fauna that have been slowly reclaiming the estate to be protected. Rather, some years before her disappearance, she bequeaths Xanadu to a cousin she hardly knows. Her "legatee and relative," Eustace Cleugh, promptly sells the property to a real estate developer and he no less expediently "demolish[es] and subdivide[s]" the estate (White, *Riders in the Chariot* 519).

Riders in the Chariot, as with the writings that precede it, *The Aunt's Story, The Tree of Man*, and *Voss*, refuses to give us a character capable of effecting an ecologic on a level broad enough to have significant social and political impact. The ecological vision of individual characters is doomed to remain unrealized at a larger, societal, level. Scholars have persuasively and eloquently made this point about the figure of the alienated individual in White's fictions (Wilding). This figure includes Mary Hare, who represents marginalized ecocentric as opposed to anthropocentric values, and another character in *Riders in the Chariot*, Ruth Godbold.

Similar to Mary Hare, and to Theodora Goodman in the novel *The Aunt's Story*, individuals who "have not the ... vanity" of the intellectual or the artist (White, *The Aunt's Story* 56), Godbold is unprepossessing, hardly noticed by the human members of her community. The narrative nonetheless makes clear that she is a figure to be reckoned with. (Even Mary, because she is not without "arrogance" [*Riders in the Chariot* 72], pales in comparison with Ruth Godbold.) To the townspeople of Sarsaparilla, Godbold is a *persona non grata*, a woman who lives in "a shed" below the Sarsaparilla post office and "takes in washing" (*Riders in the Chariot* 70). In actuality, Godbold is the humblest, most plebian, and "most positive evidence of good" in her community (72). She is touched by "wings of love and charity" (549). She does not hold herself above or separate from any other being, human or nonhuman. She respects all "Living Creatures," both those she has known and those she has not (551–552). She shows "love and respect" for the most "common objects and trivial acts" (536). She "goes about" such labor as planting a row of beans, like the much more celebrated eco-visionary Henry David Thoreau, or admiring a row of cabbages, like Patrick White at Castle Hill, "as if she were learning a secret of immense importance, over and over" (536). When she "indulge[s] herself at all in her almost vegetable existence," it is "to walk and look [...] at the ground" (536–537). She does not aspire to transcend the ecogenic object-subject world; rather she seeks intimate contact with it. When she walks, she does not look skyward, *transcendentally*, but downward and "smile[s] at the ground" (8). To her fellow townspeople, Godbold is an inferior human being. She is "[p]hysically [...] too massive [...] too coarse, too flat of face, thick-armed, big of breast, waxy-skinned, the large pores opened by the steam from the copper" (72). They only begrudgingly recognize the aspects of the Greek goddess of wisdom, Athena, in Godbold:

"Nobody could deny Mrs Godbold her breadth of brow. She wore her hair in thick and glistening coils, and her eyes were a steady grey" (72). She is the least "isolated and inward looking" of the characters in the novel (Mark Williams 83).

Mary Hare and Ruth Godbold speak more for than against the local environment, subjugated by Norbert Hare and Hare's colonial forbears in the nineteenth century and by postcolonial forces in the twentieth. Real estate developers have "shaved" Xanadu's "green hill" down to a "bald, red, rudimentary hill" (*Riders in the Chariot* 545). Rows of semi-prefabricated "fibro homes" now stand where Xanadu had once stood (545). *Riders in the Chariot* exposes the ugly aspects of the Australian suburb and middleclass suburban imagination. This "anti-suburbanism" has been commented upon by critics (Kinnane, McCann).[7] Yet, if *Riders in the Chariot* takes a stab at the anti-environmentalism of Australia's middle classes and their suburbs, then it also criticizes the anti-environmental imagination of an older ruling class symbolized by the figure of Norbert Hare.

Carolyn Bliss, in *Patrick White's Fiction: The Paradox of Fortunate Failure*, makes the case that principal characters in White's novels are figures of failure. Considering this argument from an ecocritical perspective, one could add that such characters constitute two types: those that fail in spectacular terms and demonstrate indifference or hostility toward the ecogenic object-subject world (the so-called natural world) and those that default under relatively unremarkable, undistinguished circumstances but express humility in their relations with the ecogenic object-subject world. Theodora Goodman in *The Aunt's Story*, Stan Parker in *The Tree of Man*, and Mary Hare and Ruth Godbold in *Riders in the Chariot* belong to the second type. Peter Beatson, in *The Eye in the Mandala. Patrick White: A Vision of Man and God*, notes that White's principal characters have "a living, organic relationship with the sensuous world that surrounds them"; there is a sense of their "'being there' in the phenomenal world"; and they manifest "an openness to the pulsations and emanations of places and things" (133). By the words "world," "places," and "things" Beatson mostly refers to nature and the environment. The principal characters that he discusses are mostly those that show reverence for the natural world, sensitivity toward it, and acceptance that the natural world is equal to, not less than, the anthropogenic worlds that humans build around them.

Final Remarks: "Openness from Closure"

In bringing this study to an end, I briefly comment on a concern that Cary Wolfe addresses in his book on posthumanism. The concern refers to literary and cultural studies scholars who foray into other disciplines in their work of reading and analyzing literature. Wolfe discusses this concern by drawing on the work of scholars in systems theory and by making what seems to be but is not an arch-conservative defense of disciplinarity. His defense of disciplinarity, indeed, is also, seemingly paradoxically so, a defense of transdisciplinarity.

In "'Animal Studies,' Disciplinarity, and the (Post)Humanities," one of the chapters in *What Is Posthumanism?*, Wolfe argues that it is "only through disciplinary specificity," or through the discursive protocols of scholars' fields of disciplinary expertise, that one can "contribute something specific and irreplaceable" to knowledge about the world (117). Although this "something specific" is not "something *accurate*," it is, nonetheless, as Wolfe continues, "something *specific*" (114). He goes on to elaborate this point in his argument in defense of disciplinarity by referring to the work of Niklas Luhmann in systems theory and to Jacques Derrida's theory of deconstruction. Systems theory (more broadly known as complexity theory) and deconstruction theory, two of the most important theories to emerge in the last 50 years in literary and cultural studies, both emphasize difference or "radical heterogeneity," a term and concept that appears in Wolfe's study in an earlier chapter entitled "Meaning and Event" (14). Systems theory specifically holds that any system (e.g., an ecosystem, an animal species, an organization, an academic discipline, a city, or a poem) functions *as* such—as a more or less discrete or autonomous or distinctive functioning entity—because of, not in spite of, its engagements with neighboring or adjacent systems, which constitute its "environment." So long as these engagements do not cause excessive or irredeemable loss of or do not overdetermine the systems adjacent to it, the result is more (not less) systemic complexity, difference, and autonomy. In other words, the system's, or organism's, or body's, or brain's, or object's independence (of operation or function), or capacity for autopoiesis—a term that Wolfe takes from Luhmann and Luhmann takes in turn from the work (in biology) of Humberto Maturana and Francisco Varela—is a reflection of the "seemingly paradoxical fact" that the system must be "both open *and* closed" (Wolfe 111). In order to exist and reproduce itself, the system must maintain "[its] boundaries and integrity through a process of self-referential closure" (111). Paradoxically, it is only on that basis of closure that the system can "then engage in 'structural coupling' with [its] environment" (111).

As Wolfe continues to argue, disciplinary knowledge is strengthened by scholars who work quite narrowly within the boundaries of their own discipline. Referring to the work of Luhmann in systems theory, he characterizes this work as a commitment to the fundamental principle of existence of "openness from closure" (117). Yet, as Wolfe also argues, in order to do this kind of disciplinary work, scholars must engage with knowledge claims being generated outside of their disciplines. This part of his argument offers an especially powerful provocation to literary and cultural studies scholars who are resistant to bringing into literary and cultural studies knowledge claims generated out of other disciplines. Many see such claims as being ancillary to literary and cultural studies—not essential to the study and teaching of literature—or worse, as being irrelevant. Wolfe's argument foregrounds the fact that these scholars may be reducing, and making insular, obsolete, and dependent what they could be expanding and making magnanimous, viable, and autonomous. Literary and cultural studies are not necessarily doomed because their scholars are responding to external pressures from adjacent or more distant disciplines such as social systems, ecology, geophysics, climatology, and ethology. Literary and cultural studies are being challenged, not threatened, by scholars who are addressing concerns that in the "humanist" lamplight of traditional literary and cultural studies appear unseemly and unfitting to them.

Wolfe uses systems theory to defend transdisciplinarity, paradoxically so, by arguing for the systems theory principle of "openness from closure" (113). He does this to defend scholars who bring questions of animal rights into the halls of literary studies and to attack scholars who argue that animal rights is ancillary to and so should not be addressed by literary studies scholars. What Wolfe foregrounds is how literary studies can shed light on and contribute to animal rights questions because its scholars use different tools of inquiry than do animal rights activists to address the subject of the animal. In other words, literary studies scholars' disciplinary-specific forms of addressing the subject of the animal are potentially useful precisely because they are different from the forms of address and the rhetorical strategies that one sees elsewhere. For sure, literary studies scholars' theorizing of the subject of the animal might not always be "transparent" (or instantly so) to people situated outside of literary studies inclusive of people who are first and foremost animal rights activists. Literary studies scholars' theorizations of the animal might not be readily accessible even to scholars working in more or less adjacent disciplinary areas of inquiry; yet these theorizations, which illustrate the "fundamental principle" of systems theory of "openness from closure" and distinguish the areas of literary studies of ecocriticism, ecofeminism, feminist ecocriticism, ecophilosophy, environmental justice studies, postcolonial ecocriticism, and posthumanism, are important and perhaps even necessary. By no means are they worth defending merely in order to fabricate and sustain literary studies. They are worth defending in the sense that when scholars engage with the subject of the animal and animal rights issues and debates *within* the normative bounds of or according to the protocols of their own discipline or vocational area of expertise, they generate potentially unique and irreproducible claims about normative distinctions between human animals and nonhuman animals.

In this book, I have relied on ecocritical theory and closely intersecting theoretical perspectives to read a small selection of Australian literature, a canon of literature produced in a country that has been arguably detrimentally overdetermined by people who first settled in and colonized Australia less than 300 years ago. Many of those immigrants' descendants and many other Australians benefited from the pastoral practices that Anglo-Europeans brought with them in 1788. Ecocriticism—which includes such work as Simon C. Estok's focused and sustained address of ecophobia, Greta Gaard's equally sustained and committed contribution to ecofeminism, Bill Gammage's *The Biggest Estate on Earth: How Aborigines Made Australia*, Bruce Pascoe's postcolonial ecocritical study, *Dark Emu. Black Seeds: Agriculture or Accident?*, John Ryan's critical plant studies projects, Wendy Wheeler's work in biosemiotics, and Cary Wolfe's critique of mainstream transhumanist posthumanist projects—offers insights into what those practices unfairly nicked from Australia. Ecocriticism and animal studies, plant studies, indigenous studies, and posthumanism studies constitute the critical questioning of and engagement with the taken-for-granted assumption that Australian beings other than humans can be sacrificed, with minimal reflection or debate, to the goal of improving, so-called perfecting, human life. Such assumption betrays a profound moral failure, the reluctance to acknowledge that the oldest environments and species of Australia and the animals and plants that were brought to Australia after 1788 deserve the kinds of moral consideration granted to humans. Contributing to and participating in the given theoretical work include foregrounding it when reading, studying, and teaching Australian literature.

Notes

1 For a list of many other studies published in the last ten years that theorize or otherwise engage with ecophobia, see Estok, *Ecophobia* (5–7).

2 Morton or Alaimo do not eschew the term "ecophobia." Indeed, they both embrace the potentials it offers. Those relate to the term's edginess and to how it evokes raw, visceral responses (hence, the "Estok-Robisch Controversy").

3 Adorno's esteem for Hegel should not be underestimated. However, he questioned Hegel's logic, which was "'fastened' to a transcendental subject" that lay outside of the so-called objective condition of history (human and nonhuman) (Adorno, "Introduction" 114).

4 Williams does not make an environmental argument for White. Nonetheless, his insights, like those of other critics whom I mention, point toward such an argument. Both he and Carolyn Bliss, for example, consider it significant to include in their brief introductions to their studies of White, White's active environmental opposition during the 1960s and 1970s to the nuclear industry and uranium projects (Bliss xi; Williams 6).

5 Human condescension toward the nonhuman-made so-called natural world is found in nineteenth-century Romantic-Symbolist literature in the stock literary trope, the pathetic fallacy. This literary device attributes human traits to the nonhuman world and describes a world in which the human communicates with the nonhuman in the language of the human. Richard

Caddel (modernist scholar and author of *Ezra Pound: Nature and Myth*) points to some "straightforward examples" of the pathetic fallacy in Wordsworth's poetry and discusses the "Romantic exception" of John Clare, the "'peasant poet' of Helpston" (141). Unlike his contemporaries, Clare did not "literally, Romanticise" the nonhuman world but instead represented an ecology that was based on "real observation, as opposed to spectator status," and allowed "no separation between the 'human' and 'natural' world" and "no concept of eternity" (143). The ecocritic J. Scott Bryson also discusses the pathetic fallacy and the rejection of this trope in the context of twentieth-century Anglo-American "anti-romantic" literature. For ecocritical defenses of the pathetic fallacy see Chapter 5.

6 When Mrs. Jolley slanders Mordecai, calling him "dirty Jew!" (331), the anger that "rises" in Mary is "green" anger (331). "Then I am offal, offal [too]! Green, putrefying [...]" (331), she hurls at Mrs. Jolley. The "brown word," "plaster[s]" her offender Mrs. Jolley's back (332). Mary's rebuke of Mrs. Jolley reflects Mary's identification with the ecogenic nonhuman maligned by humans as well as a human subject reviled by another human subject. Essentially a figure for the "green" world marginalized by her father's colonial order, Hare is the green analogue to Alf Dubbo, the marginalized Aboriginal person and the alienated artist figure; Ruth Godbold, the working-class individual whom the middle- and upper-middle-class individual condescends to as being unintelligent, hardly sensate, mere "dumb beast"; and Mordecai Himmelfarb, another social pariah, a Jew crucified by a World War II–era, neocolonial, suburban, Anglo-Australian order (represented in the novel by the figures of Mrs. Jolley and her coconspirator Mrs. Flack).

7 McCann analyzes White's "vehemently anti-suburban" themes ("Decomposing Suburbia" 59) and "at times paranoid fear of suburbia" ("The Ethics of Abjection" 145).

Works Cited

Acocella, Joan. "Rich Man, Poor Man: The Radical Visions of St. Francis." *The New Yorker*, 14 January 2013, pp. 72–77. https://www.newyorker.com/magazine/2013/01/14/rich-man-poor-man.

Adams, Carol J. *The Sexual Politics of Meat*. Continuum, 1990.

Adamson, Joni, William A. Gleason, and David N. Pellow, editors. *Keywords for Environmental Studies*. New York UP, 2016.

Adorno, Theodor. "The Melancholy Science." *The Adorno Reader*, edited by Brian O'Connor. Blackwell, 2000, pp. 79–83.

———. "Subject and Object." *The Essential Frankfurt School Reader*, edited by Andrew Arato and Eike Gebhardt. Continuum, 1978, pp. 497–511.

Agamben, Giorgio. *The Open: Man and Animal*. Translated by Kevin Attell. Stanford UP, 2004.

"Ag-gag." *Voiceless*. The Animal Protection Institute, n.d. https://www.voiceless.org.au/hot-topics/ag-gag.

Agriculture Protection Board. "State Barrier Fence of Western Australia, 1901–2001." Department of Agriculture, Western Australia, n.d. http://pandora.nla.gov.au/pan/43156/20040709-0000/agspsrv34.agric.wa.gov.au/programs/app/barrier/intro.htm.

Ahuja, Neel. "Rhetorics of Endangerment: Cultural Difference and Development in International Ape Conservation Discourse." *Postcolonial Green: Environmental Politics and World Narratives*, edited by Bonnie Roos and Alex Hunt. U of Virginia P, 2010, pp. 118–134.

Alaimo, Stacy. *Bodily Natures: Science, Environment, and the Material Self*. Indiana UP, 2010.

Albright, Daniel. "Exhibiting Modernism: A View from the Air." *The Rise of Modernism: Make It New*, edited by Kurt Heinzelman. Harry Ransom Humanities Research Center, 2003, pp. 30–59.

Althusser, Louis. "Marxism and Humanism." *Posthumanism*, edited by Neil Badmington. Palgrave, 2000, pp. 30–33.

"Animal Rights Activists 'Akin to Terrorists,' Says NSW Minister Katrina Hodgkinson." *ABC News*. Australian Broadcasting Corporation, 12 November 2016. http://www.abc.net.au/news/2013-07-<18/animal-rights-activists-27terrorists272c-says-nsw-minister/4828556.

AnimalsAustralia. "Koalas are being bulldozed in Queensland." *AnimalsAustralia*, 18 October 2017. http:// animalsaustralia.org/features/koalas-queensland-bulldozed-tree-land-clearing-beef.php.

(A)pollonia. Directed by Krzysztof Warlikowskim, Warsaw, Poland, 2009; Taipei, Taiwan, 2011.

Armstrong, Philip. *What Animals Mean in the Fiction of Modernity*. Routledge, 2008.

Arthur, Jay. *The Settler-Colonial Default Country: A Lexical Cartography of Twentieth-Century Australia*. U of New South Wales P, 2003.

Babe. Directed by Chris Noonan. Produced by Bill Miller, George Miller, and Doug Mitchell, Universal Pictures, 1995.

Badmington, Neil, editor. *Posthumanism*. Palgrave, 2000.

Baker, Kim. "Home and Heart, Hand and Eye: Unseen Links between Pigmen and Pigs in Industrial Farming." *Why We Eat, How We Eat*, edited by Emma-Jayne Abbots and Anna Lavis. Ashgate, 2013, pp. 53–73.

Baker, Mona. "The Changing Landscape of Translation and Interpreting Studies." *A Companions to Translation Studies*, edited by Sandra Bermann and Catherine Porter. John Wiley and Sons, 2014, pp. 15–27.

Baker, Steve. *The Posmodern Animal*. Reaktion Books, 2000.

Bassnett, Susan. *Translation Studies* (1980), revised edition. Routledge, 1991.

Beatson, Peter. *The Eye in the Mandala, Patrick White: A Vision of Man and God*. Elek Books, 1976.

Bell, Diane. *Ngarrindjeri Wurruwarrin: A World That Is, Was, and Will Be*. Spinifex Press, 2014.

Bennett, Bruce. *Australian Compass: Essays on Place and Direction in Australian Literature*. Fremantle Arts Centre Press, 1991.

Bermann, Sandra and Catherine Porter. "Introduction." *A Companion to Translation Studies*, edited by Sandra Bermann and Catherine Porter. John Wiley and Sons, 2014, pp. 1–11.

Blair, Ruth. "Hugging the Shore: The Green Mountains of Southeast Queensland." *The Littoral Zone: Australian Contexts and Their Writers*, edited by CA. Cranston and Robert Zeller. Rodopi Press, 2007, pp. 177–197.

Blanchette, Alex. *Porkopolis: American Animality, Standardized Life, and the Factory Farm*. Duke UP, 2020.

Bliss, Carolyn. *Patrick White's Fiction: The Paradox of Fortunate Failure*. Macmillan, 1986.

Bobis, Merlinda. *Fish-Hair Woman*. Spinifex Press, 2011.

———. *Locust Girl*. Spinifex Press, 2015.

Boom, Keely, Dror Ben-Ami, David B. Croft, Nancy Cushing, Daniel Ramp, and Louise Boronyak. "'Pest' and Resource: A Legal History of Australia's Kangaroos." *Animal Studies Journal*, vol. 1, no. 1, 2012, pp. 17–40. http://ro.uow.edu.au/asj/vol1/iss1/3/.

Bourdieu, Pierre. *Language and Symbolic Power*. Translated by Gino Raymond and Matthew Adamson. Polity, 1991.

Bradley, James. "Introduction." *Wish* by edited by Peter Goldsworthy (1995). Text Publishing, 2013, pp. vii–xiii.

Brady, Veronica. *South of My Days: A Biography of Judith Wright*. Harper Collins, 1998.

———. "Towards an Ecology of Australia: Land of the Spirit." *Worldviews: Environment Culture Religion*, vol. 3, 1999, pp. 139–155.

Brayton, Dan. Rev. of *Ecocriticism and Shakespeare: Reading Ecophobia*, by Simon Estok. *ISLE: Interdisciplinary Studies in Literature and Environment*, vol. 19, no. 1, 2012, pp. 205–206.

Bristow, Tom. *The Anthropocene Lyric: An Affective Geography of Poetry, Person, Place*. Palgrave Macmillan, 2015.

Brodzki, Bella. *Can These Bones Live? Translation, Survival, and Cultural Memory*. Stanford UP, 2007.

Bryson, J. Scott. "Introduction." *Ecopoetry: A Critical Introduction*, edited by J. Scott Bryson. The U of Utah P, 2002, pp. 1–13.

Buck-Morss, Susan. *The Origins of Negative Dialectics: Theodor W. Adorno, Walter Benjamin, and the Frankfurt Institute*. The Free Press, 1977.

Butler, Judith. *Gender Trouble: Feminism and the Subversion of Identity*. Routledge, 1990.

Caddel, Richard. "Secretaries of Nature: Towards a Theory of Modernist Ecology." *Ezra Pound: Nature and Myth*, edited by William Pratt. AMS Press, 2002, pp. 139–150.

Calarco, Matthew. *Zoographies: The Question of the Animal from Heidegger to Derrida*. Columbia UP, 2008.

Carney, Matthew. "Tokyi WWII Firebombing, the Single Most Deadly Bombing Raid in History, Remembered 70 Years On." *ABC News*. Australian Broadcasting Corporation, 9 March 2015. https://mobile.abc.net.au/news/2015-03-09/tokyo-wwii-firebombing-remembered-70-years-on/6287486.

Carr, Rachel. "100% Pure Pigs: New Zealand and the Cultivation of Pure Auckland Island Pigs for Xenotransplantation." *Animal Studies Journal*, vol. 5, no. 2, 2016, pp. 78–100. ro.uow.edu.au/asj/vol5/iss2/5.

Casteel, Sarah Phillips. "Pastoral." *Keywords for Environmental Studies*, edited by Joni Adamson, William A. Gleason, and David N. Pellow. New York UP, 2016, pp. 158–161.

Caulfield, Malcolm. *Animals in Australia: Use and Abuse*. Vivid Publishing-Fontaine Press, 2018.

Chapman, Edgar L. "The Mandala Design of Patrick White's *Riders in the Chariot*." *Critical Essays on Patrick White*, edited by Peter Wolfe. G. K. Hall, 1979, pp. 107–122.

Chen, Peter. *Animal Welfare in Australia*. Sydney UP, 2016.

Chiasson, Dan. "Fire Down Below. The Poetry of Les Murray." *The New Yorker*, 11 and 18 June 2007, pp. 136–139.

Chrichton, Michael. *Congo*. Ballantine Books, 1980.

Chrulew, Matthew and Dinesh Wadiwel, editors. *Foucault and Animals*. Brill, 2016.

Clancy, Laurie. Rev. of *Oink, Oink, Oink*, by Eric Yoshiaki Dando. *Readings*, Readings Pty Ltd, 7 October 2008. https://www.readings.com.au/review/oink-eric-yoshiaki-dando.

Clark, Timothy. *The Cambridge Introduction to Literature and the Environment*. Cambridge UP, 2011.

Coetzee, J. M. *Elizabeth Costello* (2003). Penguin Books, 2004.

———. "The Lives of Animals." *The Lives of Animals*, edited by Amy Gutman. Princeton UP, 1999, pp. 13–69.

Cohen, Jeffrey Jerome. "Posthuman Environs." *Environmental Humanities: Voices from the Anthropocene*, edited by Serenella Iovino and Serpil Oppermann. Rowman and Littlefield, 2017, pp. 25–44.

Coleridge, Samuel Taylor. "Kubla Khan." *The Norton Anthology of English Literature*, 6th edition, vol. 2, edited by M. H. Abrams (general editor). W. W. Norton, 1993, pp. 346–349.

———. "The Subjective & Objective" (1817). *The Green Studies Reader: From Romanticism to Ecocriticism*, edited by Laurence Coupe. Routledge, 2000, pp. 21–22.

Coupe, Laurence. "Introduction." *The Green Studies Reader: From Romanticism to Ecocriticism*, edited by Laurence Coupe. Routledge, 2000, pp. 13–15.

Cranston, CA. and Robert Zeller, editors. *The Littoral Zone: Australian Contexts and Their Writers*. Rodopi Press, 2007.

Crosby, Alfred W. *Ecological Imperialism: The Biological Expansion of Europe, 900–1900*. Cambridge UP, 1986.

Cudworth, Erica. *Developing Ecofeminist Theory: The Complexity of Difference*. Palgrave Macmillan, 2005.

Cummins, Ronnie. "How Factory Farming Contributes to Global Warming." Ecowatch. ecowatch.com/how-factory-farming-contributes-to-global-warming-1881690535.amp.html.

Dando, Eric Yoshiaki. *Oink, Oink, Oink*. Hunter Publishers, 2008.

Davidson, Robyn. *Tracks* (1980). Vintage Books, 1995.

Day, Gregory. Rev. of *Drowning in Wheat: Selected Poems 1980–2015*, by John Kinsella. *The Best Australian Essays 2016*, edited by Geordie Williamson. Black Inc. (Schwartz Publishing), 2016, pp. 173–177.

DeLoughrey, Elizabeth and George B. Handley, editors. *Postcolonial Ecologies: Literatures of The Environment*. Oxford UP, 2011.

DeLoughrey, Elizabeth, Jill Didur, and Anthony Carrigan, editors. *Global Ecologies and the Environmental Humanities: Postcolonial Approaches*. Routledge, 2015.

Department of Agriculture. "Dairy." Australian Government. http://www.agriculture.gov.au/about/commitment/portfolio-facts/dairy.

———. "Wool." Australian Government. http://www.agriculture.gov.au/ag-farm-food/meat-wool-dairy/wool.

Derrida, Jacques. "The Animal That Therefore I Am (More to Follow)." Translated by David Wills. *Critical Inquiry*, vol. 28, no. 2, 2002, pp. 369–418.

———. *The Beast and the Sovereign. The Seminars of Jacques Derrida, Volume. 1*. Translated by Geoffrey Bennington. U of Chicago P, 2009.

———. "'Eating Well,' Or the Calculation of the Subject." *Who Comes After the Subject?*, edited by Eduardo Cadava, Peter Conor, and Jean-Luc Nancy. Routledge, 1991, pp. 96–119.

———. "Force of Law. The 'Mystical Foundation of Authority.'" *Cardozo Law Review*, vol. 11, no. 5–6, 1990, pp. 919–1045.

Diamond, Cora. "The Difficulty of Reality and the Difficulty of Philosophy." *Philosophy and Animal Life*, edited by Cary Wolfe. Columbia UP, 2008. pp. 43–89.

Douglas, Alfred Lord. "Two Loves." *The Chameleon*, vol. 1, no. 1, 1894, pp. 26–28.

"Dryandra State Forest." Australian National Parks, n.d. http://www.australiannationalparks.com/westernaustralia/dryandra/default.htm.

Eather, Warwick and Drew Cottle. "The Rabbit Industry in South-East Australia, 1870–1970." *Proceedings of the 14th Biennial Labour History Conference*, edited by Phillip Deery and Julie Kimber. Australian Society for the Study of Labour History, 2015, pp. 1–20.

Estok, Simon C. "Activist Ecocriticism: An Introduction." *Forum for World Literatures*, vol. 6, no. 2, 2014, pp. 261–271.

———. *Ecocriticism and Shakespeare: Reading Ecophobia*. Palgrave Macmillan, 2011.

———. *The Ecophobia Hypothesis*. Routledge, 2018.

———. "Theorizing in a Space of Ambivalent Openness: Ecocriticism and Ecophobia." *ISLE: Interdisciplinary Studies in Literature and Environment*, vol. 16, no. 2, 2009, pp. 203–225.

———. "Virtually There: 'Aesthetic Pleasure of the First Order,' Ecomedia, Activist Engagement." *ISLE: Interdisciplinary Studies in Literature and Environment*, vol. 24, no. 1, 2017, pp. 4–21.

Fanon, Franz. "The Wretched of the Earth." *Posthumanism*, edited by Neil Badmington. Palgrave, 2000, pp. 23–26.

Flannery, Tim. *The Future Eaters*. Reed Books, 1994.

Flood, Tom. *Oceana Fine*. Allen and Unwin, 1988.

Flys-Junquera, Carmen and Carmen Valero-Garcés. "Translation." *Keywords for Environmental Studies*, edited by Joni Adamson, William A. Gleason, and David N. Pellow. New York UP, 2016, pp. 189–191.

Foster, John Bellamy. *Marx's Ecology: Materialism and Nature*. Monthly Review Press, 2000.

Franklin, Adrian. *Animal Nation: The Story of Animals and Australia*. U of New South Wales, 2006.

Freeman, Carol, Elizabeth Leane, and Yvette Watt, editors. *Considering Animals: Contemporary Studies in Human–Animal Relations*. Ashgate, 2011.

Gaard, Greta. *Critical Ecofeminism*. Rowman and Littlefield, 2017.

———. "Ecofeminism." *Keywords for Environmental Studies*, edited by Joni Adamson, William A. Gleason, and David N. Pellow. New York UP, 2016, pp. 68–71.

———. "New Directions for Ecofeminism: Toward a More Feminist Ecocriticism." *ISLE: Interdisciplinary Studies in Literature and Environment*, vol. 17, no. 4, 2010, pp. 643–665.

Gaard, Greta, Simon C. Estok, and Serpil Oppermman, editors. *International Perspectives in Feminist Ecocriticism*. Routledge, 2013.

Gagliano, Monica. "Breaking the Silence: Green Mudras and the Faculty of Language in Plants." *The Language of Plants: Science, Philosophy, Literature*, edited by Monica Gagliano, John C. Ryan, and Patricia Vieira. U of Minnesota P, 2017, pp. 84–100.

Gammage, Bill. *The Biggest Estate on Earth: How Aborigines Made Australia*. Allen and Unwin, 2012.

Garimara, Nugi (Doris Pilkington). *Follow the Rabbit-Proof Fence*. U of Queensland P, 1996.

Garnett, D. *A Man in the Zoo* (1924). Vintage, 2000.

Garrard, Greg. *Ecocriticism*. Routledge, 2004.

Gelder, Ken and Rachael Weaver. "The Australian Kangaroo Hunt Novel (1830–1858) as *Bildungsroman*." *ALS: Australian Literary Studies*, vol. 34, no. 1, 2019. doi:10.20314/als.e4d03b4165.

———. "Killing and Sentiment in the Colonial Australian Kangaroo Hunt Narrative." *Ecocritical Concerns and the Australian Continent*, edited by Beate Neumeier and Helen Tiffin. Lexington, 2019, pp. 191–202.

Giffin, Michael. *Arthur's Dream: The Religious Imagination in the Fiction of Patrick White*. Spaniel Books, 1996.

Gifford, Terry. *Pastoral*. Routledge, 1999.

———. "Pastoral, Anti-pastoral, Post-pastoral." *The Cambridge Companion to Literature and Environment*, edited by Louise Westling. Cambridge UP, 2014, pp. 17–30.

Golding, William. *Lord of the Flies*. Faber and Faber, 1954.

Goldsworthy, Peter. *Wish* (1995). The Text Publishing Company, 2013.

"Gondwana." *Encyclopædia Britannica. Encyclopædia Britannica Online*. Encyclopædia Britannica Inc., 2012. http://www.britannica.com/EBchecked/topic/238402/Gondwana.

Goodbody, Axel and Adeline Johns-Putra, editors. *Cli-Fi: A Companion*. Peter Lang, 2019.

Government of Western Australia. "Camels in Western Australia." 12 June 2014. https://www.dpaw.wa.gov.au/management/pests-diseases/202-camels-in-western-australia.

Graham, Don. Rev. of *Like Nothing on this Earth: A Literary History of the Wheatbelt*, by Tony Hughes-d'Aeth. *ALS: Australian Literary Studies*, vol. 34, no. 1, 2019. doi:10.20314/als.e487f5777e.

Gravil, Richard. "Imagining Wordsworth: 1797–1807–1817." *Coleridge's Imagination: Essays in Memory of Pete Laver*, edited by Richard Gravil, Lucy Newlyn, and Nicholas Roe. Cambridge UP, 1985, pp. 129–142.

Greenblatt, Stephen, general editor. *Norton Anthology of English Literature, Volume 2*, 9th edition. W. W. Norton, 2012.

Gutman, Amy, editor. *The Lives of Animals*. Princeton UP, 1999.

Haebich, A. and R. H. W. Reece. "Neville Auber Octavius, 1875–1954" (1988). *Australian Dictionary of Biography*, n.d. http://adb.anu.edu.au/biography/neville-auber-octavius-7821.

Halberstam, Judith. *Female Masculinity*. Duke UP, 1998.

Haraway, Donna. "A Cyborg Manifesto: Science, Technology, and Socialist-Feminism in the Late Twentieth Century." *Posthumanism*, edited by Neil Badmington. Palgrave, 2000, pp. 69–84.

Harper, Jane. *The Dry*. Pan Macmillan Australia, 2017.

Hawthorne, Susan. *Cow*. Spinifex Press, 2011.

Hazzard, Shirley. *The Great Fire*. Picador, 2003.

Heise, Ursula. "Afterword. Postcolonial Ecocriticism and the Question of Literature." *Postcolonial Green: Environmental Politics and World Narratives*, edited by Bonnie Roos and Alex Hunt. U of Virginia P, 2010, pp. 251–258.

———. "Hitchhiker's Guide to Ecocriticism." *PMLA: Publications of the Modern Language Association of America*, vol. 121, no. 2, 2006, pp. 503–516.

———. *Sense of Place and Sense of Planet: The Environmental Imagination of the Global*. Oxford UP, 2008.

Heiss, Anita and Peter Minter, editors. *Macquarie Pen Anthology of Aboriginal Literature*. Allen and Unwin, 2008.

Herbert, Xavier. *Capricornia* (1938). HarperCollins, 2001.

Hewitt, Helen Verity. *Patrick White, Painter Manque: Paintings, Painters and their Influence on His Writing*. Miegunyah Press, 2000.

Hitchens, Christopher. *Hitch-22: A Memoir*. Atlantic Books, 2010.

Horowitz, Richard P. *Hog Ties: What Pigs Tell Us about America*. U of Minnesota P, 1998.

Housman, A. E. “XL.” *A Shropshire Lad* (1896). *The Collected Poems of A. E. Housman*. Project Gutenberg. http://www.gutenberg.org/files/5720/5720--h/5720-h.htm.

Huang, Peter I-min. “Canon Formation in the Study of the Environment in China and Taiwan.” *CLCWeb: Comparative Literature and Culture*, vol. 16, no. 6, 2014. doi:10.7771/1481-4374.2534.

Huggan, Graham. *Australian Literature: Postcolonialism, Racism, Transnationalism*. Oxford UP, 2007.

Huggan, Graham and Helen Tiffin. *Postcolonial Ecocriticism: Literature, Animals, Environment*. Routledge, 2010.

Hughes, Robert. *The Fatal Shore: A History of the Transportation of Convicts to Australia, 1787–1868*. Vintage Books, 2003.

Hughes-d'Aeth, Tony. *Like Nothing on this Earth: A Literary History of the Wheatbelt*. University of Western Australia (UWA) Publishing, 2017.

———. “Salt Scars: John Kinsella's Wheatbelt.” *ALS: Australian Literary Studies*, vol. 27, no. 2, 2012, pp. 18–31.

Invasive Animals Ltd. “Large Populations of Feral Camels in Australia.” https://www.feralscan.org.au.

Jakobson, Roman. “On Linguistic Aspects of Translation” (1959). *The Translation Studies Reader*, third edition, edited by Lawrence Venuti. Routledge, 2012, pp. 126–131.

James, Erin. “Teaching the Postcolonial/Ecocritical Dialogue.” *Teaching Ecocriticism and Green Cultural Studies*, edited by Greg Garrard. Palgrave Macmillan, 2012, pp. 60–71.

Johns-Putra, Adeline. *Climate Change and the Contemporary Novel*. Cambridge UP, 2019.

Johnson, Sian. “Budj Bim Cultural Landscape Fire Reveals New Sections of Ancient Aquatic System.” *ABC News*. Australian Broadcasting Corporation, 19 January 2019. http://www.abc.net.au/news/2020-01-19/fire-reveals-further-parts-of-6600-year-old-aquatic-system/11876228.

Jolly, Elizabeth. *The Well*. Viking Press, 1986.

Kafka, Franz. “A Report for an Academy (1917).” Translated by Ian Johnston. http://openmods.uvic.ca/islandorg/object/uvic%3A606/datastream/pdf/view.

Kane, Paul. *Australian Poetry: Romanticism and Negativity*. Cambridge UP, 1996.

Kellert, Stephen R. and Edward O. Wilson, editors. *The Biophilia Hypothesis*. Island P, 1993.

Kheel, Marti. *Nature Ethics: An Ecofeminist Perspective*. Rowman and Littlefield, 2008.

Kiernan, Brian. “Coloring in White.” *Southerly*, vol. 63, 2003, pp. 194–198.

———. “The Novelist and the Modern World.” *Prophet from the Desert: Critical Essays on Patrick White*, edited by John McLaren. Red Hill Press, 1995, pp. 1–23.

King Kong. Directed by Merian C. Cooper and Ernest B. Schoedsack, Radio Pictures, 1933.

King-Smith, Dick. *The Sheep-Pig*. Gollanz, 1963.

Kinnane, Gary. “Shopping at last!: History, Fiction and the Anti-suburban Tradition.” *Australian Literary Studies*, vol. 18, 1998, pp. 41–55.

Kinsella, John. *Contrary Rhetoric: Lectures on Landscape and Language*, edited by Glen Phillips and Andrew Taylor. Fremantle Press, 2008.

———. *Disclosed Poetics: Beyond Landscape and Lyricism*. Manchester UP, 2007.

———. *Drowning in Wheat: Selected Poems 1980–2015*. Picador, 2016.

Klein, Naomi. *This Changes Everything: Capitalism vs. The Climate*. Simon & Schuster, 2014.

Köhler, Wolfgang. "The Mentality of Apes." *Nature*, vol. 116, 1925, pp. 351–352. doi:10.1038/116351a0.

Kristal, Efrain. "Philosophical/Theoretical Approaches to Translation." *A Companions to Translation Studies*, edited by Sandra Bermann and Catherine Porter. John Wiley and Sons, 2014, pp. 28–40.

Lacan, Jacques. *Ecrits: A Selection*. Translated by Alan Sheridan. Tavistock Publications, 1977.

Lantana. Directed by Ray Lawrence, Palace Films, 2001.

Lenore, Miriel. *In the garden*. Wakefield Press, 2007.

Linnaeus, Carolus. *Systema naturae*. Lugduni Batavorum (Haak), 1735.

London, Joan. *The Golden Age*. Vintage (Random House Australia Pty Ltd), 2015.

Long, Mark. "William Carlos Williams, Ecocriticism, and Contemporary American Nature Poetry." *Ecopoetry*, edited by J. Scott Bryson. The U of Utah P, 2002, pp. 58–74.

Lynch, Tom. "Pastoralism." *The Littoral Zone: Australian Contexts and Their Writers*, edited by CA. Cranston and Robert Zeller. Rodopi Press, 2007, pp. 72–76.

———. "Strange Lands: The Lexicon of Settler-Colonial Landscapes in Charles Fletcher Lummis's and Arthur Groom's Portrayals of the American West and the Australian Outback." *ISLE: Interdisciplinary Studies in Literature and Environment*, vol. 22, no. 4, 2015, pp. 697–716.

Macbeth, ShakespeaRe-Told. Directed by Mark Brozel. Produced by BBC Northern Ireland and BBC Drama Department, Acorn Media UK, 2005.

Manes, Christopher. "Nature and Silence." *Environmental Ethics*, vol. 14, no. 4, 1992, pp. 339–350; reprinted in *The Ecocriticism Reader: Landmarks in Literary Ecology*, edited by Cheryll Glotfelty and Harold Fromm. U of Georgia P, 1996, pp. 15–29. doi:10.5840/enviroethics19921445.

Mann, Charles C. *1491: New Revelations of the Americas before Columbus*. Alfred A. Knopf, 2005.

Maran, Timo. "On the Diversity of Environmental Signs: A Typological Approach." *Biosemiotics*. Springer Science + Business Media B.V., part of Springer Nature 2017, 9 November 2017. doi:1007/s12304-017-9308-5.

Macbeth. ShakespeaRetold. Directed by Mark Brozel. Produced by BBC Ireland and the BBC Drama Department. Distributed by Acorn Media, 2005.

Marshall, James Vance. *Walkabout*. New York Review of Books Classics, 2012.

Martel, Yann. *Life of Pi*. Knopf Canada, 2001.

Massey, Charles. *Call of the Reed Warbler*. Chelsea Green Publishing, 2017.

Mathews, Freya. *Without Animals Life is not Worth Living*. Ginninderra Press, 2015.

Mathews, Freya, Kate Rigby, and Deborah Rose. "Introduction." *The Eye of the Crocodile*, edited by Lorraine Shannon. Australia National University E Press, 2012.

McCabe, Patrick. *The Butcher Boy*. Pan Books, 1992.

McCann, Andrew. "Decomposing Suburbia: *Patrick White's* perversity," *Australian Literary Studies*, vol. 18, no. 4, 1998, pp. 56–71. https://www.australianliterarystudies.com.au/articles/decomposing-suburbia-patrick-whites-perversity. doi:10.20314/als.c705e2407a.

———. "The Ethics of Abjection: Patrick White's *Riders in the Chariot*." *Australian Literary Studies*, vol. 18, no. 2, 1997, pp. 145–155. https://www.australianliterarystudies.com.au/articles/the-ethics-of-abjection-patrick-whites-riders-in-the-chariot. doi:10.20314/als.f8f294e84a.

McCooey, David. "Les Murray." *Macquarie Pen Anthology of Australian Literature*, edited by Nicholas Jose (general editor). Allen and Unwin, 2009, pp. 900–901.

McCorkie, Don and Audrey Brohy, directors. *River of Waste: The Hazardous Truth About Factory Farms*. Directed by Don McCorkie and Audrey Brohy, Cinema Libre Studio, 2009.

McGregor, Craig, David Beal, David More, and Harry Williamson, editors. *In the Making*. Thomas Nelson, 1969.

Meat and Livestock Australia. "Fast Facts: Australia's Beef Industry." Meat and Livestock Australia. https://www.mla.com.au/globalassets/mla-corporate/prices--markets/documents/trends--analysis/fast-facts--maps/mla-beef-fast-facts-2019.pdf.

———. "Fast Facts: Australia's Sheepmeat Industry." Meat and Livestock Australia. https://www.mla.com.au/globalassets/mla-corporate/prices--markets/documents/trends--analysis/fast-facts--maps/mla_sheep-fast-facts-2018.pdf.

———. "The Red Meat Industry." Meat and Livestock Australia. https://www.mla.com.au/about-mla/the-red-meat-industry/#.

Milman, Oliver. "Australian Feral Camel Population Overestimated, Says Study." *The Guardian*. Guardian News and Media Ltd, 18 November 2013. https://www.theguardian.com/environment/2013/nov/18/australian-feral-camel-population-overestimated-says-study.

Milton, Kay. "Possum Magic, Possum Menace: Wildlife Control and the Demonisation of Cuteness." *Considering Animals: Contemporary Studies in Human–Animal Relations*, edited by Carol Freeman, Elizabeth Leane, and Yvette Watt. Ashgate, 2011, pp. 67–77.

Moran, Albert and Tom O'Regan, editors. *The Australian Screen*. Penguin Books, 1989.

Morley, Patricia A. *The Mystery of Unity: Theme and Technique in the Novels of Patrick White*. McGill-Queen's UP, 1972.

Morrison, Blake. Rev. of *Housman Country*, by Peter Parker. *The Guardian*, 6 July 2016. https://www.theguardian.com/books/2016/jul/16/housman-country-heart-of-england-peter-parker-review.

Mortimer-Sandilands and Bruce Erickson, editors. *Queer Ecologies: Sex, Nature, Politics, Desire*. Indiana UP, 2010.

Morton, Timothy. "Deconstruction And/As Ecology." *The Oxford Handbook of Ecocriticism*, edited by Greg Garrard. Oxford UP, 2014, pp. 291–304.

———. *The Ecological Thought*. Harvard UP, 2010.
———. "Here Comes Everything: The Promise of Object-Oriented-Ontology." *Qui Parle*, vol. 19, no. 2, 2011, pp. 163–190. http://www.academia.edu/934518/Here_Comes_Everythig_The_Promise_of_Object_Oriented_Ontology.
Murray, Les. *Subhuman Redneck Poems* (1996). Farrar, Straus and Giroux, 1998.
———. *Translations from the Natural World*. Isabella Press, 1992.
Murray, Scott, editor. *Australian Cinema*. Allen and Unwin, 1994.
My Fair Lady. Music by Frederick Loewe. Lyrics and Script by Alan Jay Lerner, 1956.
Mystery Road. Directed by Ivan Sen, Transmission Films, 2013.
Narraway, Guinevere and Hannah Stark. "Vital Plants and Despicable Weeds in Ray Lawrence's *Lantana*." *The Green Thread: Dialogues with the Vegetal World*, edited by Patricia Vieira, Monica Gagliano, and John Ryan. Rowman and Littlefield, 2016, pp. 183–198.
Newlyn, Lucy. "'Radical Difference': Coleridge and Wordsworth, 1802." *Coleridge's Imagination: Essays in Memory of Pete Laver*, edited by Richard Gravil, Lucy Newlyn, and Nicholas Roe. Cambridge UP, 1985, pp. 117–128.
Nowra, Louis. *Walkabout*. Currency Press, 2003.
O'Connor, Brian, editor. *The Adorno Reader*. Blackwell, 2000.
Okja. Directed by Joon-ho Bong. Produced by Dede Gardner, Jeremy Kleiner, et al. Distributed by *Netflix*, 2017.
Oppermann, Serpil. "How the Material World Communicates: Insights from Material Ecocriticism." *Routledge Handbook of Ecocriticism and Environmental Communication*, edited by Scott Slovic, Swarnalatha Rangarajan, and Vidya Sarveswaran. Routledge, 2019, pp. 108–117.
Oppermann, Serpil and Serenella Iovino. "Introduction: The Environmental Humanities and the Challenges of the Anthropocene." *Environmental Humanities: Voices from the Anthropocene*, edited by Serpil Oppermann and Serenella Iovino. Rowman and Littlefield, 2017, pp. 1–21.
O'Sullivan, Siobhan. "Ag gag' Laws: The Battle for Animal Welfare is a Battle Over Information." Guardian News and Media Limited, 5 May 2014. http://www.theguardian.com/commentisfree/2014/may/05/ag-gag-laws-the-battle-for-animal-welfare-is-a-battle-over-information.
Pascoe, Bruce. *Dark Emu. Black Seeds: Agriculture or Accident?* Magabala Books, 2016.
———. "The Slaughters of the Bulumwaal Butcher." *Macquarie Pen Anthology of Australian Literature. Macquarie Pen Anthology of Australian Literature*, edited by Nicholas Jose (general editor). Allen and Unwin, 2009, pp. 1124–1139.
Paterson, Banjo. "It's Grand." *Classic Australian Short Stories and Verse*, edited by M. Pinkney. Summit Press, 2002, p. 374.
Pepys, Samuel. *The Diary of Samuel Pepys*. https://www.pepysdiary.com/diary/1661/08/24.
Plumwood, Val. *Environmental Culture: The Ecological Crisis of Reason*. Routledge, 2001.
———. *The Eye of the Crocodile*, edited by Lorraine Shannon. Australian National University E-Press, 2012. http://epress.anu.edu.au/titles/the-eye-of-the-crocodile.

———. *Feminism and the Mastery of Nature.* Routledge, 1993.

Pople, Tony and Gordon Grigg. "Commercial Harvesting of Kangaroos in Australia." Department of Environment, Water, Heritage and the Arts, n.d. http://www.environment.gov.au/biodiversity/wildlife-trade/publications/kangaroo/harvesting/index.html.

Pughe, Thomas, Benedicte Chorier-Fryd, and Charles Holdefer, editors. "Pastoral: Past, Present, Future." *Green Letters: Studies in Ecocriticism*, vol. 20, no. 1, 2016, pp. 1–118.

Pulé, Paul M. "Caring for Society and Environment: Towards Ecological Masculinism." Paper presented at the Villanova University Sustainability Conference, April 2009. http://www.paulpule.com.au/Ecological_Masculinism.pdf.

———. "Ecology and Environmental Studies." *Routledge International Encyclopedia of Men and Masculinities*, edited by Michael Flood, Judith Kegan Gardiner, Bob Pease, and Keith Pringle. Routledge, 2007, pp. 158–162.

Rabbit-Proof Fence. Directed by Phillip Noyce, Becker Entertainment, 2002.

Raber, Karen. "Vermin and Parasites: Shakespeares's Animal Architectures." *Ecocritical Shakespeare*, edited by Lynne Bruckner and Dan Brayton. Ashgate, 2011, pp. 13–32.

Ralph, Iris. Book Rev. of *Ecocriticism and Shakespeare: Reading Ecophobia*, by Simon C. Estok. *Tamkang Review*, vol. 44, no. 2, 2014, pp. 191–199.

———. "Ecophobia and the Porcelain Porcine Species." *ISLE: Interdisciplinary Studies in Literature and Environment*, vol. 16, no. 2, 2019, pp. 401–412. doi:10.1093/isle/isz050.

———. "Performing Others, Other Performers, Mark Twain, and Elizabeth Costello." *Cowrie: A Journal of Comparative Literature and Culture*, no. 2, 2014, pp. 40–58.

Rattigan, Neil. "*Walkabout.*" *Images of Australia: 100 Films of the New Australian Cinema.* Southern Methodist UP, 1991, pp. 308–311.

Readings. "Oink, Oink, Oink: A Savage Modern Fable." Readings Pty Ltd. readings.com.au/products/3092082/oink-oink-oink-a-savage-modern-fable.

Rendle-Short, Francesca. *Bite Your Tongue.* Spinifex Press, 2011.

———. "Permissions." *Bite Your Tongue.* Spinifex Press, 2011, pp. 242–244.

Rigby, Kate. *Dancing with Disaster: Environmental Histories, Narratives, and Ethics for Perilous Times.* U of Virginia P, 2015.

———. "The Poetics of Decolonization: Reading *Carpentaria* in a Feminist Ecocritical Frame." *International Perspectives in Feminist Ecocriticism*, edited by Greta Gaard, Simon C. Estok, and Serpil Oppermann. Routledge, 2013, pp. 120–136.

Rise of the Planet of the Apes. Directed by Rupert Wyatt, 20th Century Fox, 2011.

Ritvo, Harriett. "Animal Planet." *Environmental History*, vol. 9, no. 2, 2004, pp. 204–220.

Robin, Libby. "The Eco-Humanities as Literature: A New Genre?" *Australian Literary Studies*, vol. 23, no. 3, 2008, pp. 290–304.

Robin, Marie-Monique. *The World According to Monsanto: Pollution, Politics and Power.* Translated from the French by George Holoch. Spinifex P, 2010.

Robertson, Joshua. "'Alarming' Rise in Queensland Tree Clearing as 400,000 Hectares Stripped." *The Guardian*, 2019 Guardian News and Media Limited,

5 October 2017. https://www.theguardian.com/environment/2017/oct/05/alarming-rise-in-queensland-tree-clearing-as-400000-hectares-stripped.

Rolls, Eric. *A Million Wild Acres*. Nelson, 1981.

Roos, Bonnie and Alex Hunt, editors. *Environmental Politics and World Narratives*. U of Virginia P, 2010.

Rose, Deborah Bird. *Nourishing Terrains: Australian Aboriginal Views of Landscape and Wilderness*. Australian Heritage Commission, 1996.

———. "Val Plumwood's Philosophical Animism: Attentive Inter-Actions in the Sentient World." *Environmental Humanities*, vol. 3, 2013, pp. 93–109.

———. *Wild Dog Dreaming: Love and Extinction*. U of Virginia P, 2013.

Rose, Deborah Bird, Thom van Dooren, and Matthew Chrulew, editors. *Extinction Studies: Stories of Time, Death, and Generations*. Columbia UP, 2017.

Rosser, Debra, preparer. "Moore River Native Settlement (1918–1951)." *Find & Connect*, n.d. https://www.findandconnect.gov.au/ref/wa/biogs/WE00948b.htm.

Rothwell, Nicholas. "The Mirror that Creates." *Meanjin*, vol. 72, no. 2, 2013, pp. 18–36.

Rozelle, Lee. Rev. of *Dark Nature: Anti-Pastoral Essays in American Literature and Culture*, edited by Richard J. Schneider. *ISLE: Interdisciplinary Studies in Literature and Environment*, vol. 24, no. 2, 2017, pp. 376–377.

Ryan, John. *Green Sense: The Aesthetics of Plants, Place and Language*. Trueheart P-Oxford P, 2012.

———. *Posthuman Plants: Rethinking the Vegetal through Culture, Art, and Poetry*. Common Ground Publishing, 2015.

———. "Sunday Zamia Swagger." *Perilous Adventures*. n.d. https://www.perilousadventures.net/1004/ryanzamia.html.

Salemme, Nadia. "'Sickening' Australian Wool Practices Revealed in New PETA Footage." *News.Com.Au*. News Corp Australia, 14 December 2017. https://www.news.com.au/lifestyle/fashion/sickening-australian-wool-practices-revealed-in-new-peta-footage/news-story/7646f795ca1b22e831017b4df87573d6.

Samuels, Gabriel. "Chimpanzees Have Rights, Says Argentine Judge as She Orders Cecilia Be Released from Zoo." *Independent*, 7 November 2016. https://www.independent.co.uk/news/world/americas/argentine-judge-says-chimpanzee-poor-conditions-has-rights-and-shold-be-free-from zoo-a7402606.html.

Schulman, Audrey. *Theory of Bastards*. Europa Editions, 2018.

Scigaj, Leonard M. *Sustainable Poetry: Four American Ecopoets*. The UP of Kentucky, 1999.

Scott, Kim. *Benang: From the Heart*. Fremantle Arts Centre Press, 1999.

Senate Rural and Regional Affairs and Transport Committee. *Commercial Utilisation of Australian Native Wildlife*. Parliament of the Commonwealth of Australia, 1998.

Senate Select Committee on Animal Welfare. *Kangaroos*. Parliament of the Commonwealth of Australia, 1988.

Serventy, Vincent. *Dryandra. The Story of an Australian Forest*. A. H. & A. W. Reed, 1970.

Sesame Street. Created by Joan Ganz Cooney and Lloyd Morrisett. Produced by Samuel Gibbon and Jon Stone, 1969–2015.

Shaw, George Bernard. *Pygmalion* (1913). Dover Publications, 1994.

Siegel, Lee. Rev. of *Walkabout*, by James Vance Marshall. *The New York Review*, 12 January 2012, pp. 34–35. http://www.nybooks.com/articles/2012/01/12/two-walkabouts/.

Singer, Peter. "Introduction." *In Defense of Animals: The Second Wave*, edited by Peter Singer. Blackwell, 2006, pp. 1–10.

Slezak, Michael. "3 Billion Animals Killed or Displaced in Black Summer Bushfires, Study

Estimates." *ABC News*. Australian Broadcasting Corporation, 28 July 2020. https://www.abc.net.au/news/2020-07-28/3-billion-animals-killed-displaced-in-fires-wwf-study/12497976.

Soper, Kate. *Humanism and Anti-Humanism*. Open Court Publishing Company, 1986.

Spenser, Edmund. *The Faerie Queene*. Project Gutenberg. http://www.gutenberg.org/files/15272/15272-h/15272-h.htm#canto_1.

Spiegel, Marjorie. *The Dreaded Comparison: Human and Animal Slavery*. Mirror, 1988.

Spinifex Press. n.d. http://www.spinifexpress.com.au/Bookstorebook/id306/.

Steffen, Will. "The Angry Summer." Australian Climate Commission Report, February 2013. http://climatecommissiongov.au/report/the-angry-summer.

The Sydney Morning Herald. "Daughter Dies with Her Story Still Incomplete." The Sydney Morning Herald, 15 January 2004. https://www.smh.com.au/national/daughter-dies-with-her-story-still-incomplete-20040115-gdi5s5.html.

Taylor, Andrew. "Introduction." *Contrary Rhetoric: Lectures on Landscape and Language*, edited by John Kinsella, Glen Phillips, and Andrew Taylor. Fremantle Press, 2008, pp. 8–11.

Taylor, Matthew A. "The Nature of Fear: Edgar Allan Poe and Posthuman Ecology." *American Literature*, vol. 84, 2012, pp. 353–379.

Taylor, Rebe. "The National Confessional." *Meanjin Quarterly*, vol. 71, no. 3, 2012, pp. 22–36.

Thorsborne, Margaret. "Foreword." *The Coral Battleground* by Judith Wright. Spinifex Press, 2014, pp. xvii–xx.

Tiffin, Helen. "The Speech of Dumb Beasts." *Considering Animals: Contemporary Studies in Human–Animal Relations*, edited by Carol Freeman, Elizabeth Leane, and Yvette Watt. Ashgate, 2011, pp. 137–151.

Tindall, Ashley. "Hindmarsh Island." Sacred Land Film Project. Earth Island Institute, 12 March 2007. http://www.sacredland.org/hindmarsh-island/.

Tredinnick, Mark. "Under the Mountains and Beside a Creek: Robert Gray and the Shepherding of Antipodean Being." *The Littoral Zone: Australian Contexts and Their Writers*, edited by CA. Cranston and Robert Zeller. Rodopi Press, 2007, pp. 124–143.

———. *A Place on Earth: An Anthology of Nature Writing from Australia and North America*, edited by Mark Tredinnick. U of New South Wales P, 2003.

Treloar, Lucy. *Salt Creek* (2015). Pan Macmillan, 2017.

Trexler, Adam. *Anthropocene Fictions: The Novel in a Time of Climate Change*. U of Virginia P, 2015.

Turner, Graeme. *National Fictions: Literature, Film and the Construction of Australian Narrative*. Allen and Unwin Academic, 1993.

Twine, Richard. *Animals as Biotechnology. Ethics, Sustainability and Critical Animal Studies*. Earthscan, 2010.

Venuti, Lawrence. *The Scandals of Translation*. Routledge, 1998.

———. *The Translator's Invisibility: A History of Translation* (1995). Routledge, 2008.

Vieira, Patrícia, Monica Gagliano, and John Ryan. "Introduction." *The Green Thread: Dialogues with the Vegetal World*, edited by Patrícia Vieira, Monica Gagliano, and John Ryan. Rowman and Littlefield, 2016, pp. ix–xxviii.

Walkabout. Directed by Nicolas Roeg, Max. L. Raab-Si Litvinoff Films, 1971.

Warren, Karen. "The Power and the Promise of Ecological Feminism." *Environmental Ethics*, vol. 12, 1990, pp. 125–144.

Watt, Yvette. "Making Animals Matter: Why the Art World Needs to Rethink the Representation of Animals." *Considering Animals: Contemporary Studies in Human–Animal Relations*, edited by Carol Freeman, Elizabeth Leane, and Yvette Watt. Ashgate, 2011, pp. 119–134.

Weiss, Tony. *The Ecological Hoofprint: The Global Burden of Industrial Livestock*. Zed Books, 2013.

Wheaton, Claire. "Black Summer Fires Royal Commission Receives 400 Submissions, Victims Call for Extension." *ABC News*. Australian Broadcasting Corporation, 20 April 2020. https://www.abc.net.au/news/2020-04-20/bushfire-victims-plead-for-delay-to-royal-commission-timeline/12163224.

Wheeler, Wendy. "The Biosemiotic Turn: Abduction, or, the Nature of Creative Reason." *Ecocritical Theory: New European Approaches*, edited by Axel Goodbody and Kate Rigby. U of Virginia P, 2011, pp. 270–282.

———. "Natural Play, Natural Metaphor, Natural Stories." *Material Ecocriticism*, edited by Serenella Iovino and Serpil Oppermann. Indiana UP, 2014, pp. 67–79.

———. "'Tongues I'll Hang on Every Tree': Biosemiotics and the Book of Nature." *The Cambridge Companion to Literature and the Environment*, edited by Louise Westling. Cambridge UP, 2014, pp. 121–135.

———. *The Whole Creature: Complexity, Biosemiotics and the Evolution of Culture*. Lawrence and Wishart, 2006.

White, E. B. *Charlotte's Web*. Harper & Brothers, 1952.

White, Neil. "The Historical Roots of our Ecological Crisis." *Environmental Ethics: Readings in Theory and Application*, 4th edition, edited by Louis P. Pojman. Thomson Learning Wadsworth, 2005, pp. 19–25.

White, Patrick. *The Aunt's Story*. Viking Press, 1948.

———. "Australians in a Nuclear War." *Patrick White Speaks*, edited by Paul Brennan and Christine Flynn. Primavera Press, 1989, pp. 113–126.

———. *Voss*. Penguin, 1961.

Wilding, Michael. "The Politics of Modernism." *Prophet from the Desert: Critical Essays on Patrick White*, edited by John McLaren. Red Hill Press, 1995, pp. 24–33.

Williams, Jacqueline. "Obituary: Daisy Kadibil, 95, Whose Australia Trek Inspired a Film, Dies." *New York Times*, 27 June 2018. https://www.nytimes.com/2018/06/27/obituaries/daisy-kadibil-95-whose-ausstralia-trek-inspired a-film-dies.html.

Williams, Mark. *Patrick White*. Macmillan Press, 1993.

Wilson, E. O. *Biophilia: The Human Bond with Other Species*. Harvard UP, 1984.

———. *The Diversity of Life*. Harvard UP, 1992.

Wohlleben, Peter. *The Hidden Life of Trees: What They Feel, How They Communicate* (2015). Translated by Jane Billinghurst. Black Inc. (Schwartz Publishing), 2016.

Wolfe, Cary. *Animal Rites: American Culture, the Discourse of Species and Posthumanism*. U of Chicago P, 2003.

———. *What Is Posthumanism?* U of Minnesota P, 2010.

"The Wollemi Pine: A Very Rare Discovery." The Royal Botanic Gardens and Domain Trust. http://www.rbgsyd.nsw.gov.au/plant_info/wollemi_pine.

Wright, Alexis. "Seeking the Silenced Voice." Rev. of *Walkabout*, by Louis Nowra. *RealTime*, vol. 58, 2003, p. 23. http://www.realfitimearts.net/article/issue58/7297.

Wright, Judith. *Coral Battleground*. Spinifex Press, 2014.

Wyld, Evie. *All the Birds, Singing*. Jonathan Cape, 2013.

Zapf, Hubert. *Handbook of Ecocriticism and Cultural Ecology*. Walter De Gruyter, 2016.

Index

Note: Page numbers followed by "n" denote endnotes.

For Product Safety Concerns and Information please contact our EU representative GPSR@taylorandfrancis.com
Taylor & Francis Verlag GmbH, Kaufingerstraße 24, 80331 München, Germany

www.ingramcontent.com/pod-product-compliance
Lightning Source LLC
Chambersburg PA
CBHW071521100726
47908CB00004B/1248